Concepts and Semantics of Programming Languages 2

Series Editor
Jean-Charles Pomerol

Concepts and Semantics of Programming Languages 2

*Modular and Object-oriented Constructs
with OCaml, Python, C++, Ada and Java*

Thérèse Hardin
Mathieu Jaume
François Pessaux
Véronique Viguié Donzeau-Gouge

WILEY

First published 2021 in Great Britain and the United States by ISTE Ltd and John Wiley & Sons, Inc.

ISTE Ltd
27-37 St George's Road
London SW19 4EU
UK

www.iste.co.uk

John Wiley & Sons, Inc.
111 River Street
Hoboken, NJ 07030
USA

www.wiley.com

Library of Congress Control Number: 2021935827

British Library Cataloguing-in-Publication Data
A CIP record for this book is available from the British Library
ISBN 978-1-78630-602-9

Contents

Foreword

Computer programs have played an increasingly central role in our lives since the 1940s, and the quality of these programs has thus become a crucial question. Writing a high-quality program – a program that performs the required task and is efficient, robust, easy to modify, easy to extend, etc. – is an intellectually challenging task, requiring the use of rigorous development methods. First and foremost, however, the creation of such a program is dependent on an in-depth knowledge of the programming language used, its syntax and, crucially, its semantics, i.e. what happens when a program is executed.

The description of this semantics puts the most fundamental concepts into light, including those of value, reference, exception or object. These concepts are the foundations of programming language theory. Mastering these concepts is what sets experienced programmers apart from beginners. Certain concepts – like that of value – are common to all programming languages; others – such as the notion of functions – operate differently in different languages; finally, other concepts – such as that of objects – only exist in certain languages. Computer scientists often refer to "programming paradigms" to consider sets of concepts shared by a family of languages, which imply a certain programming style: imperative, functional, object-oriented, logical, concurrent, etc. Nevertheless, an understanding of the concepts themselves is essential, as several paradigms may be interwoven within the same language.

Introductory texts on programming in any given language are not difficult to find, and a number of published books address the fundamental concepts of language semantics. Much rarer are those, like the present volume, which establish and examine the links between concepts and their implementation in languages used by programmers on a daily basis, such as C, C++, Ada, Java, OCaml and Python. The authors provide a wealth of examples in these languages, illustrating and giving life to the notions that they present. They propose general models, such as the *kit* presented in Volume 2, permitting a unified view of different notions; this makes it easier for readers to understand the constructs used in popular programming languages and facilitates comparison. This thorough and detailed work provides readers with an understanding of these notions and, above all, an understanding of the ways of using the latter to create high-quality programs, building a safer and more reliable future in computing.

Gilles DOWEK
Research Director, Inria
Professor at the École normale supérieure, Paris-Saclay

Catherine DUBOIS
Professor at the École nationale supérieure
d'informatique pour l'industrie et l'entreprise

January 2021

Preface

This two-volume work relates to the field of programming. First and foremost, it is intended to give readers a solid grounding in the bases of functional or imperative programming, along with a thorough knowledge of the module and class mechanisms involved. In our view, the semantics approach is most appropriate when studying programming, as the impact of interlanguage syntax differences is limited. Practical considerations, determined by the material characteristics of computers and/or "smart" devices, will also be addressed. The same approach will be taken in both volumes, using both mathematical formulas and memory state diagrams. With this book, we hope to help readers understand the meaning of the constructs described in the reference manuals of programming languages and to establish solid foundations for reasoning and assessing the correctness of their own programs through critical review. In short, our aim is to facilitate the development of safe and reliable software programs.

Volume 1 presented a broad overview of the functional and imperative features of programming, from notions that can be modeled mathematically to notions that are linked to the hardware configuration of computers themselves.

Volume 2 is dedicated to the study of language features (modules, classes, objects) that are known to ease the development of software systems. It builds on the foundations laid down in Volume 1 since modules, classes and objects are, in essence, the means of organizing functional or imperative constructs.

Chapter 1 first analyzes some of the needs of developers in terms of tools for building large software. Based on these requirements, an original semantic model is drawn up, jointly presenting all of the features of modules and classes that can meet these needs. We introduce our own structure, a *kit*, to describe this model, a word chosen to avoid any confusion with the usual denominations (structure, module, package, class, etc.) used by languages. These *kits* serve to explain naming management, export and import mechanisms, access restrictions, extension and parametrization (genericity, functors), subtyping and subclassing. In contrast to the mathematical study of semantics of functional and imperative features, the semantics of these kits remains rather informal, as research has not yet led to a relatively simple mathematical model. In this chapter, we have therefore prioritized intuition and simplicity, which inevitably leads to approximations and a lack of rigor, to some degree. Chapter 1 also proposes a set of questions to guide the acquisition of a language, with some answers given in the subsequent chapters. Chapter 2 first presents an implementation of *kits* with the modules of Ada and then a richer implementation of *kits* with the modules of OCaml. It ends with a much more succinct implementation of *kits*, referred to as weak *kits*, using the header files and the mechanisms of import–export of C. Chapter 3 takes up the *kit* model to handle classes and objects and their tools, for example inheritance, late binding and subclassing. This model is exemplified in Chapter 4, which presents the classes of Java, C++, OCaml and Python from a unified perspective.

This work is aimed at a relatively wide audience, from experienced developers – who will find valuable additional information on language semantics – to beginners who have only written short programs. For beginners, we recommend working on the semantic concepts described in Volume 1 using the implementations in OCaml or Python to ease assimilation. All readers may benefit from studying the reference manual of a programming language, while comparing the presentations of constructs given in the manual with those given here, guided by the questions mentioned in Volume 2.

Note that we do not discuss the algorithmic aspect of data processing here. However, choosing the algorithm and the data representation that fit the requirements of the specification is an essential step in program development. Many excellent works have been published on this subject, and we encourage readers to explore the subject further. We also recommend using the standard libraries provided by the chosen programming language. These libraries include tried and tested implementations for many different algorithms, which may generally be assumed to be correct.

Namespaces: Model and Operations

Most programming languages currently in use offer tools to facilitate the construction and maintenance of large software. Two approaches coexist, that of languages with modules and that of object-oriented languages; approaches that are different or even historically opposed but which in fact share many characteristics. This is why this chapter elaborates on a unique model of these two approaches by introducing a structure, referred to here as *kit*, as well as operations on these *kits*. We have chosen to introduce our own vocabulary for this study as programming languages sometimes use the same words to designate tools whose meanings differ significantly. The notion of a *kit* will be progressively enriched during its presentation. It will serve as a common framework to reflect the division of software into sub-systems, to explain management of names, export and import mechanisms, different possibilities of restricting access to elements of these *kits*, and extension mechanisms. Modules, classes and objects will be presented using this framework in the following chapters.

This chapter introduces a large number of notions which may seem difficult. It can be read in two passes. The first pass will give the reader an overview of the contents and may be followed by reading at least one of Chapters 2 or 3. This can be seen as a real exercise if, at the same time, the reader illustrates the notions with a few examples in the language they use. The second pass will then be an opportunity for the reader to deepen their understanding of these concepts.

At the end of each section, we pose a few questions that the reader can ask themselves when reading the reference manual of their favorite programming language. We call this language MYL in the statement of the questions. Chapters 2 and 3 will provide some examples of answers to these questions.

1.1. Reusing, dividing, confining

1.1.1. *Analysis of some developer needs*

We hope the contents of Volume 1 – at least in part – met the developer's need to produce programs that conformed to their specifications and that did not contain programming errors. The study of typing, execution semantics and the presentation of tools, such as constructed types and pattern matching, exceptions, etc., provided them with some responses. Developing a software system at a certain scale additionally requires that the programming languages used be able to satisfy some other *developer needs*; globally, these can be described by the words "reuse", "divide", "confine".

1.1.1.1. *Reusing*

Reusing parts of a software system is perhaps the developer's primary need. This reduces the cost and time for development, debugging and software maintenance (bug correction, performance improvement, etc.). Functions and procedures provide a first response to this need; but they are not suitable for reusing whole sections of code, if possible in a compiler-controlled manner.

1.1.1.2. *Dividing*

If a software specification is large enough, it is best to *divide* it into relatively independent parts, the communications between them being precisely stated and, if possible, automatically controlled. Today's programming languages provide tools to reflect this division of the specification into components, which can be separately developed then assembled to achieve a consistent software satisfying the specification. Very schematically, it is possible to split a specification by being guided by the nature of the data to be manipulated or by the actions to be performed. The first choice is that which is said to have led to the notions of class and object. The second would have rather led to the notion of module and then to the notion of functor. In the object-oriented framework, a data is usually strongly linked to the set of tools dedicated to its manipulation. In the modular framework, a data has an independent existence, without direct links to the tools that handle it, other than the typing ones. These two approaches are reminiscent of the notion of *abstract type*, introduced early on in both semantics and programming. In programming, an abstract type is a syntactic structure grouping together a data type and its manipulation tools. The theory of *Abstract Data Types* (ADT) gives a formal model of these structures; it is briefly presented in Chapter 2.

1.1.1.3. *Confining*

Maintaining program properties is not always easy, for example if several developers interact on the same software or, in the case of maintenance, if the software documentation is imprecise about these properties. We saw in section 6.5.2 of Volume 1 that typing allows us to define data structures respecting some invariants: for instance, a binary tree cannot have three branches starting from the same node. But these structures remain free in the sense that one cannot introduce restrictions on the values of a type. Some languages do allow such restrictions but their validity can only be checked at runtime which can lead to unscheduled, and therefore dangerous, execution aborting. Let us take the following example: how to encode binary trees in OCaml whose leaves can only be even natural integers. The following type is naturally defined.

EXAMPLE 1.1.–

```OCaml
type even_tree = Node of (even_tree * even_tree) | F of int
```

The values of type `even_tree` are binary trees whose leaves are integers: there are no means of restricting the possible values of leaves to even natural integers in this type declaration. The developer of this data representation can certainly offer tools for manipulating these trees which guarantee this invariant. But the user of type `even_tree` can build values of this type directly with leaves being odd integers, so without using the developer's offered tools. A mechanism is needed to make this type definition inaccessible – to *confine* it – and give only the information needed to use the developer's tools. The user of this type will be obliged to use only these tools to manipulate the `even_tree` values. Therefore the invariant will be respected. The control, in particular by static typing, done by the compiler can guarantee that this confinement will not be abused.

1.1.2. *Meeting developer needs*

Let us analyze some possible answers to divide, confine or reuse program fragments to identify rigorous and systematic construction methods for the development of software applications.

1) To help preservation of invariants, a programming language can have a syntactic structure devoted to grouping together definitions of types, functions, exceptions, etc., and to confine some of them by only providing the information necessary for their use outside this structure. This syntactic structure can even completely prevent the external use of certain names, making them invisible from the outside. Most languages offer such structures, named abstract types, modules, classes, packages, objects, etc. In order to study their common characteristics, maintaining a fairly general point of view, in this chapter we introduce our own syntactic construct called a *kit*. It will appear in the examples with the keyword Kit. In return, readers interested in modules, classes, etc., of a given language will be able to appropriate their semantics with the help of this notion of *kit*. Chapters 2 and 3 will present, respectively, modules, classes and objects from the *kit* approach.

The study of reuse leads to two distinct visions of the same functionality: that of its developer and that of its users. The developer creates a *kit* with a group of definitions (of types, expressions, procedures, exceptions, etc.). Thanks to the *export* mechanism (presented later), they can *confine* some of these definitions within the *kit* or decide to export them. Thanks to an *import* mechanism, a user of a definition exported by the *kit* can use its name and, according to the functionality of this definition, its parameters, its type, etc. In their code, the importer denotes an imported definition using a notation often called *dot-notation*, constructed with the name of the *kit* and the name of the definition.

Distinguishing between the roles of the importing user and the exporting developer allows us to better state certain questions. What specification needs does the developer have to satisfy? What are the reusable components for a new development? Is it possible to modify them? What are the consequences of these modifications for other uses? In other words, to borrow software engineering terminology, the developer sees a *kit* as a "white box" and the user sees it (rather) as a "black box".

It is essential that the compiler guarantees the consistency between the definitions in the *kit* and their export, the non-export of confined entities, the proper use of the exported definitions by their importers, and, in particular, the absence of any confinement bypassing. This can be done by the compilation process, making different so-called *static analyses*, and at least by typing analyses that extend those seen in Volume 1.

2) The introduction of such *kits* may only be allowed within the same program, which will be compiled into a single block. However, it is possible to go a little further by rendering these *kits* more autonomous:

a) The system architecture can be reflected in the software structure by representing each sub-system by a *kit*. This will provide the other sub-systems with the functionalities they need, but only those they need in order to respect the partitioning between sub-systems. The support for the maintenance of invariants will be facilitated.

b) Depending on languages' choices, confinement of parts of a *kit* can be directly integrated into its definition, or can be introduced after this definition to be well-tuned to every importer's needs.

c) The programming language can propose to compile each of these *kits* separately, making the object codes of these *kits* totally autonomous. This makes it possible to create libraries of object codes, thus facilitating reuse.

d) Confinement facilitates software maintenance. The effects of changing a definition are circumscribed to the *kit* introducing it if, however, the guidelines for using it remain unchanged. If the export is not modified, if the modifications have not changed the semantics of the definitions, the importer has nothing to modify in their own code.

e) The compiler can perform consistency checks at each step of creation/export/import of these *kits*, as parts of a complete development.

We begin our list of questions to help and guide learning of a language and the reading of its reference manual. The first question concerns some characteristics of the language and those that follow will address points discussed in this chapter. In the following chapters, during the presentation of a particular language, the simple mention of (Ans. *n*) will indicate that elements of the answer have just been given for question *n*.

QUESTION 1.1.– *How is the source language under consideration – referred to here as* MYL *– translated into binary code: is it compiled, interpreted or compiled to bytecode and then interpreted on a virtual machine? Does it offer both a compiler and an interpreter of the source code? Is* MYL *a typed language? Is it strongly typed (i.e. does every expression have one unique type)? Is it statically typed (typing done only by the compiler)? If not, does the language offer a notion of a type that prohibits certain operations or that determines the size of memory allocation?*

QUESTION 1.2.– *Does* MYL *offer at least one syntactic construct for the notion of* kit*? If not, how can this notion emerge from the functionalities of the language, using for example its file management, as we would do in C? (see the introduction of the concept of a* weak *kit in section 2.3.2)*

1.2. Namespaces

In the Chapters 3, 4 and 5 of Volume 1, a unique notion of identifier was used to introduce variables, new data types, exceptions, etc. Each of the analyses presented was implicitly aware of the role of the identifiers under consideration. The binding of an identifier present in an environment could only be masked during the evaluation of a local declaration. The identifier scopes were easy to determine by proofreading the program source.

The division of software into *kits* requires better explanation of the role of identifiers. What happens if a *kit* exports an identifier already used in the program being written by the importer? Can two occurrences of an identifier in the same expression have different bindings? Is it possible that several bindings are potentially usable for the same occurrence of an identifier? Answering these questions requires more complex modeling of the environment and the memory than the one given in Volume 1. We will describe this modeling in a more or less formal way, relying on the notions already studied in the first volume. The model allows us to determine precisely the bindings of each of the occurrences of an identifier of an expression during its typing and its execution. It will then be enough to apply the rules already seen in Volume 1 to complete typing and evaluation of this expression.

Examples will often be given with a syntax à *la* OCaml, using sum types and definitions by pattern matching introduced in Volume 1, simply to reduce the length of the codes presented.

1.2.1. *Namespaces definition*

In the compilation framework, the term *namespace* denotes the set of identifiers occurring in a program. The names occurring in the bindings of typing or execution environments, the record labels, etc., are elements of this namespace. In fact, most programming languages have a structured namespace, which is divided into several (sub) namespaces. Syntactic constructs provided to the user to declare their identifiers are also used to determine the namespace to which a given identifier should belong. These constructs can use keywords type, exception, var or syntactic conventions, such as putting the name of modules in uppercase. So the compilation process is simplified and code proofreading is made easier because the role of the identifiers is more easily recognizable. Programming languages can thus allow the use of the same identifier to name a type, an exception, a variable, a function, a procedure, etc. In other words, the same identifier can appear several times in the same expression, each of its occurrences being related to a type or value that may differ from those of the other occurrences. Note immediately that these possibilities sometimes make it easier to write source code but help proofreading only if they are used judiciously. We can see this in example 1.2, written in OCaml and quite exaggerated. The comments in the source code allow us to clarify the different uses of t.

EXAMPLE 1.2.–

```
OCaml
# type t = { t : int } ;;    (* type t1 = { t2 : int } *)
type t = { t : int; }
# let t t =                  (* let t3 t4 = *)
    let t = t + 1 in         (* let t5 = t4 + 1 in *)
    { t = t } ;;             (* t2 = t5 *)
val t : int -> t = <fun>     (* val t3 : int -> t1 = <fun> *)
# t 3 ;;                     (* t3 3 *)
- : t = {t = 4}             (* -: t1 = {t2 = 4} *)
```

This example uses the same identifier t for the name of a type, the name of a record field, the function name and the variable name. It even exploits name hiding by local definitions, and the fact that, it is possible to use the same name for the function and its argument, without conflict, as function t is not declared recursive. This kind of code writing is of course to be proscribed. However, the compiler of OCaml is able to process this example because each occurrence of t can only be accepted by a single rule of syntax analysis (presented in section 1.2.3 of Volume 1).

In the remainder of this chapter, the model that includes *kits* uses three namespaces:

– N_T the namespace of types;

– N_V the namespace grouping names denoting values, thus, constant identifiers, variables, functions, exception identifiers, etc;

– N_K the namespace of *kits*.

Example 1.3 is written assuming the language accepts that the same identifier can appear in several namespaces. To express this example, we use a hypothetical language, remaining just at the intuition level.

EXAMPLE 1.3.–

```
1 type person = (string * int)
2 Kit person = { ... }
3 exception person
4 person person = ("a", 20)
5 bool person = false
6 person := 25
```

Compiling example 1.3 in this way extends the namespaces as follows:

– adding person from line 1 to N_T since it is the name of a type;

– adding person from line 2 to N_K since it is the name of a *kit*;

– adding person from line 3 to N_V since it is the name of an exception value;

– adding person from line 4 to N_V since this line declares a variable by giving first its type, then its name and finally its definition. Will the name of the exception be hidden by the name of the variable or not? It depends on the language, the compiler can recognize that person declared in line 3 is an exception thanks to the keyword introducing it and can remove the ambiguity. It can also consider an exception just as a value of a known type (exn by example), which will be hidden by the declaration/definition of line 4;

– adding person from line 5 to N_V since it is the name of a variable. Is the name of the variable entered on line 4 being hidden or not? Again, it depends on the language. If this one accepts variable overloading, then the definitions of lines 4 and 5 are accepted because their types are different;

– will the compiler accept line 6? No, if the type declaration is mandatory, line 6 would then be interpreted as an assignment to one of the declared variables and would be considered ill-typed, unless the language accepts that 25 denotes a boolean value. Yes, if, on the one hand, the language accepts the introduction of a variable without type declaration and, on the other hand, if it accepts overloading because it can determine the type of 25. Line 6 (by replacing := by =) will then be understood as the introduction of a new variable person of type int and added to N_V.

The developer is thus led to refine the scope rules seen in Volume 1 in order to take into account the existence, or not, of different namespaces. If the same identifier is introduced by several declarations/definitions, there is not always masking of its previous bindings by the last declaration made. Techniques for removing ambiguities can be used. However, readers are advised to be careful when relying on them: it is necessary to make sure that they will clarify what the binding is of each occurrence of the multi-declared identifier throughout the source code. Remember that the presence of multi-declared identifiers does not ease proofreading.

Note that the expression "namespace" is used by some authors to actually denote the execution environment and to describe the scope of the identifiers. This can create confusion. The determination of the membership of an identifier to a namespace is made during the syntactic analysis by the compiler. The execution environment (also called the evaluation environment) evolves during execution, in accordance with the study in the Chapters 3 and 4 of Volume 1, which also explain the notions of scope of an identifier and masking (also called hiding).

1.2.2. *Extending notions of environment and binding*

Partitioning the global namespace into three (sub) namespaces induces the partition of any environment into three sub-environments (which are also called *environments*) described below.

Within this model, an environment Env $\in$ **E** is partitioned into Env$_T$, Env$_V$ and Env$_K$:

– Env$_T$ contains the binding of type names belonging to N_T to their definition;

– Env$_V$ contains the bindings of names of N_V to their value (resp. their type) during execution (resp. during typing) in Env;

– Env$_K$ contains the bindings of names (of *kit*) belonging to N_K to their values (or their types) introduced below.

Values and types were studied in Volume 1 using the notion of environment and memory. The notion of memory is left unchanged while that of environment is extended. With this extension, a typing analysis done in Env uses:

– bindings of Env$_T$;

– bindings to their type of names in N_V appearing in Env$_V$;

– typing information bound to the names of the *kits* appearing in Env_K.

If the language is statically typed, an execution (also called an evaluation) made in Env does not use the bindings of Env_T. It uses:

– bindings in Env_V of names (belonging to N_V) to their values;

– bindings in Env_K of names of *kits* to their values (defined further).

If type checking is (at least partly) done at runtime, the runtime typing-evaluation uses:

– bindings of Env_T;

– bindings in Env_V of names (belonging to N_V) to their types and to their values;

– bindings in Env_K of names of *kits* to their types and their values.

Programming languages differ not only in their typing verification methods but also by their notion of scope (lexical or dynamic or adapted according to the syntactic constructs). The distinction between the typing environment and the evaluation/execution environment is fading as typing can be started at compile-time and completed at runtime. To simplify the description of the semantics of these languages, we extend the notion of binding.

A binding will now be a tuple (identifier, information$_1$, information$_2$, etc.), the information simply being separated by commas, the first information being, by convention, the type of the identifier. If the type is not a given information (because the type is confined, for example), it will be noted by $\perp_t$. If a value is unknown (not yet initialized by example), it will be denoted by $\perp_v$. For example, in an untyped language, the binding of the identifier x can be $(x, \perp_t, \perp_v)$ if x is only declared, then will become $(x, \perp_t, v)$ after the evaluation of its definition having returned the value v. In a typed language, the type t of x will replace $\perp_t$ in both bindings.

The definition `let x = 1` introduces the binding (x, int, 1) in OCaml. The definition `type t = K of int` introduces two bindings (t , K of int) in Env_T and (K , int $\rightarrow$ t, Constructor) in Env_V. Here, mention of Constructor means that the compiler is aware of the particular status of K, as shown by example 1.4 reminding use of the distinction made by the OCaml compiler between a function f and a value constructor K.

EXAMPLE 1.4.–

```
OCaml
# type t = K of int ;;
type t = K of int
# K ;;
Error: The constructor K expects 1 argument(s),
       but is applied here to 0 argument(s)
# K 1 ;;
- : t = K 1
# let f x = 1 ;;
val f : 'a -> int = <fun>
# f ;;
- : 'a -> int = <fun>
```

With our extended definition of binding, we have only one kind of binding in our model, therefore one kind of environment. Depending on the nature of the analysis performed and the namespace to which an identifier belongs, the subset of information used for an analysis may be empty, may contain only type information, or only the (execution) value, or confinement modifiers, etc. If we use only typing information then we retrieve the typing environment used for static typing. If we use only the value, we retrieve the execution (or evaluation) environment. Ultimately, the important thing is that the developer or the user can model, within the bindings, all the information available on a given identifier at any moment of compilation or execution they are considering. This extension of bindings can help in grasping the meaning of the source code, along writing and proofreading.

Let us look at example 1.5, which uses the dot-notation for the identifiers of the *kit* P supposed to be imported. The types are not explicitly listed in the definitions to lighten the example.

EXAMPLE 1.5.–

```
1  Kit P
2    type person = A of (string * int)
3    fun age = function A (s, a) -> a
4    ...
5  end P

6  type client = C of P.person
7  var a_client = C (P.A ("Pierre", 14))
9  exception too_young
9  fun accept = function C (P.A (s, a)) ->
10   if (P.age (P.A (s, a)) < 12) then raise too_young
11   else s
```

After typing and evaluation of this fragment of program, using the previous notations for the three components of the environment, we have:

– after line 5, the binding (P, type_P, val_P) is added to Env$_K$, type_P and val_P being the type and the execution value of P described below;

– from line 6, the identifiers of P are visible with the dot-notation P.person and P.age. We will see later that the binding of P in Env$_K$ also provides access to the bindings (person, A of (string * int)) and (age, person -> int, FP), FP being the closure (value) of the function P.age;

– after line 7, the environment Env$_T$ has been extended with the binding (client, C of P.person);

– after line 11, Env$_V$ has been extended with the three bindings below. F is the value of accept, so a closure, containing the definition environment of F if the language is lexically scoped.

```
(a_client, client, C (P.A ("Pierre", 14)))
(too_young, exception, val_too_young)
(accept, client -> string, F)
```

We suppose that in example 1.6 the developer decides to confine the definition of the type person by marking confine as its definition.

EXAMPLE 1.6.–

```
1  Kit P
2    confine type person = A of (string * int)
3    fun age = function A (s, a) -> a
4    fun name = function A (s, a) -> s
5    fun build = function (s, a) -> A (s, a)
6  end P
7  type client = C of P.person
8  var a_client = C (P.build ("Pierre", 14))
9  exception too_young
10 fun accept = function C (x) ->
11   if P.age (x) < 12 then raise too_young else P.name (x)
```

The developer of P continues to see the binding (person, A of (string * int)) until the end of the definition of P. This is necessary so that, for example, they can correctly define the function age of type person -> int. At the end of the execution of line 6, the export mechanism applied to P is in place and provides importers (in other words, the users) of P, on the one hand, the binding (person, ⊥$_t$), ⊥$_t$ meaning this type is confined and, on the other hand, the functions of P with their types.

From line 7, the developer becomes the *importer* of P. The current environment Env$_K$ of line 7 gives access to the binding (P.person, ⊥$_t$), the identifier person being visible only as P.person. It also gives access to the binding of the functions of P since they are not confined. The definition of the variable a_client uses the function

P.build, provided by P, to define values of the confined type. The definition of the function accept is modified as – the definition of the type person being confined – it is no longer possible to decompose the actual parameter of the call to P.age by pattern matching (see line 10 of example 1.5). Therefore, the formal parameter of accept can no longer be completely decomposed, the constructor A of the type person being no longer visible.

In example 1.6, it was necessary to add to the *kit* P the function name to give access to the first argument of the constructor A and also the function age and the function build. If the name of this type person was also confined, then no binding of person would be offered to the user: the name of this type would be kept secret outside of P. The importer could no longer use the name person and therefore could not define the type client.

To conclude this section, we formulate two questions.

QUESTION 1.3.– *Does* MYL *have multiple namespaces? How is the membership of an identifier of a given namespace determined (syntactic construct, naming convention, etc.)?*

QUESTION 1.4.– *What is the general mechanism of scoping adopted by* MYL*? What forms of masking are accepted by* MYL*? Write – if needed – a program such as (exaggerated) example 1.2 to show prohibited/allowed masking.*

1.3. *kit* development

In this section, we define the notions of types and the values of *kits*. Here, we borrow a lot from different type theories, introduced to give a formal account of modular and object features, however these theories go far beyond the scope of this book. Although precise, our presentation remains informal in the sense that it does not allow for the proof of partial correction of typing. The limits and possible extensions of this model will be commented upon at the end of the chapter.

Let Lang_K be a language offering declarations/definitions of types and variables, functions, procedures, exceptions, etc., that is, all the features studied in Volume 1. This language also offers a syntactic construct introduced by the keyword Kit which defines a named entity, referred to here as *kit*. A *kit* name begins with an uppercase letter. The concrete syntax is defined as follows:

```
Kit K_ident = { component_1 ... component_n }
```

A *kit* component is introduced as follows:

1) a type declaration: type ident, for example, type person;

2) a type definition: `type ident = deftype`, for example, `type person = A of (string * int)`;

3) a variable declaration: `var ident: type`, for example, `var un_client: client`;

4) a variable definition: `var ident: type = def`, for example, `var un_client: client = ("Alan", 25)`;

5) a function (or procedure) declaration: `fun ident: type`, for example, `fun age: person -> int`;

6) a function (or procedure) definition: `fun ident : type = def`, for example, `fun age: person -> int = function A (n, a) -> a`;

7) an exception declaration: `exception ident`;

8) a definition of *kit*, called "internal *kit*", for example, `Kit Kit_ident = { component_a ... component_n }`.

In our concrete syntax, the introduction of a component begins with a keyword which specifies its nature, simply to facilitate reading and writing of the book. This is not always the case in programming languages. Example 1.7 illustrates this syntax. It is an implementation of a stack of integers that only memorize positive integers and ignore push requests of negative or null integers. It contains only definitions of types, variables and functions.

EXAMPLE 1.7.–

```
Kit Stack = {
  type t_stack = H of int list
  var floor : int = 0
  exception empty_stack : exn
  fun top : t_stack -> int =
    function p ->
      match p with
      | H [] -> raise empty_stack
      | H (h :: _) -> h
  fun push : (int * t_stack) -> t_stack =
    function (elt, (H l)) ->
      if elt > floor then H (elt :: l) else H l
  fun create_stack : unit -> t_stack = function () -> H []
}
```

The abstract syntax adopted for *kits* is as follows:

$$P = \{ \; l_1 : t_1 = e_1; \; \cdots; \; l_n : t_n = e_n \; \}$$

The components of a *kit* are of the form $l : t = e$ where l is the identifier of the component, referred to as the *field* of the component. All of the fields are supposed to be distinct and we suppose that this syntactic condition is always fulfilled, for example it can be verified by the compiler. t is the name of a type of $\mathbf{Lang}_K$ and e denotes an expression of $\mathbf{Lang}_K$ or a definition of type in $\mathbf{Lang}_K$. In example 1.7, the component expressed in the concrete syntax var floor : int = 0 is translated into the abstract syntax in floor : int = 0 where floor is the field of the component; the indication var is not integrated in the abstract syntax.

The text fragment "the component of field 1" will often be abbreviated to "the field 1" and the word component will be replaced with field when there is no need to distinguish between the component and its name.

Some definitions (represented by e_i in the abstract syntax) of components may be absent in the definition of a *kit*. In this case, the field is said to only be *not-defined* (or just declared). A *kit* is said to be *complete* if all of its components have received a definition. Otherwise, it is said to be *incomplete*. For example, the kit Stack of example 1.7 is complete.

WARNING.– The abstract syntax could lead to the conclusion that the notion of *kit* is just a kind of generalization of records, the components of the *kit* being the fields of these records. However, record fields, even if they can be of any type – including a functional type (as in OCaml, for example) – cannot be definitions of types, nor can they contain local declarations of variables or be defined by expressions using the names of the other fields. Records are only designed to encode structured data. The above example illustrates the difference between a *kit* and a record: the definition of the component whose field is push uses the field floor.

The syntax used to name imported components in a development is the dot-notation *P.l*, *P* being the name of the *kit* and *l* one of its fields. For example, importers of the *kit* Stack in example 1.7 can use the type t_stack denoting it by Stack.t_stack, call the function Stack.top, etc.

1.3.1. *Namespace of a* kit

In our model, we assume that every *kit*, say P, has its own namespace that we call $N(P)$, itself divided into sub-spaces of names, denoted $N(P)_T$, $N(P)_V$ and $N(P)_K$. Allowing a *kit* to have fields which are themselves *kits* leads to a kind of recursivity in the definition of $N(P)$ since $N(P)_K$ is the namespace of the "internal *kits*" defined in P, each of these *kits* having its own namespace, which is also divided into three namespaces, and so on.

In example 1.7, the *kit* Stack has 6 fields. The first field t_stack introduces the definition of the type t_stack. The second field, floor, defines a variable and so on. The namespace associated with Stack is divided into:

– $\text{N}(\text{Stack})_T = \{\, \texttt{t\_stack} \,\}$;

– $\text{N}(\text{Stack})_V = \{\, \texttt{floor},\ \texttt{empty\_stack},\ \texttt{top},\ \texttt{push},\ \texttt{create\_stack} \,\}$;

– $\text{N}(\text{Stack})_K = \emptyset$.

1.3.2. *Order of fields introduction*

Programming languages differ in their strategies for analyzing dependencies between declarations and definitions of *kit* components. The choice is twofold: either components can only use the fields of the components previously introduced in the *kit*, or any component can use any field of any component. Therefore, the chosen strategy defines what the allowed dependencies are between fields of the same *kit*.

The first possibility can be imposed on the developer of a *kit*, who must choose an order in which to introduce fields in the *kit*, according to the dependencies between them. This choice may also be left to the compiler, which will try to reorder fields to satisfy the strategy. The second possibility leads all definitions being considered mutually recursive definitions, this simplifies source coding but can complicate the static analyses performed by the compiler. In this section, for the sake of simplicity, we opt for the first choice. More precisely we make the hypothesis that the order of components in abstract syntax is such that a component depends only on those introduced previously. This allows us to give very simple definitions of the type and the value of a *kit*, without the need to introduce fixpoints for these definitions (see Chapter 4 of Volume 1 where fixpoints are studied). These simple notions of type and value will be developed later in the chapter, when some operations will be added to the *kits*. For example, in the case of confinement, it is also necessary to associate to a *kit* the information on the types and values it exports, i.e. the information made available to users.

1.3.3. *Typing* kits

In this section, we only consider *complete kits*, thus with all components defined. *Incomplete kits* will be studied in section 1.4.

Let Env be the current environment partitioned into Env_T, Env_V and Env_K. Any binding present in one of these environments associates an identifier with a set of information. Supposing that the language is statically typed and that types are declared by the user, the typing analysis will use the typing information enclosed in the different bindings. We just retrieve the typing environments of Chapter 5 of Volume 1. Our hypothesis on the order of fields in the source code of a *kit* induces the typing strategy. Typing of a *kit* is done by applying the typing rules given in Chapter 5 of Volume 1 to each field, following their order in the source code. As soon as a component of the *kit* has been typed, the binding of its field to its type is added to the (corresponding component of the) current environment and typing of the next component is done in this extended environment. So this strategy assumes that the types figuring in the *kit* are introduced before the components using them (such as those introduced by `var`, `fun` etc.).

Let P be a *kit* defined as follows: $P = \{\, l_1 : t_1 = e_1; \ldots; l_n : t_n = e_n \,\}$. The type of P, denoted P_{Type}, is defined by the collection of associations of its fields belonging to $N(P)_T$ with their type definitions and the associations of its other fields with the types of their definitions. It is described as follows:

$$P_{Type} = \{\, l_1 : t_1; \ldots; l_n : t_n \,\}$$

If $l_i \in N(P)_T$, then $t_i = e_i$ (we take the type definitions figuring in P), otherwise t_i is the type of e_i which is obtained by the typing algorithm used by the language $\mathbf{Lang}_K$. The typing rule of a *kit* is stated as follows:

$$(R_T)\, \frac{\forall i \in [1, n]\ (l_1, t_1) \boxplus \cdots \boxplus (l_{i-1}, t_{i-1}) \boxplus \mathrm{Env} \vdash e_i : t_i}{\mathrm{Env} \vdash P : P_{Type}}$$

where $\boxplus$ is an operation which adds the binding of the field l to the right component of Env, according to the contents of l.

As soon as the type of P is determined, the binding associating P to P_{Type} is added to Env_K. It allows us to find the types of components of P thanks to the dot-notation $P.l$, which gives access to the binding of P in Env_K so to P_{Type} and then to the type of the field l.

Again, let us take example 1.7 which defines the *kit* `Stack`. The type of this *kit* contains, among others, the association of `t_stack` with the definition `H` of `int list` and the association of `top` with the type `t_stack -> int`. With a concrete syntax similar to the one adopted for *kits*, this type is written:

```
type Stack = {
   type t_stack = H of int list
   var floor : int
   exception empty_stack : exn
   fun top : t_stack -> int
   fun push : int -> t_stack  -> t_stack
   fun create_stack : unit -> t_stack
}
```

The strategy of typing presented above will be reused for the evaluation of a *kit* and will be detailed there.

In our model, fields are an integral part of the type of a *kit*. Two *kits* having components of the same type but differing in their fields do not have the same type. We also make the hypothesis that two *kits* having different names are not equal. So the chosen typing system is *nominal* (also called *named-based*). Type equality was discussed in section 6.6 of Volume 1.

WARNING.– In fact, this presentation of *kit* types and typing, reminiscent of record typing, is far too simple to completely handle all the features and operations on *kits* (functors, inheritance, etc.). It has the advantage only of providing an intuitive approach to *kit* typing and more or less corresponding to the typing discipline of most typed object-oriented languages. But it may also seem too complicated to be applied to some languages such as Python, which do not require declarations of fields to be typed and which do not make type inference but perform certain type checks at runtime. See example 1.8, using the interactive mode of Python.

EXAMPLE 1.8.–

```
Python
$ python3
>>> class C:
...     x = 5
...
>>> print ("value of the field C.x:", C.x, "; type of C.x:", type (C.x))
value of the field C.x: 5;type of C.x: <class 'int'>

>>> C.x = 'aa'
>>> print ("After assignment, the value of C.x is:", C.x, "; its type is:", \
    type (C.x))
After assignment, the value of C.x is: aa ; its type is: <class 'str'>

>>> 3 + C.x
Traceback (most recent call last):
  File "<stdin>", line 1, in <module>
TypeError: unsupported operand type(s) for +: 'int' and 'str'
```

The assignment C.x = 'aa' apparently changes the type of the field x. Python is dynamically typed and the type of a field may change at runtime. On the other hand, the operator + cannot be applied to an integer and a string (which is the value of C.x after the assignment) because + is not bound in the current environment to any functional value able to do this addition.

Of course, no one writes such code right away. But these modifications of *kit* fields can be made in any code which has access to the class C. This example, conforming to the semantics of Python, will be reviewed in section 4.4 to detail the meaning of this assignment operation, which explains and justifies the answers of Python. In any case, maintaining a typing discipline, even if the language does not require it, is a good practice in writing *kits* because it ensures some logical consistency of the written source code. This leads to some questions.

QUESTION 1.5.– *Does* MYL *possess a notion of type of a kit? If so, what is the link between the name of a* kit *and the name of its type?*

QUESTION 1.6.– *Are the fields of* kits *typed? Are their types declared by the developer or synthesized by the compiler?*

QUESTION 1.7.– *Let* P1 *and* P2 *be two* kits *having the same fields associated with the same types. Do* P1 *and* P2 *have the same type? Or, is* MYL *typing strictly nominal?*

QUESTION 1.8.– *This question covers all types (if any) in* MYL. *Is it possible to make explicit a conversion of a type* t_1 *to a type* t_2? *Does* MYL *perform implicit conversion of types, at least in some cases? Identify these cases.*

QUESTION 1.9.– *May two components of a* kit *having different types be named by the same field? In other words, if* MYL *accepts some form of overloading of fields, is it allowed?*

1.3.4. kit *values*

We continue to consider only *complete kits.* So far, in our model, the evaluation of a syntactic construct produces either a side effect or a value, sometimes called the *execution value* (or *runtime value*). This value is not always a *first class value*, that is, a value that can, for example, be returned as a result (see Volume 1 for a precise definition of all these kinds of values). We extend this model with the notion of *kit value*. In some languages, *kit* values are not first-class, they are only runtime values. This is quite often the case with modules and classes. But these *kit* values can also be first class values and it is quite often the case with objects. The intuitive presentation which follows can be applied to both kinds of values; the issues specific to first class *kit* values will be discussed in Chapters 2 and 3.

Let us first consider a *kit* P whose fields are not type definitions nor *kit* definitions. The value of this *kit* is then built as the collection of the values of its components denoted by:

$$P_{Value} = \{ \ l_1 = v_1; \ \ldots; \ l_n = v_n \ \}$$

where v_i is the value of the component whose field is l_i.

Let us detail the evaluation of P, assuming the field definitions are evaluated in the order of its abstract syntax. Let us also assume that the language is statically typed. The typing has therefore already been done. The evaluation does not perform any type checking and therefore uses only the accessible values in the bindings of the current environment. To evaluate a *kit*, we follow the strategy used for typing, each step of evaluation being done with the evaluation/execution rules of Chapters 3 and 4 of Volume 1.

Let $E = (\text{Env}_0, \text{Mem}_0)$ be the current state at the beginning of the evaluation of the *kit* P where $\text{Env}_0 = (\text{Env}_T, \text{Env}_V, \text{Env}_K)$.

The evaluation of the first field, say $l_1 \in P_V$, in $(\text{Env}_0, \text{Mem}_0)$ with our convention, returns a value v_1 and modifies the state E which becomes the new state:

$$((\text{Env}_T, (l_1, v_1) \oplus \text{Env}_V, \text{Env}_K), \text{Mem}_1)$$

Mem_1 will differ from Mem_0 if the evaluation of e_1 produces side effects. The value v_i of each field l_i is then obtained in the same manner, by following the order of the fields in the source code. Every evaluation extends the current environment and possibly modifies the memory.

At the end of the evaluation of P, bindings added to Env_V disappear and the binding (P, P_{Value}) is added to Env_K. The resulting environment is therefore $(\text{Env}_T, \text{Env}_V, (P, P_{Value}) \oplus \text{Env}_K)$. The memory remains in the state reached at the end of the complete evaluation, as the execution of some components may cause side effects.

However, the components of a *kit* can also be type definitions, for which no (runtime) value has been defined. We then have the small difficulty of writing values bypassed as follows. Strictly speaking, fields belonging to N_T should not figure in a *kit* value. But this requires the renumbering of the l_i fields. To avoid this and thus maintain a uniform presentation of *kits* in abstract syntax, we assign a fictive value $\emptyset_t$ to any field introducing a type.

Moreover, some fields of a *kit* P can be *kits* themselves. Their evaluation is done in the current state reached by evaluation of the fields written before them in the source code of P and follows the strategy we have just described.

Note that, if the language has lexical scope, if the definition of a field $P.l_i$ is a function whose body contains an occurrence of the field $P.l_j$, then the value of $P.l_i$ is a closure that contains the binding of $P.l_j$ to its value.

Under lexical scope, the evaluation rule of a *kit* is as follows:

$$(R_E)\frac{\forall i \in [1, n] \; (l_1, v_1) \boxplus \cdots \boxplus (l_{i-1}, v_{i-1}) \boxplus \text{Env} \vdash e_i \rightsquigarrow v_i}{\text{Env} \vdash P \rightsquigarrow P_{Value}}$$

In the case of dynamic typing, the evaluation of a field l_i starts by the typing verification of its definition, followed by the evaluation itself, and it uses the type information present in the bindings of the current environment. The description of the evaluation made for statically typed languages can be taken over but the result is twofold: the type t_i and the value v_i are returned and the name l_i is bound to the two sets of information t_i and v_i.

We have not yet detailed the evolution of the environment alongside the evaluation of *kits*. We do so now, considering only the evaluation of *kit* Stack from example 1.7. We assume that the language uses lexical scope and that the current state is $(\mathrm{Env_0}, \mathrm{Mem_0})$. Let $\mathrm{Env_{0T}}$, $\mathrm{Env_{0V}}$, and $\mathrm{Env_{0K}}$ be the components of $\mathrm{Env_0}$:

1) evaluation of field type t_stack = H of ... extends the environment $\mathrm{Env_{0T}}$ to $\mathrm{Env_{1T}} = (\texttt{t\_stack}, \emptyset_t) \oplus \mathrm{Env_{0T}}$. The other components of the environment $\mathrm{Env_1}$ so obtained are those of $\mathrm{Env_0}$: $\mathrm{Env_{0V}} = \mathrm{Env_{1V}}$ and $\mathrm{Env_{1K}} = \mathrm{Env_{0K}}$;

2) evaluating exception empty_stack extends the environment $\mathrm{Env_{1V}}$ to $\mathrm{Env_{2V}} = (\texttt{empty\_stack}, \texttt{exception}) \oplus \mathrm{Env_{1V}}$;

3) evaluating var floor = 0 extends $\mathrm{Env_{2V}}$ to $\mathrm{Env_{3V}} = (\texttt{floor}, 0) \oplus \mathrm{Env_{2V}}$;

4) in the same way, evaluation of the definition fun top p = match p with ... returns the closure $F_1 = \langle \texttt{p}, \texttt{match p}, \ldots, \mathrm{Env_3} \rangle$ and extends $\mathrm{Env_{3V}}$ to $\mathrm{Env_{4V}} = (\texttt{top}, F_1) \oplus \mathrm{Env_{3V}}$;

5) and evaluating fun push elt H l = if ... in $\mathrm{Env_4}$ returns the closure $F_2 = \langle \texttt{elt, H (l), if}, \ldots, \mathrm{Env_4} \rangle$ and extends $\mathrm{Env_{4V}}$ to $\mathrm{Env_{5V}} = (\texttt{push}, F_2) \oplus \mathrm{Env_{4V}}$;

6) The evaluation of the last field fun create_stack () = H [] in $\mathrm{Env_5}$ returns the closure $F_3 = \langle \_, \texttt{H ([])}, \mathrm{Env_5} \rangle$ and extends $\mathrm{Env_{5V}}$ to $\mathrm{Env_{6V}} = (\texttt{create\_stack}, F_3) \oplus \mathrm{Env_{5V}}$.

The evaluation of the *kit* Stack is finished. The value of Stack is:

$$\mathrm{Stack}_{Value} = \{\, \texttt{t\_stack} = \emptyset_t;\ \texttt{empty\_stack} = exception;\ \texttt{floor} = 0; \\ \texttt{top} = F_1;\ \texttt{push} = F_2;\ \texttt{create\_stack} = F_3 \,\}$$

During this evaluation, the source code of Stack was *de facto* considered as a sequence of local definitions in the *kit*, thus placing this execution analysis within the framework defined in Volume 1, Chapters 3 and 4. The environments built during the evaluation of Stack disappear but remain stored in the closures, which are values of functional fields of Stack, to conform to lexical scoping. The evaluation of the definition of Stack extends the current environment into:

$$\mathrm{Env}_T, \mathrm{Env}_V, (\mathrm{Stack}, \mathrm{Stack}_{Type}, \mathrm{Stack}_{Value}) \oplus \mathrm{Env}_K$$

In this example with no side effects, the memory remains the same throughout the evaluation of the *kit*.

We recall that this evaluation was carried out under the assumption that fields are evaluated in the order of their presentation in the source code. This is the case in OCaml: the first line of example 1.9 has been rejected because the field y is used before being introduced.

EXAMPLE 1.9.–

```
OCaml
# module M = struct let x = y + 1 let y = 3 end ;;
Error: Unbound value y
# module M = struct let y = 3 let x = y + 1 end ;;
module M : sig val y : int val x : int end
```

Example 1.10 shows that Java makes the same choice.

EXAMPLE 1.10.–

```
Java
class MC {
  int x = y + 1 ;
  int y ;
  MC (int a , int b) {
    this.x = a ; this.y = b ;
  }
  public static void main (String args[]) { ... }
}
```

```
$ javac MC.java
MC.java:4: error: illegal forward reference
    int x = y + 1 ;
            ^1 error
```

Here follow some questions about the definition and evaluation of a *kit*.

QUESTION 1.10.– *In* MYL, *is the order of the fields of a* kit *important? Can a field use a field that is defined after it in the source code?*

QUESTION 1.11.– *May a field have a recursive definition without mentioning it using a keyword like* rec*? Is there a possibility of mutual recursivity between several fields?*

QUESTION 1.12.– *Apart from its fields, can a* kit *contain a block of instructions declaring, for example, local variables to the* kit *and performing any side effects? When is this block executed?*

QUESTION 1.13.– *Are the functions of* MYL *first class values?*

QUESTION 1.14.– *Are the* kits *of* MYL *first class values? (see Chapters 2 and 3 to for further explanation).*

1.3.5. kit *export, confining fields*

The frontier between development and usage of a *kit* was discussed in section 1.1. Remember that any operation on a *kit* is the responsibility of the developer. The importer can only use the fields of the imported *kit* (even if the developer and the importer are the same person). In this section, we study the confinement operation and the resulting mechanism of exports. We will see in section 1.7 that this confinement operation does not only serve to restrict exports. It is also used to control certain operations on *kits*, such as the addition of fields. It is important to make a clear distinction between these two different roles, as explained in the following.

We have seen in Volume 1 that the evaluation of a local declaration can hide a binding already present in the current environment. This masking concerns the whole code written by the developer in the scope of this declaration and ceases at the end of this scope. When the local binding disappears, the hidden binding is again visible. In general, no syntactical mark points out this hiding. The confinement of a type definition, of a value, etc., is a very different kind of operation, its objective is to restrict access to some *kit* fields to importers. It is denoted in the source code by a syntactic construct. The confinement operation of a *kit* P acts on the visibility of P fields after the export operation. Depending on the language, it can be carried out in two different ways.

– Restricting export possibilities of a field can be done by adding a mark on it, which can be a keyword or a modifier like `protected`, `private`, etc. The confinement achieved by marking some fields of a *kit* depends on the language: the marks `private` of Ada, Java or OCaml do not have the same meaning.

A field `type ident = deftype` can be marked so as to authorize the export of `ident` and to prohibit the export of `deftype`. The name `ident` can also remain confined by using another mark.

A mark on a field that defines a value can prohibit the export of the field name which is therefore not usable outside of the kit (see the mark `private` of Ada in Chapter 2).

Confining by marking fields in this way is typical of object-oriented languages (see Chapter 3). The exporter sets the conditions of field exports directly into the source code of the *kit*, according to categories of importers defined by the language. For example, in Java, a field of a class C marked `protected` can only be used to define classes belonging to the same group of files (called a *package*) as C. So the mark `protected` has some consequences on later stages of Java software developments importing C.

– Confinement can be conceived in a more flexible way in order to meet the needs of different importers. This implies that the confinement is defined outside the source code of the *kit*. One can either indicate which fields are to be confined or which fields are to be exported to comply with importer requirements. The confinement can be expressed by a type or a dedicated syntactic construct, sometimes called the *interface*. This is the case, for example, for the OCaml modules (see section 2.2), which can adapt field visibility to each importer's needs, as will be seen in Chapter 2. Incidentally, note that the word "interface" is used by many programming languages, but with quite different meanings.

We now consider the confinement mechanism(s) that can be used to export a *kit*. Let M be the confinement information which we are making explicit. For example, for the *kit* P of example 1.6, $M = \texttt{confine type person}$. In OCaml, we study the confinement obtained by the restriction put on the type t_1 of a *kit* P defined by a "more constraining" type t_2 and M will then be $M = \{P : t_2\}$ (see Chapter 2).

We note $RP = \mathsf{From(P,M)}$ the export operation of P, according to the confinement indication M, RP is the name given to the result of this export. For the moment, denoting the confinement information by M is sufficient, there is no need to know its contents explicitly. We will distinguish between the two possibilities of confinement when necessary.

With or without confinement, the export of a *kit* P should allow importers to use exported fields without needing to access the source code of P. In return, importers must not make any assumptions about the implementation of exported fields from P. This is the very principle of the "off the shelf" component software libraries.

Export does not build a new *kit* but provides the importer with access to the P exported "part", named RP, consisting of a set of component names, associated with their types (if the language requires type declaration). An importer can use a field l exported by P by naming it $RP.l$. In some languages (often in object languages) the P and RP identifiers are identical. In other languages, RP is considered to be a new *kit*, which is not totally correct because there is always some sharing at object-code level between P and RP components.

The definition of any component of a *kit* P can, without restriction, use the name (field), the type and the value of another component totally or partially confined in P: the export operation does not constrain the developer of the *kit* themselves. As soon as the *kit* P has been completely defined, its fields can be used immediately with the dot-notation in the source code, provided it is done in accordance with the confinement: once the *kit* P is built, the developer becomes an importer of P for the continuation of source writing.

The operation $RP = \mathsf{From(P,M)}$ produces, from the field $P.\texttt{ident}$, a set of information in accordance with the mention M of confinement. We describe below the information that is provided by the confinement of a field, according to its nature and M requirements. We denote by From(1) the result of the confinement operation applied to a field 1 and we use the concrete syntax to informally describe it. Of course From(l) returns 1 if this field is not confined:

1) if ident $\in N(P)_T$, we can only confine the definition of the type. Only the name of the type ident is then exported:

From(type ident = typedef) $=$ type ident

In this case, importers cannot directly define values of this type ident nor can they define functions by pattern matching on the values of ident. Only the fields exported by the *kit* P can be used to manipulate values of type ident;

2) the restriction on ident $\in N(P)_T$ may be stronger: the name ident of the type can be confined:

From(type ident = typedef) produces nothing.

The importer will have no way of knowing this type. In addition, if the type of a field l contains occurrences of ident, then l must also be confined because an expression of the importer using l could not be typed;

3) an exception ident can be confined. The importer will not be able to raise it or catch it with the name ident. Be careful, this exception can, however, be caught up by an exception handler with a case *by default* intercepting all exceptions raised (see section 8.2 of Volume 1):

From(exception ident) produces nothing;

4) If the name ident of a component which is a variable (var in our concrete syntax) or a function (fun) is confined, then the field ident is not exported:

From(var ident :   type = def) produces nothing;

5) Otherwise, the name ident and the type of a not-confined component, which is a variable or a function var (or fun), are provided to importers who can use all of the information:

From(var ident :   type = def) $=$ var ident :   type

6) If ident $\in N(P)_K$, ident is the name of a *kit*, which can be confined: this internal *kit* ident is not exported:

From(kit ident :   type = def) produces nothing;

7) Alternatively the developer may confine some fields of the internal *kit* ident by applying the operation From on the fields of ident.

The importer is not aware of the existence of a totally confined field. In other words, this field is not visible to the importer. *This does not necessarily mean that the value of this field is inaccessible because any other field of P can use the confined field and reveal its value.*

If the field l is not exported, if instead there is an occurrence of the name $P.l$ in the importer's source code, we make the hypothesis that the compiler will reject this source through a preliminary analysis (syntactic analysis, scope analysis) or ultimately by a typing analysis, and we do not handle this case in the following.

The export operation computes the type RP_{Type} and the value RP_{Value} of RP taking into account confinement indications. Let P be a *kit*, whose type is $P_{Type} = \{ l_1 : t_1; \ldots; l_n : t_n \}$ and value is $P_{Value} = \{ l_1 = v_1; l_n = v_n \}$. Let us consider the question of expressing the type and value of RP. The only way is to refer to types and values of P fields. Mentioning in the RP type and value all the P fields cannot be correct. Simply removing those fields of P which are not exported would create some "holes" in the numbering of the RP fields if we keep the numbering of P fields. For example, if $P = \{ l_1 ; l_2 ; l_3 \}$, if l_2 is not exported, then writing $RP = \{ l_1 ; l_3 \}$ requires mention of the absence of l_2 and this solution is not easily generalized to n fields. Our solution is as follows.

If m fields among the n fields of P are exported, we define a set of indices $\{ a_1, a_2, \ldots, a_j, \ldots, a_m \}$ and we note $RP = \{ l_{a_1} \ldots; \ldots; l_{a_m} \}$ making the hypothesis that for any $j \in [1, m]$, there is a unique $k \in [1, \ldots, n]$ such that the field $RP.l_{a_j}$ is obtained by exporting the field $P.l_k$. Therefore the export operation builds the collection of exported fields $\{ l_{a_j} \mid j = 1, \cdots, m \}$ named RP, which are defined as follows:

– Let us suppose that the indication of confinement M is given independently of the definition of P:

- if the field l_k introduces the definition of a type t_k and if this definition is confined, then the type associated with $RP.l_{a_j}$ is $\perp_t$ otherwise it is t_k;

- if l_k introduces the definition of a value of type t_k, if this definition is not confined then the type associated to $RP.l_{a_j}$ is t_k and its value is v_k;

Therefore, the type and value exported by P can be written:

$$RP_{Type} = \{ l_{a_1} : t_{a_1}; \ldots; l_{a_m} : t_{a_m} \} \quad \text{where } t_{a_j} = t_k \text{ if } l_{a_j} = l_k$$
$$RP_{Value} = \{ l_{a_1} = v_{a_1}; \ldots; l_{a_m} = v_{a_m} \} \quad \text{where } v_{a_j} = v_k \text{ if } l_{a_j} = l_k$$

– if the confinement marks are carried by the fields, then they must be stored in the type and/or value of P to be used when verifying import operations (and extension operations, studied later) either at compile-time or runtime. We note this marks c_i and include them in the type of P, by placing them before the fields. Therefore, in our model, a field of P is now bound to a set of information build up with its type, its value and its confinement mark. The type of a *kit* P is now written: $P_{Type} = \{ c_1 \, l_1 : t_1; \ldots; c_n \, l_n : t_n \}$. The export operation keeps the marks on fields of RP. The type of RP is therefore written: $RP_{Type} = \{ c_{a_1} \, l_{a_1} : t_{a_1}; \ldots; c_{a_m} \, l_{a_m} : t_{a_m} \}$. The value of RP is identical to the one given in the previous point.

Note that, unless the definition of the type of a field is confined, the type of an exported field is the same in P and in RP.

An expression e in the source code of the importer can use an exported field $RP.l_2$, even though the definition of l_2 in P uses a confined field l_1 (which is not in RP). Indeed, the value of $RP.l_2$ is that of $P.l_2$ and was obtained by the evaluation of P. Refusing such an indirect use of l_1 would in fact amount to prohibiting the use of l_2. More fundamentally, this refusal would force us to modify the notions of type and execution value of a field, which would depend not only on the current typing and evaluation environments of P, but also on any decision taken later on other fields. Therefore, during typing and evaluation of the importer's code, any expression containing the field $RP.l_2$ can be typed and evaluated, even if the definition of the field $P.l_2$ uses the confined field $P.l_1$.

Example 1.11 continues example 1.7; we confine the definition of the type t_stack by marking it with confine-def and the field floor by marking it with confine. So, $M =$ (confine-def t_stack, confine floor).

EXAMPLE 1.11.–

```
Kit Stack = {
  confine-def type t_stack = H of int list
  confine var floor = 0
  exception empty_stack
  fun top p =
    match p with
    | H [] -> raise empty_stack
    | H (h :: _) -> h
  fun push elt (H l) =
    if elt > floor then H (elt :: l) else H (l)
  fun create_stack () = H []
}
```

The type of Stack is now written:

$$Stack_{Type} = \{ \text{confine-def t\_stack} : \text{H of int list}; \text{confine floor} : \text{int}; \\ \text{empty\_stack} : \text{exn}; \text{top} : \text{t\_stack} \to \ldots ; \\ \text{push} : \text{int} \to \ldots ; \text{create\_stack} : \text{unit} \to \text{t\_stack} \}$$

Let RStack = From(Stack,M). The type of RStack is the following

$$\text{RStack}_{Type} = \{\, \texttt{t\_stack} : \perp_t \,;$$
$$\texttt{empty\_stack} : \texttt{exn}\,; \texttt{top} : \texttt{t\_stack} \rightarrow \dots\,;$$
$$\texttt{push} : \texttt{int} \rightarrow \dots\,;\ \texttt{create\_stack} : \texttt{unit} \rightarrow \texttt{t\_stack}\,\}$$

We recall the value of Stack:

$$\text{Stack}_{Value} = \{\, \texttt{t\_stack} = \emptyset_t;\ \texttt{empty\_stack} = \texttt{exception};\ \ \texttt{floor} = 0;$$
$$\texttt{top} = F_1; \texttt{push} = F_2;\ \texttt{create\_stack} = F_3\,\}$$

The value of RStack is the following:

$$\text{RStack}_{Value} = \{\, \texttt{empty\_stack} = \texttt{exception};$$
$$\texttt{top} = F_1\,; \texttt{push} = F_2\,;\ \texttt{create\_stack}, F_3\,\}$$

The types and values of fields of a *kit* are computed by the compilation/runtime process and are not modified by confinement. Exported fields that are not types keep their type and value. Remember that if one of the fields of a *kit* P is a type t with a confined definition, the importer can do nothing with the mere knowledge of this name t. So P must export creation and manipulation tools for the values of type t. If the name t is also confined, making its values accessible to importers requires the export of components accessing it indirectly, in such a way that the type t does not appear explicitly in the exported component types (a point to handle if confining t is done to keep secret the values of t). Section 2.2.3 will resume all of these points using OCaml.

WARNING.– Confining a type or a value does not guarantee that this type or value cannot be indirectly recovered by importers. In addition, some languages provide tools to get information on confined types or values, a point which can lead to serious security problems.

We extend the list of questions to be raised when reading a reference manual, as follows:

QUESTION 1.15.– *The file management made jointly by the language and the operating system may offer some form of export/import. Does* MYL *allow for confining values or types apart from a kit mechanism? See the definition of weak kits in Chapter 2.*

QUESTION 1.16.– *How is confinement of kits defined in* MYL*? Is there some interaction between confinement and the management of language libraries through some marks (as* protected*, for example)?*

QUESTION 1.17.– *Is the name of the confined* kit *different to that of the original* kit? *Is it possible that the two names are identical?*

QUESTION 1.18.– *Is it possible to define several confinements for the same* kit?

QUESTION 1.19.– *Does* MYL *consider that the type of the confined* kit *is the same as that of the original* kit?

1.3.6. kits *import*

In this section, we adopt the importer's point of view on the result of the operation $RP = $ From(P,M). Remember that the importer has no way of performing an operation on the imported *kit*: they have no access to the source text of P. This vision of the importer allows for positioning the frontier between pure reuse and continuation of *kit* development, started earlier (for extending it, by example).

1.3.6.1. *Import operation*

The import of RP is done by an operation referred to here as With(RP). The name RP must be known to the importer: either RP has already been defined in the source program being written or it belongs to an external library and its name is known after *loading*.

This import can be made explicit in the source itself, for example using the keyword with in Ada, from/import in Python, or it may remain implicit, the simple use of the complete name of the *kit* indicating the import request. This complete name may mention, in addition to the name of the *kit* itself, the path to the *kit* in the system libraries. For example, in Java, one can access the class array by naming it java.util.array, the *package* (i.e. the library) util being included in the standard library, named java, which the compiler can access through the Java installation.

Any field l of a *kit* P can be used in importer programs under two conditions: on the one hand, the name P must be visible to the importer, on the other hand, the developer of P must have decided to export this field l. In the expressions of his source code, the importer denotes the field l by a *qualified* identifier, formed with the name of the *kit*, a separator and the name of the field. The separator is often a dot, hence the name "dot-notation" for qualified identifiers. In this case, the qualified name of l is $P.l$.

We now describe our model of the import operation. Let $\text{Env} = (\text{Env}_T, \text{Env}_V, \text{Env}_K)$ be the current typing/evaluation environment. The import operation With(RP) extends Env_K with the binding of RP to its type RP_{Type} and to its value RP_{Value}, in accordance with the following rule:

$$((\text{Env}_T, \text{Env}_V, \text{Env}_K), \text{Mem}_0) \xrightarrow[\text{With}(RP)]{} \textbf{Def}_6$$
$$(\text{Env}_T, \text{Env}_V, (RP, (RP_{Type}, RP_{Value})) \oplus \text{Env}_K, \text{Mem}_1)$$

This operation makes the fields of RP and their types visible to the importer, they can use them in their code using the dot-notation. It ensures consistency between import and export, with or without confinement. A compiler can check this consistency, for example, by typing.

Let us go back to the type of RP, from the importer's point of view. We recall this type seen in the previous section:

$$RP_{Type} = \{\, c_{a_1}\, l_{a_1} : t_{a_1};\ \ldots;\ c_{a_m}\, l_{a_m} : t_{a_m} \,\}$$

Let us assume that the field l_{a_1} is a type whose definition is confined (and that, to simplify the description, this field is the only confined type). The types of the other fields of RP_{Type} can contain occurrences of l_{a_1} (for example, the type of a field l that prints a value of type l_{a_1} is $l_{a_1} \rightarrow$ unit). Let e be an expression of the importer using l_{a_1}. To type e, the compiler cannot make any hypothesis on l_{a_1} since the only information available on l_{a_1} is that this type exists because it has a name. To account for this meaning of the name l_{a_1}, we can extend the syntax of the type language by an existential quantifier $\exists$, abstracting all occurrences of l_{a_1} in the types t_{a_j}. The type of RP can then be expressed as follows:

$$RP_{Type} = \exists\, l_{a_1} \cdot \{\, c_{a_1}\, l_{a_1};\ \ldots;\ c_{a_m}\, l_{a_m} : t_{a_m} \,\}$$

We also have to add an introduction rule and an elimination rule of this existential quantifier to the typing rules studied in Chapter 5 of Volume 1 and modify the typing algorithm to apply these rules. The algorithm will then be able to check the *consistency of import towards export*, that is, to ensure that uses of the exported fields of P in the source code of an importer are compliant with the confinement semantics.

Adding existential types to the family of types makes it possible to precisely model and verify type confinement. The presentation of this extension is beyond the scope of this book but it is well studied in type theories for programming languages. To intuitively analyze typing in the case of confinement, the importer can consider that the field denoting a confined type is the unique constructor of a constant type, completely opaque in the sense that no information is available on values of this type.

Let us justify the evolution of memory in the import rule. Some fields in a *kit RP* can be mutable. In this case, a memory area is allocated to each mutable field by the operation With(RP), so the current memory is modified. The initialization of this memory area can be done during the With(RP) operation. Otherwise, it is imperative to do so before the first reading of these fields (as for any mutable variable). Similarly, a *kit P* may have fields whose evaluation performs a side effect. The evaluation of With(RP) triggers these side effects, sometimes with very surprising consequences (see article [JAE 14]). As a general rule, side effects in the *kits* are not recommended. The Example 1.12 in OCaml illustrates this point and demonstrates the consequences of an omission of () in the definition of show. The "involuntary" side effect displaying loading of S: 25 after loading of the module S is not reproduced by loading the module Sbis, the addition of a parameter () to show modifying the type of show.

EXAMPLE 1.12.–

```
OCaml
# module S = struct
  let v = 25
  let show = Format.printf "chargement de S : %d\n" v
  end ;;
chargement de S : 25
module S : sig val v : int val show : unit end
# module Sbis = struct
  let v = 25
  let show () = Format.printf "chargement de Sbis : %d\n" v
end ;;
module Sbis : sig val v : int val show : unit -> unit end
```

The following questions concern the names of the *kits* imported from the same *kit*.

QUESTION 1.20.– *In* MYL, *can a* kit P *be imported under two different names* RP_1 *and* RP_2 *in the same source code?*

QUESTION 1.21.– *If the answer to the previous question is yes, does the typing consider that the type of the* kit RP_1 *is different from the type of the* kit RP_2?

QUESTION 1.22.– *Does* MYL *accept some form of compatibility between types* RP_1 *and* RP_2?

QUESTION 1.23.– *If P exports a type t whose definition is confined, does the typing consider that the type* $RP_1.t$ *is different from the type* $RP_2.t$? *Apply the same question to other exported fields.*

1.3.6.2. *Flattening import*

Let P be the name of an *imported kit* and l_i be one of its fields. The notation $P.l_i$ unambiguously designates this field l_i, which makes it easier to review programs. Some developers find it a bit heavy. Some languages thus offer the operation $\mathsf{Flat}(P)$ which places, in the current environment Env, bindings of P fields with their type and/or value.

Let P_T, P_V, and P_K be the namespaces introduced by P. Let Env_T, Env_V, and Env_K be the three parts of an environment Env. To execute $\mathsf{Flat}(P)$ in Env, the name P of the imported *kit* must be bound in Env_K. The operation $\mathsf{Flat}(P)$ acts as follows:

– the fields l_i belonging to P_T are bound to their type definitions and these bindings are added to the environment Env_T;

– the fields l_i belonging to P_V and P_K are bound to their type, their value (and to any information needed to analyze them) and these bindings are added to Env_V and Env_K, respectively.

The following rule shows the insertion – in each of the components of the environment – of the bindings built from the type and value of P, and the structure of its namespace. We do not distinguish between typing environments and execution environments, as explained above, and omit the confinement mentions to lighten writing:

$$(\text{Flat}(P)) \frac{(P, \{(l_1, t_1, v_1); \ldots; (l_n, t_n, v_n)\}) \in \text{Env}_K}{\text{Env}_T, \text{Env}_V, \xrightarrow{\text{Flat}(P)} Pl_T \oplus \text{Env}_T, Pl_V \oplus \text{Env}_V,} \\ \qquad\qquad\qquad \text{Env}_K \qquad\qquad\qquad Pl_K \oplus \text{Env}_K$$

knowing that:

$$Pl_T = \{(l_i, t_i) \mid l_i \in P_T\} \\ Pl_V = \{(l_i, t_i, v_i) \mid l_i \in P_V\} \\ Pl_K = \{(l_i, t_i, v_i) \mid l_i \in P_K\}$$

The bindings of l_i inserted by the operation $\text{Flat}(P)$ make the bindings of P fields directly accessible, avoiding to use the dot-notation.

The question now is to decide where this insertion takes place. By continuing to consider that an environment is a list (in fact, a stack), they can be placed at the head of the list. But if the program has already introduced a name identical to a field, then there is a risk of masking. Suppose that Env_V already contains a binding (l, t, v) and that l is also a field of P. Suppose that $l \in P_V$, its type being t_l and its value v_l. The operation $\text{Flat}(P)$ adds the binding (l, t_l, v_l) to Env_V and, if this insertion is done in the head of the environment, this binding (l, t_l, v_l) hides the binding (l, t, v). The current value of l becomes v_l. This is the case in OCaml, as shown in the following example. After the definition of a, Env_V is extended with the binding (a, int, 36). After the definition of S, Env_K is extended with the binding (S, {a : int = 25 }). The binding of a in Env_V is not modified. Then, the module S is flattened (by open S). The binding (a, int, 25) is inserted in the head of (a, int, 36)$\oplus\text{Env}_V$, hence masking of this last binding.

EXAMPLE 1.13.–

```
OCaml
# let a = 36 ;;
val a : int = 36
# module S = struct
  let a = 25
end ;;
module S : sig val a : int end
# a ;;
- : int = 36
# open S ;;
# a ;;
- : int = 25
```

Other choices can be made. In Ada, for example, the rule is that the operation Flat() can never lead to hiding an identifier already occurring in the source code. The field l of P is therefore not directly visible but can be used with the qualified notation $P.l$.

Let us note that the very notion of library imposes acceptance of the fact that the same field l can be exported by several *kits*. Flattening all of these imports with the operation Flat() can lead to some maskings. It is necessary to consult the reference manual of your programming language to determine how these potential maskings are managed. Involuntary masking by the operation Flat() can lead to a runtime error which is difficult to find.

QUESTION 1.24.– *Does* MYL *have an explicit syntactic construct for exporting a* kit? *For importing a* kit? *Otherwise, how does the language handle these operations?*

QUESTION 1.25.– *Is it possible to flatten a* kit? *Can this operation mask bindings in the source being written? Is there a way to remedy this masking?*

QUESTION 1.26.– *Can flattening a* kit *overload an identifier?*

1.3.7. *Stages of* kit *development*

The development of a software usually requires the construction of several *kits*. We have studied the construction of a complete *kit*, therefore entirely defined by its source code. This *kit* could be confined and, once its definition has been analyzed by the language compiler or interpreter, it can be exported and then imported and flattened.

A developer may wish to split the construction of a complete *kit* into several steps. There are several mechanisms for this which are studied in the following sections and which we briefly introduce here:

1) defining an incomplete *kit* only: at least one of the components is only introduced by its declaration, its definition being deferred to a later stage of development (see section 1.4);

2) generalizing the notion of *kit* by accepting that its definition may depend on type variables or value parameters, the types and actual values being provided later. We will call such a construction a *parameterized kit* (see section 1.5);

3) generalizing the notion of *kit* in a slightly different way to the one previous by introducing *functors* of *kits*, that is, functions taking a *kit* as a parameter and returning a *kit* (see section 1.6);

4) extending a *kit* by adding components to it (see section 1.7).

Creating an executable file from an incomplete (or parameterized) *kit* P can lead to execution errors if the missing definition (or an unsupplied actual parameter) is required at runtime. Compilers can detect some of these errors but the language can also deliberately accept some of them, assuming for example that the missing values will be obtained at runtime, via a URL for example. The possible absence of the expected data at runtime must of course be treated by the *kit* P. To avoid such runtime errors, the choice made by most languages is to restrict import to complete *kits* only.

1.4. Incomplete *kits*

In this section, we will disregard some of the assumptions presented in section 1.3.3. Until now, the fields of a *kit* were all introduced in the source code with a type definition for the fields of $N(P)_T$, a type and an expression defining their value for the fields of $N(P)_V$ (and $N(P)_K$).

A *kit* is said to be *incomplete* if at least one of its fields, say l of $N(P)_V$ has no definition. This field l, said to be *not-defined*, is therefore reduced to a declaration. Most languages accepting this lack of definition require a *not-defined* field to be tagged with a keyword such as `abstract`, `virtual`, etc., depending on the languages (be careful, these keywords can have very different meanings in different languages). The compiler can thus distinguish between an involuntary absence of a definition and an explicit willingness to delay a definition. Here, we mark a *not-defined* field with the keyword `decl`.

A *not-defined* field l of a *kit* P can be used in an expression e, which can be typed because typing analysis only requires type information. But e cannot be executed/evaluated since the value of l is unknown. From a runtime point of view, this field l is therefore useless and P cannot be exported. The creation of incomplete *kits* is therefore associated with the operation of field completion: the operation

$\mathsf{Def}(P, l, exp)$ introduces the definition exp of the *not-defined* field l of the *kit* P. It builds a new *kit*, noted here as $\mathsf{Def}(P, l)$.

1.4.1. *Type and value of an incomplete* kit

The *not-defined* fields being declared, the type of an incomplete *kit* is defined in the same way as that of a complete *kit*:

$$P_{Type} = \{\, l_1 : t_1; \ldots; l_n : t_n \,\}$$

The value of an incomplete *kit* differs from that of a complete *kit* since some of its fields have no execution value. By convention, we represent the absence of the value of a field l_i by the notation $\bot_i$. With this notation, the value of an incomplete P is:

$$P_{Value} = \{\, l_1 = v_1; \ldots; l_j = v_j; \ldots; l_n = v_n \,\}$$

where $v_i = \bot_i$ if l_i is tagged with `decl`.

Let l_j be a field of P defined by an expression e_j using the *not-defined* field l_i, thus marked by `decl`. The evaluation of e_j in the current environment can be done by binding l_i to $\bot_i$, producing a "value" v_j which depends on $\bot_i$. Therefore v_j is not a runtime value: it is impossible to compute with it. To become a runtime value, v_j must be substituted with the value of the field l_i when this one is defined. In summary, the fields l_j of an incomplete *kit* have either the value $\bot_j$ if l_j is *not-defined* or a value v_j which is expressed using the values $\bot_i$ of some *not-defined* fields l_i. Of course, if the definition of l_j does not use any *not-defined* field, its value can be completely calculated.

1.4.2. *Completion of an incomplete* kit

Let P be an incomplete *kit* and l_i be a *not-defined* field of P. Let us note $\mathsf{Def}(P, l_i, e)$ as the operation adding a definition to l_i with the expression e. This operation, called *completion*, builds a new *kit*, $\mathsf{Def}(P, l_i)$ as follows. The evaluation of $\mathsf{Def}(P, l_i, e)$ in the environment Env is done in three steps:

1) the evaluation of the expression e in Env produces the value v_i

2) the value $\bot_i$ of the field l_i in P_{Value} is substituted by v_i, a step which defines the value of l_i in $\mathsf{Def}(P, l_i)$;

3) the values of the other fields of $\mathsf{Def}(P, l_i)$ are updated: if the value v_j of a field l_j depends on $\bot_i$, then $\bot_i$ is substituted by v_i in v_j.

The value of $\mathsf{Def}(P, l_i)$ is:

$$\mathsf{Def}(P, l_i)_{value} = \{\, l_1 = w_1; \ldots; l_j = w_j; \ldots; l_n = w_n \,\}$$

where $w_i = v_i$ and $w_j = v_j[\perp_i \leftarrow v_i]$ if $j \neq i$.

Now let us look at the type of $\mathsf{Def}(P, l_i)$. Suppose the declaration of l_i assigned it the type t_i in P. Let t be the type of e. What could happen if $t_i \neq t$? A simple, general answer is to give only a definition having the same type as the corresponding declaration. But some languages can lighten this rule, as detailed below.

– If the language is strongly statically typed, without parametric polymorphism, without subtyping or overloading, without type parametrization, the definition of l_i will be rejected by the compiler because it would lead to a typing error in the definitions of the fields using l_i. If the system did not reject this ill-typed definition of l_i, runtime errors could occur because some expressions of the other fields would then be ill-typed.

– If the type language accepts parametric polymorphism, then there are two questions. The first one is: can the compiler accept the definition of l_i if t is an instance of t_i? In this case, type t_i is of the form $\forall \alpha.s$ and $t = s[\alpha \leftarrow t_s]$, t_s being found by the typing algorithm. For example, if $t_i = \forall \alpha.\alpha \to$ bool, if $t =$ int $\to$ bool, then $t_s =$ int. But, l_i can already be used by some fields of P, whose typing has required a different instantiation of α, string for example. So the completion will be rejected.

The other question is: can the compiler accept a definition, such that t_i is an instance of t? For example, t_i is int list $\to$ int and t is $\forall \alpha.\alpha list \to \alpha$. The definition can be accepted but the type t_i will not be generalized, it remains identical to int list $\to$ int. But there is often no benefit in this because, if a true polymorphic definition is available, it suffices to use it directly. Some examples are given in section 4.3 which studies OCaml classes.

– In the other cases, the considered language can offer some form of compatibility between types (subtyping, *ad hoc* polymorphism, which we will discuss later, etc.). The definition of l_i could be accepted, provided that t is compatible with t_i and that typing can infer that the types of P and $\mathsf{Def}(P, l_i)$ are compatible. If the completion is accepted, the type of $\mathsf{Def}(P, l_i)$ can be obtained by substituting t_i by t in P_{Type}. And the types of the other fields in $\mathsf{Def}(P, l_i)$ may or may not remain the ones they had in P. For example, if t is a subtype of t_i, then the type of another field l from $\mathsf{Def}(P, l_i)$ can be – or not – a subtype of the corresponding field l in $P.l$.

So, if $t_i \neq t$, depending on the languages and even on the contents of P, the definition may or may not be rejected. A simple general rule is to only give a definition that has the same type as the corresponding declaration.

We did not introduce a concrete syntax for the completion of an incomplete *kit*. The syntax for completion varies a lot depending on the language. The completion is often done using the syntax of the extension of a *kit*, a field being declared `abstract` or `virtual` that will receive a definition in an extension (for example by inheritance).

1.4.3. *Confining an incomplete* kit

An incomplete *kit* P cannot be exported since this operation has only been defined for complete *kits*. However, could we, by confining all the *not-defined* fields, still export P by $RP = \mathsf{From(P,M)}$? RP could thus be seen, by the importer, as a complete *kit*. It would be a dangerous practice because any execution of a component of the RP, whose definition in P uses a *not-defined* field of P, would lead to an error. Usually, languages reject this export.

Some languages, however, allow us to confine a *not-defined* field in an incomplete *kit*, without allowing it to be exported. The confinement marks are then used to control the completion of the *kit*. The *not-defined* field must remain accessible to the developer who will introduce its definition. This possibility receives various treatments according to the confinement modes offered by languages. Examples will be given in the presentations of some languages made in the following chapters.

We complete the list of questions as follows.

QUESTION 1.27.– *Does* MYL *offer the possibility to build incomplete* kits*? What is the syntax of such a construct?*

QUESTION 1.28.– *What are the uses of incomplete* kits *provided by* MYL*?*

QUESTION 1.29.– *Must the type provided in the declaration of a field and the type of its definition be the same?*

QUESTION 1.30.– *Can a* not-defined *field of an incomplete* kit *be confined? Can this confinement be modified or removed when this field is completed?*

QUESTION 1.31.– *Can an incomplete* kit *be completed in several steps? Is it needed to indicate that there are still fields to be defined?*

1.5. Parameterized *kits*

1.5.1. kits *parameterized by a type*

Let us introduce the problem by using example 1.14. Let us suppose we have a *kit* `PInt` which defines the type `tlist` of the lists of integers and tools for manipulating these lists.

EXAMPLE 1.14.–

```
Kit PInt = {
  type tlist = Nil | Cons of (int * tlist)
  fun length (l) : tlist -> int =
    match l with Nil -> 0 | Cons (h, r) -> 1 + length (r)
  fun hd (l) : tlist -> int =
    match l with Nil -> raise error | Cons (h, l) -> h
}
```

It is easy to modify the source code of PInt a little to develop *kits* implementing lists of booleans, floats, trees, etc. doing everything simply from a copy-paste-adapt process. The question is, is it possible to do better?

1.5.1.1. *Case of parametric polymorphism types*

Let us first look at the response in the case of a language that has parametric polymorphic types such as those introduced in Volume 1 of this book. We encode the *kit* Pint of example 1.15 in OCaml, choosing for the type tlist the OCaml type int list, and we encode the functions length and hd by pattern matching.

EXAMPLE 1.15.–

```
OCaml
# module Pint = struct
  type tlist = int list
  let rec length l = match l with | [] -> 0 | h :: r -> 1 + length (r)
  let hd l = match l with [] -> raise (Failure "hd") | h :: r -> h
end ;;
module Pint : sig
  type tlist = int list
  val length : 'a list -> int
  val hd : 'a list -> 'a
end
```

The fields of this module have been typed in turn. The module had to provide tools to manipulate lists of integers, but the synthesized types for the definitions are, in fact, polymorphic types.

To obtain a *kit* manipulating lists of any type in OCaml, it suffices to replace the type int with a type variable in the definition of the type tlist, as is done in example 1.16.

EXAMPLE 1.16.–

```
OCaml
# module PList = struct
  type 'a tlist = 'a list
  let rec length l = match l with | [] -> 0 | h :: r -> 1 + length r
  let hd l = match l with | [] -> raise (Failure "hd") | h :: r -> h
end ;;
module PList : sig
  type 'a tlist = 'a list
```

```
    val length : 'a list -> int
    val hd : 'a list -> 'a
end
```

Let us anticipate the presentation of the modules of OCaml by giving the type PList_{Type} of the module PList:

$$\{\,\text{tlist} : \forall\alpha_1.\alpha_1 \text{ list}\,;\; \text{length} : \forall\alpha_2 : \alpha_2 \text{ list} \to \text{int}\,;\; \text{hd} : \forall\alpha_3.\alpha_3 \text{ list} \to \alpha_3\,\}$$

Even if tlist and the types of length and hd are displayed by OCaml using only the symbol 'a, these types are independently universally quantified: there is no link – no constraint – between α_1, α_2 and α_3. The field length of PList can be used on a list of integers and hd on a list of booleans, without previously having to specialize the module PList to treat int or bool lists (see section 5.3.1 of Volume 1).

The following example, example 1.17, written in OCaml, shows that the head of the list [1, 2] and the length of the list ["aa"] can be computed just after the definition of Plist. Typing the expression Plist.hd [1, 2] recognizes that [1; 2] is a list of integers, so its type is int list. This type must "match" the type α_3 list of the formal parameter of hd. Therefore, the type variable α_3 must be substituted by int and this substitution is performed on (a copy of) the type of hd, that is, the whole expression α_3 list $\to \alpha_3$. The type of Plist is not concerned by this substitution, which is only performed on a copy of the hd type suppressed after typing Plist.hd [1, 2].

EXAMPLE 1.17.–

```
OCaml
# Plist.hd [1, 2] ;;
- : int = 1
# Plist.length ["aa"] ;;
- : int = 1
```

In a language that has parametric polymorphic types, defining the most general *kit* meeting a given specification can be done with a judicious use of parametric polymorphism. In example 1.17, the type synthesis algorithm applied to hd shows that there is no constraint on the type, say t, of the items in the list. This type t can therefore be abstracted, i.e. replaced by a variable α which is universally quantified as $\forall\alpha$, the scope of this universal quantifier being the expression defining the type of hd.

1.5.1.2. *Type variables without parametric polymorphism*

Some languages, such as Ada, which do not have parametric polymorphism, allow us to answer the question "is it possible to do better?" by introducing type variables in the definitions of types of *kit* fields. A *kit* with such types is said to be *parameterized by a type*. Some languages use the word *genericity* to speak of this possibility.

In our model, the concrete syntax for the definition of a parameterized *kit* is given below, where Ident is the name of the kit and tparam the name of the type.

```
Kit Ident (type tparam) = { component ... component }
```

The formal parameter `tparam` is a type variable and this identifier is bound in the whole definition of the parameterized *kit*: the types of the fields of the parameterized *kit* are described using (if needed) the `tparam` parameter. Example 1.18 introduces the type variable `T` and uses it in the type `tlist`.

EXAMPLE 1.18.–

```
Kit P (type T) = {
  type tlist = Nil | Cons of (T * tlist)
  fun length (l) : tlist -> int =
    match l with Nil -> 0 | Cons (h, r) -> 1 + length (r)
  fun hd (l) : tlist -> T =
    match l with Nil -> raise error | Cons (h, r) -> h
  fun create (elt) : T -> tlist = Cons (elt, Nil)
}
```

Creating a specialization of the *kit* Ident adapted to a known t_ident type consists of substituting the type variable `tparam` with `t_ident` and to name the obtained *kit*. We do this with the following concrete syntax:

```
Kit Ident_bis = Ident (type t_ident)
```

This operation, which we call the *instantiation of a type variable*, creates a new *kit* Ident_bis. It is obtained by replacing the formal type parameter `tparam` in all the types of fields of Ident with the effective parameter, `t_ident`, under the assumption that `t_ident` is known in the current environment. Let us finish example 1.18 by instantiating the variable of type `T`.

```
Kit Pint = P (type int)
Kit Pstring = P (type string)
```

Thus, `Pint` provides tools for integer lists and `Pstring` for string lists.

In abstract syntax, we denote by $P(\alpha)$ a *kit* parameterized by a type variable α. This parametrization is similar to that of a type by a type variable, studied in Chapter 5 of Volume 1. However, the type attributed to $P(\alpha)$ must express the fact that *all* the types of fields of $P(\alpha)$ have been introduced by the developer under the same hypothesis: α will be substituted *in one step in all types* of $P(\alpha)$. The parametrization of a *kit* by a type variable is here a *global* operation on the *kit*. To model this intention, we universally quantify the type variable α globally, on all types of $P(\alpha)$ components. The type of $P(\alpha)$ is therefore:

$$P(\alpha)_{Type} = \forall \alpha.\{\, l_1 : t_1 ; \ldots ; l_n : t_n \,\}$$

Note the difference with the previously reviewed parametric polymorphism typing, for which the universal quantification is done *independently and separately* on each of the components, according to the type variables they contain (see the synthesis of types in Chapter 5 of Volume 1).

Let $P(t)$ be the *kit* obtained by substituting the type variable α with the known type t in all types of components of $P(\alpha)$. This substitution is the same as the one studied in Chapter 5 of Volume 1. We note the type of $P(t)$ as follows:

$$P(t)_{Type} = \{\, l_1 : t_1[\alpha \leftarrow t] ; \ldots; l_n : t_n[\alpha \leftarrow t] \,\}$$

There is no possibility left for different local non-permanent substitutions of α, which is in opposite to what the rule in regular polymorphism is. The result of this substitution is indeed a new *kit*, whose type differs from the P type. This difference is illustrated by the comparison between the following example, example 1.19, and example 1.17. The evaluation of `hd` `[1, 2]` must be done with the field `hd` of the *kit* `Pint` while the one of `length` `["aa"]` must use the `Pstring` field.

EXAMPLE 1.19.–

```
Pint.hd [1, 2] ;;
(* Returns 1 *)
Pstring.length ["aa"] ;;
(* Returns 1 *)
```

That being said, in spite of allowing type variables, a language that does not offer parametric polymorphism means that the typing algorithm used by its compiler does not manage the local quantification of type variables. However, the fact that a *kit* $P(\alpha)$ is parameterized by a type means it is taken into account at the syntax analysis stage. It is then possible to type the definition of this kit $P(\alpha)$ using a dedicated typing algorithm, which considers α as a constant (unknown) type. The typing algorithm is therefore able to check the consistency of the definitions of the field types.

PROPOSITION 1.1.– If $P(\alpha)$ is recognized as well-typed by the compiler, then, whatever the type t, the substitution of α by the type t keeps this property: $P(t)$ is well-typed.

Only the $P(\alpha)$ field types can contain an occurrence of α. If the definitions of these fields only use identifiers bound in the current environment, the evaluation of $P(\alpha)$ can be done rather completely and the obtained value can be shared among all *kits* created by the instantiation of α in $P(\alpha)$. This sharing of object codes of components is effective in some languages.

In a language that accepts overloading, a definition can use an identifier whose type can only be determined once α instantiated. Let's think for example of a field using the identifier +, which in the used language can be overloaded and could denote either the addition of two integers or the concatenation of two strings. The typing algorithm of $P(\alpha)$ may fail if overloading constraints cannot be satisfied because of the presence of the type parameter. In this case, the compiler may just perform a first typing analysis and add to the object code of the program some typing checks to be done when the type parameter is being instantiated.

A *kit* parameterized by a type variable cannot be exported. Indeed, suppose that the *kit* P parameterized by Type T of example 1.18 is exported. How can one type P.create 1 if one only has in the current importer environment the binding of P.create to its type T $\to$ tlist and the information 1:int? The compiler should instantiate T by int but its typing algorithm does not always know to do so. This algorithm can be unable to distinguish, throughout the typing, an implicitly universally quantified type variable from an identifier of unknown type (for example, a not-defined type, a misspelled type name, for which it needs to send an error message). The import of a component of P could therefore lead to typing errors not being detected.

1.5.2. kits *parameterized by types and values*

Some languages accept some variants of the source code defined in the following example, example 1.20 (where the definitions of functions hd and tl are omitted for the sake of space).

EXAMPLE 1.20.–

```
Kit P (type T) = {
  type tlist = Nil | Cons of (T * tlist)
  fun insert (elt, l) : (T * tlist) -> tlist =
    if l = Nil then Cons (elt, Nil)
    else if elt < hd (l) then Cons (elt, l)
```

```
        else Cons (hd (1), insert (elt, tl (1)))
}
```

This example makes the implicit assumption that whatever the effective type parameter t_eff instantiating T is, there exists an identifier named < whose type is t_eff× t_eff→ bool and which can be called during execution of insert. This hypothesis is dangerous, even if it is described in the *kit* documentation. The compiler cannot always perform static checks on the use of such instantiations, which depend on syntactic constructs that can be introduced later. This way of programming can easily lead to runtime errors.

Some languages such as Ada allow constraints to be added on to types provided as effective parameters to the *kit*. For this example, the only accepted effective parameter types would be those with a comparison function named <. This point is detailed in Chapter 2.

To address the above problem more uniformly, we note that some languages allow us to parameterize a *kit* not only by type variables but also by values (of functions for example), whose types can use the type variables paramaterizing the *kit* (but only those type variables). The *kit* can also only be parameterized by values whose types are completely defined.

The concrete syntax of the definition of a *kit* parameterized by a type and a value is the following:

```
Kit Ident (type tparam) (f : tf) = { component ... component }
```

where tparam is a (formal) type parameter (so a type variable), f a (formal) value parameter whose type is tf, tf being a type expression that can use tparam. The types of components can also use tparam. The definitions of components can use the value parameter f. These definitions can be easily generalized in the case of several type and/or value parameters.

In example 1.21, we resume example 1.20. We modify it by making the *abstraction of the identifier* < in the source code of insert: the identifier < is replaced by the formal parameter f, the type of f is described with T.

EXAMPLE 1.21.–

```
Kit P (type T) (f : (T * T) -> bool) = {
  type tlist = Nil | Cons of (T * tlist)
  fun insert (elt, 1) : (T * tlist) -> tlist =
    if 1 = Nil then Cons (elt, Nil)
    else if f (elt, hd (1)) then Cons (elt, 1)
```

```
        else Cons (hd (1), insert (elt, tl (1)))
}
```

The concrete syntax of the instantiation of such a *kit* is the following:

```
Kit Ident_bis = Ident (type t_ident) (v : t_v)
```

This construct introduces a new *kit* `Ident_bis` obtained by instantiating the parameterized *kit* `Ident` with a known type `t_ident` and by a value identifier `v` of type `t_v`. The definition of `t_v` can contain occurrences of `t_ident` and must also verify some conditions set out below. If the *kit* `Ident` is only parameterized by values, then the type `t_ident` obviously does not appear in instantiation. Example 1.22 instantiates the *kit* P of example 1.21.

EXAMPLE 1.22.–

```
Kit Pint = P (type int) (compare : (int * int) -> bool)
```

Let us note, in abstract syntax, $P(\alpha, x)$ a *kit* parameterized by the type variable α and by the value variable x of type t_x. The type t_x can only depend on the variable α, otherwise P must be parameterized by all other type variables figuring in t_x. The *kit* $P(\alpha, x)$ is a function of the variable x:

$$P(\alpha, x) = \mathtt{fun}\, x \to \{\, l_1 = e_1 \,;\, \ldots \,;\, l_j = e_j \,;\, \ldots \,;\, l_n = e_n \,\}$$

where the definitions e_i of the fields are expressions that possibly contain occurrences of x. Their types can be expressed from α and t_x.

The typing of a *kit* parameterized by a type variable α has been studied in the previous section and is not resumed here. What remains is to take into account the parameter x to type $P(\alpha, x)$, which is done as follows:

1) let Env be the current typing environment. Any component l_i of $P(\alpha, x : t_x)$ is typed in Env under the assumption that α is a free type variable in Env and that t_x is the type of x. Let t_i be the type obtained for l_i, then t_i can contain occurrences of α and t_x;

2) $P(\alpha, x)$ is a function of the variable x, whose body is a collection of fields $\{ l_1 : t_1 ; \ldots ; l_n : t_n \}$. As a function, its type is: $t_x \to \{ l_1 : t_1 ; \ldots ; l_n : t_n \}$.

$P(\alpha, x : t_x)$ is well-typed if its components are well-typed under the assumption that α is a free type variable, so without any knowledge about α. This means that α can be replaced by any type, leaving the components well-typed. This property can be expressed by universally quantifying the type variable α in the type of $P(\alpha, x)$, so by a global quantification of the types of all the fields. The type of $P(\alpha, x : t_x)$ is written as follows:

$$P(\alpha, x)_{Type} = \forall \alpha.(t_x \to \{ l_1 : t_1 ; \ldots ; l_n : t_n \})$$

As already noticed, the *kit* $P(\alpha, x)$ is a function. So far, we have defined values of *kits* as the collection of the values of their fields which have execution values. We need to generalize the notion of a *kit* value by introducing functional values.

In a lexical scoped language, the evaluation of a *kit* parameterized by a value proceeds in the same way as the evaluation of a function (see section 3.2.4 of Volume 1). Hence the value of $P(\alpha, x : t_x)$ is a closure:

$$P(\alpha, x)_{value} = \langle \text{Env}, x, \{ l_1 = v_1 ; \ldots ; l_j = v_j ; \ldots ; l_n = v_n \} \rangle$$

Definitions e_i of the fields are compiled into object-codes represented by the v_i in the closure. The mention of x in the closure denotes a way to access the actual parameter which will be substituted to x in the v_i. The values of the other identifiers present in the e_i are those that they have in the Env environment of the *kit* definition, which is denoted by the presence of Env in the closure.

The *application of a parameterized* kit P to actual types and actual values, is often referred to as the *instantiation of parameters*. It can be done either in one single step that provides all the effective parameters or be split into several stages. In the latter case, each step builds a new *kit* by only instantiating certain formal parameters with actual ones, the non-instantiated parameters remaining formal. This still parameterized *kit* must be named and its (remaining) formal parameters must be totally explicited: non-instantiated type variables, occurring in the types of these remaining formal parameters, must remain explicit in these formal type parameters. Without type inference, this task is the responsibility of the developer.

We only consider the case of the application in a single step of a *kit* to all its effective parameters.

Let us note $PI(t, f)$ the *kit* obtained by applying $P(\alpha, x : t_x)$ to actual parameters t and f. Let t_f be the type of f. The type of the *kit* $PI(t, f)$ is obtained by verifying first that the type t_f of f is equal to $t_x[\alpha \leftarrow t]$ then by replacing the type variable α by t and the type t_x by t_f in the types of the fields of $P(\alpha, x : t_x)$:

$$PI(t, f)_{Type} = \{\, l_1 : t_1[\alpha \leftarrow t;\, t_x \leftarrow t_f];\, \ldots ;\, l_n : t_n[\alpha \leftarrow t;\, t_x \leftarrow t_f]\,\}$$

The value of $PI(t, f)$ is obtained by evaluating the application of $P(\alpha, x : t_x)$ to f: the formal parameter x is substituted by the value v_f of f in the values of the fields of $P(\alpha, x : t_x)$. With $w_i = v_i[x \leftarrow v_f]$, we get:

$$PI(t, f)_{Value} = \{\, l_1 = w_1 ;\, \ldots ;\, l_j = w_j ;\, \ldots ;\, l_n = w_n \,\}$$

A *kit* parameterized by a type and a value cannot be exported either. The discussion about the value of a *kit* parameterized by a type can be resumed. As soon as all actual type and value parameters have been provided, the obtained *kit* can be exported, so long as it is complete.

1.5.3. *Confinement, parametrization, incomplete* kits *and export*

Some languages allow us to define a parameterized *kit*, some fields of which are *not-defined* and some others can be confined (in this case, in our model, the confinement marks are added in the bindings and the types of *kits*). An incomplete, parameterized *kit* with confinement is often used to establish the base implementation of a whole family of data. It can then be specialized to describe sub-families by adding definitions, instantiation of parameters and, by extension, an operation like the one studied below. As long as the *kit* remains parameterized and/or incomplete, it cannot be exported.

Example 1.23 illustrates this combination of possibilities. The *kit* Stack is parameterized by the type variable T, the formal parameters valfloor of type T and compare of type $T \times T \to$ bool. It is incomplete since the variable max_size of type int, which provides the maximum stack height, is not defined. It contains two confined fields, t_stack and floor.

EXAMPLE 1.23.–

```
Kit Stack (type T, valfloor : T, compare : (T * T) -> bool) = {
  confine-def type t_stack = H of T list
  confine var floor : T = valfloor
  decl var max_size : int
  exception empty_stack
  fun top : t_stack -> T = ...
  fun push : (T * t_stack) -> t_stack =
    function (elt, (H l)) ->
      if ... max_size ... then raise ...
```

```
      else if compare (elt, floor) then ....
  fun create_stack : unit -> t_stack = ...
}
Kit IntStack = Stack (int, 0 : int, less_than : (int * int) -> bool)
Kit CStack = IntStack (max_size = 100)
```

The *kit* IntStack is obtained by applying Stack to the type int and to the actual value parameters 0 and less_than. This *kit* is still incomplete: the max_size of IntStack still remains *not-defined*. The *kit* CStack is obtained by adding the definition of this field max_size field. The result is a complete *kit*. Example 1.24 gives an illustration in concrete syntax of the value and of the type of the *kit* IntStack obtained after instantiation.

EXAMPLE 1.24.–

```
Kit IntStack = {
  confine-def type t_stack = H of int list
  confine var floor : T = 0
  decl var max_size : int
  exception empty_stack
  fun top : t_stack -> int = ...
  fun push : (int * t_stack) -> t_stack =
    function (elt, (H l)) ->
      if ... max_size ... then raise ...
      else if less_than (elt, floor) then ....
  fun create_stack : unit -> t_stack = ...
}
```

1.6. Functors of *kits*

In example 1.23 given in the previous section, the types of the formal parameters (Type T) and (fun f: T * T -> bool) generated a typing constraint which must be satisfied by the actual type and value parameters. In other words, the property expressed by this constraint, called a *type invariant*, must be maintained by actual parameters. We may wish to go further, choosing a *kit* as an actual parameter. The invariant is then defined by the whole structure of the *kit* parameter itself, which links field names and field types. Some languages offer this possibility, called here a *functor of* kit.

A functor of *kit* is, by definition, a *kit* parameterized by one (or more) *kits*, in other words, a function taking a *kit* as a formal parameter and whose body is itself a *kit*. We only deal with the parametrization by a single *kit*, the generalization in the case of several *kit* parameters being done easily. The concrete syntax used here is the following:

```
Kit Ident (Kit Pident : tpident) = { component ... component }
```

`Pident` is the formal parameter that should be instantiated by a *kit*. Constraints on *kits* used as effective parameters are described by the type `tpident`, which must be a type known in the definition environment of `Ident`. Definitions of components of `Ident` can use the names of components and the types of `Pident` provided by `tpident`, denoting them with their dot-notation.

Example 1.25 resumes example 1.21 using a functor, which returns a *kit* manipulating sorted lists of integers, when applied to an effective parameter which is a *kit* (adding definitions of `hd` and `tl` is still left to the reader).

EXAMPLE 1.25.–

```
Kit P (Kit F : { type T = int ; fun order : (T * T) -> bool}) = {
   type tlist = Nil | Cons of (F.T * tlist)
   fun insert (elt, l) : (F.T * tlist) -> tlist =
     if l = Nil then  Cons (elt, Nil)
     else if F.order (elt, hd (l)) then Cons (elt, l)
          else Cons (hd (l), insert (elt, tl (l)))
   fun foo (x) : int -> int = succ x
}
```

The invariant, maintained by any functor application, is thus defined by the type of the *kit* parameter `F` and by the names of the components of `F`. Therefore, to maintain this invariant, any actual *kit* parameter of a functor must have components that have the same names and types as `Pident`: their type must be `tpident`. However, this condition can sometimes be lightened, only requiring that the types of the fields of the actual parameter are compatible with the types of the corresponding fields of `Pident`.

Note that, in the definition of parameterized *kits* by types and values, given in section 1.5.2, there is no mandatory link between the type parameter `tf` and the value parameter `tparam`. This link can be imposed by the developer who chooses the same type parameter to type some value parameters, as we did in example 1.21. However, the language may not verify this concordance.

Typing a functor of *kit* can be seen as a generalization of typing a *kit* parameterized by a type and a value. The type constraints binding the type variable α and the formal parameter x of the parameterized *kit* $P(\alpha, x)$ from the previous section are replaced by the type constraints imposed by the type `tpident` of the formal parameter `Pident` of the functor.

The value of a *kit* functor is a functional value, which can be seen as an adaptation of the notion of closure. To build it, all the identifiers present in the components of the body of the functor must be bound in the evaluation environment of the definition of the functor, because they come from the formal parameter, or because they are present in this current environment, or because they are themselves formal parameters of a functional component of the functor body. In example 1.25, order comes from F, succ in foo must be bound in the typing and evaluation environment of P and elt is a formal parameter of insert.

The application of a *kit* functor P to a complete *kit* K is denoted by P(K). For P(K) to be well-typed, the *kit* K must have the same type (or a compatible type) as the formal parameter Pident. The type and value of *kit* P(K) are obtained via a simple generalization of typing and evaluation of the application of a parameterized *kit* to its actual parameters. If the components of the *kit* constituting the body of the Ident functor have confinement marks, those will be reported on the corresponding components of all the *kits* resulting of an application of this functor.

Example 1.25 raises the following questions. The type of the formal parameter F shows the definition of the field type T. This greatly restricts the interest of functor P in this example. Hence the questions: can the type tpident of parameter Pident contain type variables? Can Pident be a parameterized *kit*? In example 1.25, F would be parameterized by T. There is nothing impossible about that. In a language with parametric polymorphism, this will certainly be the most common situation (see the examples in OCaml of Chapter 2). This will also be possible in a language without parametric polymorphism, but it must allow the use of type variables and have a typing algorithm that is able to handle constraints generated by the use of these variables, at least during typing of the functor and of its applications.

Could we go further in the generalization and also consider the component names of the *kit* parameter Pident as formal parameters, as we did for the name f of the function in the case of a *kit* parameterized by a function? For example, can we pass as an effective parameter to P a *kit* K defined by Kit K = { type A = int; fun compare ... }? This question requires us to examine links between the fields of the *kit* and the type of the *kit*. The field, which is, let us recall, the name of a component of the *kit*, is constitutive of the *kit* type and the suggested generalization is not possible as is.

Examples of functors will be given in Chapter 2. A more in-depth presentation of functors is beyond the scope of this work.

Below are a few questions about the parametrization of a *kit* that can guide the reading of MYL's reference manual.

QUESTION 1.32.– *Which forms of parametrization of* kits *are offered by* MYL?

QUESTION 1.33.– *If it is possible to parameterize by a type, is it also possible to parameterize by a value? What are the dependencies between type and value parameters?*

QUESTION 1.34.– *Does* MYL *offer a notion of functor? If it does not, but if parametrization of a* kit *is possible, how do we maintain the invariants that would have been guaranteed by a* kit *passed as an actual parameter to a functor?*

QUESTION 1.35.– *Is it possible to use an incomplete* kit *as an actual parameter to a functor? Can the result of the application of a functor be an incomplete* kit*? A parameterized* kit*?*

QUESTION 1.36.– *What are the interactions between confinement and parametrization?*

1.7. *kit* extension

Is it possible to create a new *kit* R by adding components to a *kit* P, complete or incomplete, parameterized or not, while keeping P and R distinct (their types and values being different)? Of course the idea is to avoid building R by cutting and pasting the source code of P into the R source; we want the subsequent changes made on P to be automatically carried over into R by the language tools. For example, we would like to construct a *kit* P describing the semantics of a purely functional language; then we would add to the language some imperative constructs and we would "enrich" P by adding the semantic description of the imperative features to obtain a *kit* R dealing with a functional and imperative language. The extension should also allow compilers to avoid duplicating the object-code of components shared by P and R.

1.7.1. *Presentation of extension*

The extension of a *kit* requires a syntactic construct introducing the name of the *kit* to be extended. It is often defined by tagging this name with a mark, which can be include, inherits, extends, etc. Here we choose the word extending : R extending P. As usual, for this statement to be analyzed, the name P must be bound in the typing and/or evaluation environment of the R definition. If the language is statically typed, the type of P and therefore of its fields are known. The definition of P having been analyzed, the confinement status of its fields is known and the *not-defined* fields have been identified. All fields of P are visible in R during the extension definition, unless they undergo a form of confinement that prevents their use in an extension.

An important point: the extension does not require the source code of P to be accessible by the developer, who needs only to know the type of P and the confinement marks put on the fields of P (if these marks are also used for the extension). This allows us to subsequently modify the source code of P without needing to modify the code of R. To explain the extension, however, we need to show the source code of P.

1.7.1.1. *Extension of a complete* kit

Let P be a complete *kit*. P can be extended by adding new fields, which may or may not be defined and may or may not be confined. The *kit* R resulting from the extension is therefore either complete or incomplete. P and/or R may have confinement marks.

1.7.1.2. *Extension of an incomplete* kit

Let P be an incomplete *kit* and l one of its fields that is *not-defined*. A first form of extension is given by adding in R a *definition* for l (see section 1.4). A second form of extension is the addition of a new field in R, which can use l in its definition. This second form is presented below. If the language uses a syntactic mark to notify *kit* incompleteness, as long as there is a *not-defined* field in R, this *kit* must remain (most often) tagged with this mark.

The incomplete *kit* P to be extended may only contain declarations of fields with their type, a point already mentioned in the confinement presentation. Such a *kit* is often referred to as an *interface* in object and modular languages (see Chapters 2 and 3). Some languages require that the extension of an interface defines all fields of the interface at the same time. As the word *interface* has several meanings in computer science, we will call this kind of interface a *declaration interface*.

1.7.1.3. *Extension of a parameterized* kit

The instantiation of a parameterized *kit* P is not strictly speaking an extension. This has already been discussed in section 1.5.

Some languages accept that a parameterized *kit* P is extended by adding new fields, without instantiation of all P parameters in R. Thus, R remains a parameterized *kit*. The definitions of the fields added in R can use P parameters. The identifiers of the formal parameters of R and P are not necessarily identical, but there must be an exact match between the formal parameters of R and the corresponding parameters given to P in this extension. These R parameters are in fact just the renaming of the corresponding formal parameters of P. Example 1.26 resumes example 1.21. It shows this correspondence between parameters.

EXAMPLE 1.26.–

```
Kit P (type T) (f : T * T -> bool) = {
  type Tlist = Nil | Cons of (T, Tlist) ...
}
Kit R (type T1) (g : T1 * T1 -> bool) extending
    P (type T1) (g : T1 * T1 -> bool) = {
  fun hd : Tlist -> T1 = ...
}
```

The type parameters of the extension R and the instantiation of the type parameters of P have been provided *via* the syntactic construct `extending`. The type `Tlist` of R is the same as the type `Tlist` of P, but its definition should be textually understood as `Tlist = Nil | Cons of (T1, Tlist)`. Indeed, the universal quantification on T in P is replaced by the universal quantification on T1 in R. The scope of this last one includes the sub-expression `extending P (type T1) (g:    T1 * T1 -> bool)` occurring in R.

Note that this replacement of a formal parameter T by an effective parameter T1, which is itself a formal parameter of a surrounding structure, is often encountered in mathematics. Let `f = fun x -> x + 2` and `g = fun y -> f (y) + 1`. The formal parameter y of g plays the role of an actual parameter for f in the sub-expression `f (y)`, this occurrence of y being abstracted by `fun y` in the surrounding function g.

1.7.1.4. *Adding components*

We first assume that no P fields are confined nor submitted to extension restriction. Thus all fields of P are fields of R and can therefore be used to declare/define components in R.

The extension is a relatively simple operation provided that all the fields added in R to extend P differ from the fields of P. In this case, everything happens as if these new components of R were simply added to the sequence of components of P. Example 1.27 has no problem: the value of R.h (x) is 11.

EXAMPLE 1.27.–

```
Kit P = {
    type t = C of int
    var x : t = C 1
    fun get (C y) : t -> int = y
}

Kit R extending P = {
    fun h (z) = (get (C z)) + 10
}
R.h (x)
```

1.7.1.5. *Reintroduction of fields*

The extension becomes a more complicated operation if the fields added in R can be identical to (already) defined P fields. It is usually possible to add a component to R which has the same name as a component of P, say l. We will say that l is *reintroduced* in R and we will denote by $P.l$ the field l of P and by $R.l$ the one of R. Let us examine the possible limits and consequences of this reintroduction:

– the reintroduction in R of a field l of P must not change the type nor the value of $P.l$, because P can be used elsewhere;

– if the types of *P.l* and of the newly added field *R.l* differ, and if the language accepts field overloading, then this reintroduction can be considered as an overloading of the field *l* in *R*. In this case, *R* has two fields *l* of different types, the one coming from *P* and the one freshly added in *R*;

– otherwise, if the language proposes a notion of compatibility between types (equality, subtyping, etc.), then the type of *R.l* may differ from that of *P.l* but the types *R.l* and *P.l* must be compatible;

– without overloading, the reintroduction of the field *l* in *R* hides *P.l*: the field *P.l* becomes invisible in *R*: this reintroduction of *l* gives a new definition to *l* in *R*. In this case, the reintroduction is sometimes called *redefinition* or *overriding*. Despite its hiding, the field *P.l* remains accessible in *R*. In addition, some languages agree to denote by *P.l* in *R* the field *l* of *P*, if *l* is redefined in *R*. In object-oriented languages, where the extension is called the *inheritance*, the hidden field *l* in *R* can sometimes remain visible under the name *super.l*.

There is another question. With the notations of the previous discussion, any field *m* of *P* can use the field *P.l* in its definition. This field *m*, which we assume was not reintroduced, is therefore present in *R*. Can the reintroduction of *l* in *R* update the type and the value of *m* in *R*? There are two possible answers to this question, thus there are two possible semantics for this extension. They are described by two possible strategies for typing and for the evaluation of extensions. If there is no update of the type and value of *m* in *R*, then we refer to the strategy as an "extension without a back-update", and if the type and value of *m* are updated in *R*, then we refer to the strategy as an "extension with a back-update". Let us examine these two possible strategies.

1.7.1.6. *Extension without a back-update*

In a strongly typed language that only accepts lexical scoping, the type and the value of *P.m* are determined when compiling *P*, prior to the compilation of *R*. Reintroducing *l* in *R* has no influence on the type and value of *m* in *R*. The type and value of *R.m* are those of *P.m*. There is no *back-update* on the fields issued of *kit P*, which are not reintroduced in *R*. For example, C++ allows some form of extension *without back-update* (see section 4.2). Example 1.28 is written in OCaml. The modules of OCaml are *kits* (see section 2.2). The modules R and Q are extensions of the module P, which reintroduce the field y. Q adds the field u which uses y.

EXAMPLE 1.28.–

```
OCaml
# module P = struct let y = ref 3 let z = !y + 2 end ;;
module P : sig val y : int ref val z : int end
# (P.y, P.z) ;;
- : int ref * int = ({contents = 3}, 5)
```

```
# module R = struct include P let y = ref 25 end ;;
module R : sig val z : int val y : int ref end
# (R.z, R.y, P.y) ;;
- : int * int ref * int ref = (5, {contents = 25}, {contents = 3})

# module Q =
  struct include P let y = true let u = !y end ;;
Error: This expression has type bool but an expression was expected of
type 'a ref

# module Q =
  struct include P let y = true let u = !P.y end ;;
module Q : sig val z : int val y : bool val u : int
# (Q.z, Q.u, Q.y, !P.y) ;;
- : int * int * bool * int = (5,3,true,3)
```

The field z is present in P and its value is not modified by the reintroduction of y in R: the extension is done *without a back-update*. The attempt to define Q shows that the reintroduction of y in Q hides the field y of P: typing field u raises an error because y is of type bool in the current environment. The "right" version of Q shows that the field P.y remains visible with the dot-notation.

1.7.1.7. *Extension with a back-update*

It is possible to adopt another semantics for the reintroduction of a field during the extension. The reintroduction of the field l in R hides the field l from P (see the previous discussion). But it also affects the type and value of all the fields of R coming from P, if they use l in their definitions: we call this modification a *back-update* of these fields. Let m be a field from P, not reintroduced in R, whose definition uses the field l reintroduced in R. The evaluation of R re-evaluates the definition of m, so in an environment where l is bound to its value in R. While m is not reintroduced in R, its semantics in R is therefore not necessarily the one it has in P. The *extension with a back-update* requires a significant modification of the typing and evaluation mechanism, at least in the case where lexical scoping is the general rule. This binding mechanism is also called *late binding* in object-oriented languages.

Let us see this in example 1.29, assuming that the extension is made with a back-update. The field f is reintroduced in R. Evaluating P.g (20) requires the evaluation of P.f (20) which returns 21. Evaluating R.g (20) requires the evaluation of R.f (20) which returns 1020.

EXAMPLE 1.29.–

```
Kit P = {
  fun f (y) : int -> int = y + 1
  fun g (z) : int -> int = f (z) + 2
}
let a = 1000
Kit R extending P = {
```

```
  fun f (y) : int -> int = y + a
}
P.f (5), P.g (20), R.f (5), R.g (20)
6, 23, 1005, 1022
```

Let us provide a little detail about this extension with a back-update. The definition of m may contain occurrences of a field l of P. We recall that we suppose that the definition of m can only use those fields l previously introduced in P. Two cases are possible: either l can be reintroduced, or l is tagged with a mark prohibiting its reintroduction (private, static or final for example according to the languages). Let Env be the environment in which the definition of P is evaluated. Let us follow the evaluation of m, which is defined by an expression b:

1) within lexical scoping, any identifier occurring inside b which is not a field of P must be bound in Env and this binding gives its value;

2) let l be a component of P whose name (i.e. field) occurs inside b, the reintroduction of l being forbidden. The value of l is obtained during the evaluation of P in Env;

3) if the field l can be reintroduced, the value of m may be different from one extension to another. It is obtained by evaluating, in *the environment present when the extension is defined*, expression $b[l \leftarrow v_l]$, where v_l is the value of l in this extension. Identifiers occurring in b which are not reintroduced keep the values they had in Env.

Note that P can be considered as its first extension. Therefore the value of m in P is the value of the expression $b[l \leftarrow w_l]$, where w_l is the value of l obtained before, during evaluation of P in Env.

In example 1.29, the evaluation of g in P uses the binding $(f, \langle \text{Env}_1, y, y + 1 \rangle)$, where Env_1 is the environment of the evaluation of the P definition. The value of g in R is obtained by using the binding $(f, \langle \text{Env}_2, y, y + a \rangle)$, where Env_2 is the evaluation environment of the R definition.

Most of the object-oriented programming languages implement an extension with a back-update. We will return to this form of extension in Chapter 3.

Let us come back to the typing of the extension with a back-update:

– If the language is statically typed, it is mandatory that an extension with a back-update does not affect the typing of P already done, otherwise there would be risks of introducing typing inconsistencies. This implies that the types of $R.l$ and of $P.l$ are identical.

Indeed, let us suppose that $P.l$ is a field of type int $\rightarrow$ int and that the definition of $P.m$ is fun x -> 2 * P.1 (x), so P.m :int $\rightarrow$ int. Without overloading, if the reintroduction of l in R is of type string $\rightarrow$ string, then m, whose definition is not modified in R, becomes ill-typed if string $\rightarrow$ string is not compatible with type int $\rightarrow$ int. In this case, this extension with a back-update cannot be accepted;

– If typing is done at least partially during execution, type constraints on reintroduction can be relaxed by some languages, while waiting for the typing of values created during the execution. The system may accept that the type of $R.l$ is different from that of $P.l$ and may possibly interpret this reintroduction as an overloading. But this can lead to typing inconsistencies detected at runtime and can even lead to execution errors.

1.7.2. *Confinement and extension*

So far, a *kit* P can, on the one hand be exported, and on the other hand it can be extended. The developer of the *kit* P can confine some fields for export: it restricts the use of these fields for the importer. The developer can also restrict the possibilities of the extension of P by prohibiting the use of certain fields of P to define the fields added to P or by prohibiting their reintroduction. It can even prohibit the extension of certain *kits*. For example, in some languages, the final mark set on a *kit* prohibits any extension but does not restrict in any way its export. Therefore, extending is not importing. However, programming languages often use the same vocabulary (same keywords, etc.) to restrict exports and adjust the extension. We will comply with this use by deciding that the confinement mechanism already seen for the import is also used for the extension.

From now on, we consider that the confinement of a *kit* P described for export can act on the possibilities of extension of P. Let RP created by $RP = \mathsf{From}(P,M)$ and R a *kit* created by extending P.

If the confinement M is set to P after its definition, the user can either extend RP or P (thus not confined), depending on the environment to which she/he has access. If she/he extends RP, then only the P fields left visible by this confinement can be used to define new fields or can be reintroduced.

Suppose the confinement obtained by tagging P fields. The restriction can be modulated at the level of each field as follows:

– Total invisibility of the field l (sometimes indicated by the tag private). We considered in our model that RP does not have the field l but that this field remains accessible from RP (see section 1.3.5). In the case of an extension, l remains invisible in R so cannot be directly used in R for new definitions. l can be used, however indirectly *via* the fields of P that access it. In other words, the field l is invisible to the new R fields, but it remains *accessible* from R.

– No visibility restriction (sometimes indicated by public). The field is present in RP and in R.

– A mark (like protected in some languages) can allow the import of the tagged field l by a *kit* belonging to the same library lib_1. In other words, a source file written by an importer can use l of RP depending on its location in the library hierarchy (which also depends on the management of files by the operating system). This mark can, however, give the visibility of l to certain extensions of P, placed in a library lib_2 which can be different from lib_1. But in any case, l is a field of the extension, accessible if P has provided some means of access to it.

Regardless of the technique used, confinement can either render a field invisible (its name is not accessible but its value is) or make it both invisible and inaccessible (i.e. its value is not accessible during an evaluation). Some languages accept that a field of P invisible in R is reintroduced in R.

Fields of P not reintroduced in an extension R retain their confinement mark. Those redefined in R can sometimes receive a different confinement mark, even less demanding than the original mark (which can be a problem if this is not explained well). In addition, if the extension of a *kit* is forbidden (for example by a mark final), the properties verified by its fields cannot be modified.

Confinement may seem complicated to manage, but the development environments dedicated to a given language generally help in the management of field statuses. Examples will be provided in Chapters 2 and 3.

1.7.2.1. *Sharing fields*

Let R be a *kit* extending a *kit* P. Let us see how the fields they have in common can be shared. If the extension is made without a back-update, then there is no problem in the sharing of the common fields. Let us see this in example 1.30 in OCaml:

EXAMPLE 1.30.–

```
OCaml
#1 module P = struct let y = ref 3 end ;;
module P : sig val y : int ref end
#2 module R = struct include P let z = true end ;;
module R : sig val y : int ref val z : bool end
#3 P.y = R.y ;;
- : bool = true
#4 P.y := 25 ;;
- : unit = ()
#5 R.y ;;
- : int ref = {contents = 25}
#6 module P = struct let y = ref 1000 end ;;
```

```
module P : sig val y : int ref end
#7 R.y ;;
- : int ref = {contents = 25}
```

The field y of P is not duplicated by the extension. The expression in line 3 tests the equality of the addresses $P.y$ and $R.y$, line 4 modifies the value referenced by $P.y$ and line 5 shows that $R.y$ is an *alias* of $P.y$. Finally, lines 6 and 7 confirm that OCaml uses the lexical scope: R is not modified by the definition of a new module still called P, which hides the previous definition of P.

With the extension without a back-update and lexical scoping, sharing a field which is a function is the same as sharing a closure. At the time of the application of the function, only the binding (formal parameter, effective parameter) must be created and added to the function definition environment before evaluating the (compiled) body of the function. So there is no obstacle to sharing.

With the extension with a back-update, code sharing depends a bit more on the choice of implementation of *kits* made by the compiler. Roughly speaking, if l is a field that can be reintroduced, and if m is a field using l, then the object code of m produced by the compiler must include the possibility of updating the value of l when it is reintroduced.

Quite often, reference manuals explain extension with a back-update with comments on its implementation, showing *de facto* the implementation of code sharing. The extension with a back-update will be reviewed in Chapter 3.

Regardless of the extension mode, sharing field codes is not a problem if the associated components do not include side effects. Otherwise, the developer extending *kits* must weigh the advantages and disadvantages of the possibility of *aliasing* between fields and control the side effects made by the components of the extended *kit*.

1.7.2.2. *Simultaneous extension of several* kits

Some languages accept that a new *kit* R can be built by simultaneously extending several *kits*. We only consider the simultaneous extension of two *kits*, say $P1$ and $P2$ for further explanations. This possibility corresponds to what is called *multiple inheritance* in object-oriented languages. Let R be the *kit* obtained by simultaneous extension of $P1$ and $P2$. The fields of R are either the fields of $P1$ and $P2$ if these *kits* have no fields in common or the new fields added by the extension. If $P1$ and $P2$ have a field l in common, the compiler must be able to decide which field l will be visible in R. Several solutions are possible:

– fields $P1.l$ and $P2.l$ do not have the same type. R can *a priori* contain both fields, if the language handles field overloading;

– fields $P1.l$ and $P2.l$ have the same type. Remember that a compiler cannot decide if two definitions are identical (see the discussion on equality of functions in section 6.6.3 of Volume 1). The language can adopt a syntactic rule to guide the choice of the compiler: for example, the rule can impose one to choose the field of the last *kit* in the list of extended *kits*;

– the language can also propose a rename in R of the fields common to $P1$ and $P2$ so as to remove ambiguity or allow them to be named with their qualified notation. In the case of reintroduction, a means of specifying the origin of the field reintroduced can be provided.

1.7.2.3. *Subtyping and extension*

Without confinement, the P fields are fields of its extension R, whether reintroduced or not. Under the assumption, which we call H, that the extension keeps the type of fields, the extension provides the basic cases of a subtyping preorder (subtyping has been introduced in section 5.7.1 of Volume 1): if R extends P, and if H is valid, then R_{Type} is a subtype of P_{Type}. According to the rule $T_{\preceq}$ given in section 5.7.1 of Volume 1, any expression of type R_{Type} is also an expression of type P_{Type}. From the "basic cases" created by this extension, the subtype relationship can be extended, avoiding some inconsistent interferences with *kits* operations. This is a tricky point: inconsistencies like the one brought by `ref` types in section 5.7.1 of Volume 1 can occur depending on the form of compatibility chosen with these operations.

Let us examine whether the H assumption can be lightened by replacing the condition on types of common fields of P and R by the less strong requirement: if l is a field of P, the type of $R.l$ must be a subtype of that of $P.l$. This condition is not at all harmless if the field is a function, as explained in section 5.7.1 of Volume 1. If the type of $P.l$ is $t_1 \to t_2$, if the one from $R.l$ is $s_1 \to s_2$, the language designer can choose, by interpreting types inspired by set theory, to impose that s_1 be a subtype of t_1 (contravariance of the type of the argument) and t_2 a subtype of s_2 (covariance of the result). Most languages, in the framework of extension, replace the condition of the covariance of the result with a stronger condition, the equality of s_2 and t_2. This choice is not without consequences, as will be seen in Chapter 3.

It is possible to use another form of subtyping without reference to extension. This subtyping, referred to as *structural subtyping*, is defined by the structure of the types: if a *kit* P_s contains all the fields of a *kit* P_g with compatible types, it is possible to consider that the type of P_s is a subtype of P_g, *no matter how P_s and P_g were defined*. We will come back to this point with the presentation of the modules of the OCaml language in section 2.2.2.1 (and also classes of OCaml in Chapter 4).

Here are a few more questions, examples of answers will be found in the following chapters.

QUESTION 1.37.– *In* MYL, *are the actions of definition and extension of* kits *distinguished by different syntactic constructs?*

QUESTION 1.38.– *Is it possible to extend a* kit *P by reintroducing some fields of P? Is there a syntactic mark to indicate that it is a reintroduction?*

QUESTION 1.39.– *What is the semantics of such a reintroduction: with or without back-update? Can its reintroduction hide the corresponding field of P? If so, is it possible to use a qualified identifier to denote the hidden field?*

QUESTION 1.40.– *Are certain types of fields changed during the extension? Can the type t of a field of P not reintroduced in the extension be modified in the extension (perhaps becoming a subtype of t)?*

QUESTION 1.41.– *Identify all interactions between the confinement and development of* kits. *Distinguish between the interactions of the confinement with exports/imports and those with extensions.*

1.8. Conclusion

This chapter presents a model common to several syntactic constructs, such as modules, classes and objects. These provide developers with tools to reuse, and confine and export parts of their software. This model based on *kits* remains informal in order to remain roughly intuitive. The typing does not take into account the possible recursion between fields and no quantifier has been added to the language of types. We believe that this model should be enough to help one read, step by step, a reference manual while identifying, beyond the syntax of the language, what the proposed operations on the *kits* are and how they interact. In particular, even if the syntax of the language allows us to make the instantiation of a parameterized *kit* at the same time as its extension and the confinement of some of its fields for example, it is important to identify each of these steps separately in order to grasp the semantics of code and thus, to understand the source code and to guide its proofreading.

Some languages only offer the possibility of structuring a source code by dividing it into several files. If such use of files is associated with a namespace management and export/import mechanism, then we consider that a file is a first draft of a *kit*, which may have, depending on the language, a form of confinement. Examples will be given in the following chapters.

The main obstacle to further formalization is the definition of a type theory that can account for all the interactions between extension, confinement, parametrization, the completion of definitions, export/import and subtyping. We raised the need to make our typing model more complex by evoking the possibility of an existential quantification to take into account confinement, the possibility of universal quantification to take into account parametrization, etc. The study of several theories of types and subtypes continues to be pursued to provide a formal foundation for the typing techniques used by languages implementing a *kit* concept, either within the modules or in the frame of objects and classes, or in a frame integrating modular and object/class features. To our knowledge, none of these types theories have so far succeeded in fully covering typing of all existing modular and object-oriented languages. Restrictions on development tools (parametrization, extensions, etc.) must always be made to ensure consistency and especially the decidability of the typing. The main difficulty comes from the languages themselves, whose design is not always based on a theoretical study of the relations between their tools, their typing and their evaluation semantics, the latter being sometimes simply defined by their compiler (or interpreter). Readers wishing to go further into the type theories may consult the following bibliographical references: [APO 96, BRU 96, CAU 15, KEN 06, LER 00, PIE 05].

2

Modules

The need to split source files, to confine, to reuse fragments of programs to achieve the rational development for a software system arose very early in the history of programming [PAR 72]. This has been studied in Chapter 1 where *kits* are presented as a model that is a general answer to this need. To implement this model, some programming languages provide a dedicated construct often referred to by the generic name *module*. We examine them in this chapter.

Modules appeared in the early 1980s, under the name *structure* in STANDARD ML [MIL 19], *module* in OCaml [INR 19], *package* in Ada [AUT 19] or *cluster* [LIS 81] for instance.

At the same time as module creation, the theory of *algebraic abstract data types* (ADT) [GOG 78] was under development. It formally models the notion of a *data set associated with operations* as a term algebra whose properties are stated by equations between terms. This allows one to formally reason about these sets independently from their implementation. Any model consistent with these equations defines a semantics of the ADT. ADTs have been a great source of inspiration for designing the modules of the current languages.

Modules of programming languages are implementations of *kits*. They all allow us to manipulate a collection of type definitions and values but also, depending on the language, of constants, variables, functions, procedures, classes, exceptions or modules. Thus, we find in this list all the ingredients of a *kit*. Whatever the language, modules define their own namespace and provide import, export and flattening operations, as presented in Chapter 1. Their semantics is built on that of the imperative and/or functional features of the language, especially on the notions of typing and scope. These features have been studied in Volume 1.

This chapter presents implementations of *kits* in several languages and answers, in this context, some of the questions raised in Chapter 1. These languages are the following:

– Ada is one of the first programming languages (the first compiler was released in 1983), still used today, providing constructs that allow real modular programming. Its module language is pretty simple and allows a nearly immediate illustration of the study made in Chapter 1;

– OCaml, which is more recent, offers a powerful module language: a module is a first-class value, hence it can be typed, computed, handled as any other value. The semantics of OCaml's modules is an enrichment of the *kits'* semantics;

– C is a language with no real dedicated constructs for modular programming. It only provides a few features, allowing us to implement a weak notion of a *kit*, called a *W-kit*. Section 2.3.3, dedicated to C, gives some hints on a programming discipline to follow along implementations of *W-kits* in order to achieve a modular development.

2.1. Modules in Ada

Ada is an imperative language with a static scope. Types of components must be declared. It is strongly and statically typed, with type verification. It allows the overloading of functions and constants with different types (see section 5.7.2 of Volume 1). It is compiled into native code (Ans. 1.1). Ada provides constructs for modular but also for real-time, concurrent and distributed programming. Since [ADA 95], the language supports object-oriented features and since [ADA 12], it allows contract-based development: properties are stated by pre- and post-conditions which are checked at runtime (see section 4.7.2 of Volume 1 where pre- and post-conditions are studied). The definition and management of modules were available in the first versions of the language. They were enriched as successive versions progressed. The different evolutions of this language [ADA 95, ADA 05, ADA 12] have always been internationally standardized, a point which guarantees the full compatibility of the object code produced by the various compilers on the market. To get a complete presentation of Ada, the reader may refer to the reference manuals [AUT 19]. In this book, we only present modules.

2.1.1. *Developing modules*

A module of Ada is an implementation of a *kit* (Ans. 1.2). It is introduced by the keyword package and defined in two steps, by first providing its *specification*, then its *body*. The specification (also called the *interface*) introduces the module name and the declarations of the fields the developer does not confine. These declarations of functions, procedures, variables, types, constants, modules and exceptions can also be defined at this point. Example 2.1 introduces a module to define a list of integers implemented using pointers. The specification part declares the name of the module, the types used to build values, the operations to manipulate these values and an exception. The mutual recursion between types `link` and `int_l` requires a preliminary introduction of the name `link`. The same can be said for the mutual recursion between functions. There is no dedicated keyword for recursion (Ans. 1.10 and Ans. 1.11).

EXAMPLE 2.1.–

```Ada
-- Specification part
package L_integers is
   type link ;    -- Declaration of an element's type.
   type int_l is access link ; -- Type pointer to a link.
   type link is  -- Definition of type link.
     record
     v: integer; s: int_l ;
     end record ;
   function cons (n: integer; l: int_l) return int_l ;
   function empty return int_l ;
   function is_empty (l: int_l) return boolean ;
   function head (l: int_l) return integer ;
   function tail (l: int_l) return int_l ;
   specification_error: exception ;
end L_integers ;
```

The body of the module contains the definitions of all the fields only declared in the specification part of the module and these definitions repeat the declarations of the completed fields.

New functions/procedures, variables, types, modules, etc. can be defined in the body of the module, without being declared in the specification part, and then they are confined inside the body.

Example 2.2 extends example 2.1 by defining the body of the module L_integers.

EXAMPLE 2.2.–

```Ada
package body L_integers is
   function cons (n: integer; l: int_l) return int_l is ...
   function empty return int_l is ...
   function is_empty (l: int_l) return boolean is ...
   function head (l: int_l) return integer is ...
   function tail (l: int_l) return int_l is ...
   procedure proc ( ... raise specification_error ...)
end L_integers ;
```

A module specification can be seen as an incomplete *kit*, completion being performed in one unique step by the definition of the module's body (Ans. 1.27 and Ans. 1.28). Definition and declaration types must be identical.

2.1.1.1. *Namespace*

As with any *kit*, a module introduces a namespace in which names are accessible from outside using the dot-notation. In Ada, this namespace is not divided into sub-spaces. Thus, it contains all the names of types, variables and functions, etc. introduced by this module. This implies that types, variables, functions cannot have the same names (except in the case of overloading, which is described later) (Ans. 1.3 and Ans. 1.9).

Thus, the namespace introduced by the module `L_integers` of example 2.2 is: (`link`, `int_l`, `cons`, `empty`, `...`, `specification_error`, `proc`).

2.1.1.2. *Type and value of a module*

Types and values are defined and computed as indicated for *kits* (Ans. 1.5 and Ans. 1.6). For instance, the type of `L_integers` involves the name of the module and the names and types of the fields:

```
L_integers:
  link: (v: integer; s: int_l) ;
  int_l: (access link) ;
  cons: (integer * int_l -> int_l) ;
  ...
```

If we had defined another module M containing the same fields as `L_integers`, then types `M.link` and `L_integers.link` would be different (Ans. 1.7): typing is nominal.

As for *kits*, declarations are sequentially evaluated, i.e. they follow the order of the text. Any declaration can make reference to a previous one but never to a future one. This is the reason for the preliminary declaration of `link` (Ans. 1.10 and Ans. 1.11).

Evaluating an Ada module requires two steps. First, the evaluation of the specification of `L_integers` in the current environment Env_1 binds the name `L_integers` to the result of the evaluation of the fields declared and defined in this specification. Next comes the evaluation of the module's body in the current environment Env_2, which completes the value. Beware, Env_1 and Env_2 can be different and the memory Mem may have changed between the two steps.

Let us detail the evaluation of `L_integers`. Let Env be the current environment:

1) the name `L_integers` is bound in Env to the value to be defined and denoted by ??, which produces the environment (`L_integers`, ??) $\oplus$ Env;

2) by sequential evaluation of the specification's fields, a temporary value v_L_integers = (cons: ?? ; empty: ?? ; ...; specification_error: exception) is built. This value only introduces the names of the fields, bound to "temporary" values ??;

3) the binding of L_integers in Env is then updated with the value v_L_integers, leading to the environment Env$_1$;

4) throughout the evaluation of the body, closures of functions declared in L_integers are computed in the current environment, here being Env$_1$. Let us call fcons the closure of cons, the binding (cons, fcons) is added to the environment Env$_1$ and this is the same for empty and its closure fempty, etc.;

5) at the end of the evaluation, L_integers is bound in Env to the value v_L_integers (Ans. 1.12) where all ?? have been updated with real values.

2.1.2. *Export and confinement*

Ada provides a first form of confinement: only the fields declared in the specification part are exported. Any field that is only introduced in the module's body remains confined. For instance, the procedure proc of L_integers (example 2.2) is not exported. The second kind of confinement is achieved using a mark on types. A type may be marked private or limited private in the specification. The name of the type can be exported but its definition is confined. This definition must be located in the private part of the module's specification, starting with the keyword private (Ans. 1.29).

Example 2.3 modifies example 2.1 by declaring int_1 as a private type.

EXAMPLE 2.3.–

```Ada
package L_integers is
   type int_1 is private ; -- Mark on the type.
   function cons (n: integer; 1: int_1) return int_1 ;
   ...
private    -- Private part of the specification.
   type link;   -- Declaration of the type link.
   type int_1 is access link ; -- Type pointer on link.
   type link is  -- Definition of type link.
     record
        v: integer ; s: int_1 ;
     end record ;
end L_integers ;
```

The body of the module L_integers is unchanged. In the type of L_integers, the definition of the type int_1 is replaced by $\perp_t$.

Variables and constants of a type private cannot be defined, but only declared, in the specification of the module. The only allowed operations on these variables (except operations declared in the specification part of the module) are the equality test and assignment. The clause limited private strengthens the control imposed by the developer, only allowing operations declared in the module's specification: equality tests as well as assignments are forbidden. Having no more equality, the developer is in charge of defining it. The export operation does not introduce a new name for the module (Ans. 1.17). The confinement tag is provided by the module and can be inferred from its specification and its body. The operation From is only represented by the structure of the specification (Ans. 1.16). A module is associated with only one confinement (Ans. 1.18). Only defined fields can be imported (Ans. 1.30).

2.1.3. *Nesting modules*

It is possible to nest modules. Example 2.4 defines the module P which contains two nested modules, N and M, each one having a `private` part. Fields exported by P are (D, N, N.X, E).

EXAMPLE 2.4.–

```Ada
package P is
  D: Integer ;
  package N is
     X: Integer ;
  private
     Foo: Integer ;
  end N ;
  E: Integer ;
  private
     package M is
        Y: Integer ;
     private
        Bar: Integer ;
     end M ;
  end P ;
```

2.1.4. *Importing a module*

The keyword `with` followed by a module name M defines the import operation called With(M) in Chapter 1. Components exported by M can be manipulated by importers via the dot-notation.

Ada provides a standard library made of predefined modules that must be individually loaded. It also offers many other libraries. The initial environment of an Ada program is built by importing elements from libraries using the clause `with`. For instance, `text_io` is a module of the standard library containing input/output operations and must be explicitly loaded. The clause `with text_io` must be evaluated before any input/output operation is performed.

In example 2.5, the module `L_integers` is imported then a list with three elements is built.

EXAMPLE 2.5.–

```Ada
with L_integers ;
begin
  declare
    l: int_l := L_integers.empty () ;
  begin
    l := L_integers.cons (5, L_integers.cons (7, L_integers.cons (9, 1))) ;
  end ;
end ;
```

Recent versions of the language refine the import clause with by restricting the scope of the import, as for instance with the clause private with [AUT 19].

2.1.5. *Flattening an import*

The clause use M defines the flattening operation $\mathrm{Flat}(M)$ (Ans. 1.24). Example 2.6 continues example 2.5 by using the use clause.

EXAMPLE 2.6.–

```Ada
with L_integers ;
use L_integers ;
begin
  declare
    l: int_l := empty () ;
  begin
    l := cons (5, cons (7, cons (9, 1))) ;
  end
end ;
```

In Ada, an environment Env is split in two parts Env_c and Env_u. Env_c is the environment built from the declarations of the program. Env_u is built by flattening imported modules. The environment Env_c, built from the declared entities, behaves in a usual way: each identifier has one unique binding (except in the case of masking or overloading), the declaration of an identifier may mask an already existing binding in Env_c. The order of declarations is important. This is not the case for the import environment Env_u: several imported modules P_1, P_2 may quite normally contain different declarations for a same identifier ident. The compiler warns about the ambiguity, which can be resolved using the dot-notation P_1.ident or P_2.ident. The order in which the imports are performed does not matter (Ans. 1.25 and Ans. 1.26).

The look up of an identifier in an environment is achieved by first searching in Env_c then in Env_u.

2.1.6. *Generic modules*

A module can be parameterized by variables, types, functions, objects, procedures or modules. Such a module is referred to as *generic*. The syntax used to define a generic is:

> generic *g_1, g_2, ... g_n*
> package *id_generic_module* is
> *declarations list*
> end *id_generic_module*

where *g_i* are the formal parameters of this generic. Evaluated in a current environment, the value of this construct is a functional value (closure) whose parameters are those of the generic. Thus, its type is a functional type.

2.1.6.1. *Instantiation of a parameterized module*

The instantiation of a generic module is obtained by:

> package *created_module* is new *id_generic_module* (*e_1, e_2, ... e_n*)

This construct defines the module *created_module* as the result of the application of *id_generic_module* to some effective parameters. Fields of this module are instantiations of the generic's ones. The confinement installed in the generic is maintained in the created module. Typechecking the instantiation parameters is sufficient to ensure the type consistency of the instantiated unit. Any instantiation must be named and each instance is different from the other instances of a same generic. In particular, if the generic defines types, then two instances of this module will generate different types, thus they will be incompatible together.

2.1.6.2. *Module parameterized by a type*

Let us continue the example implementing lists with the code snippet in example 2.7. We define a module to process lists implemented by pointers, with the type of the elements being parameterized by the type variable a_t.

EXAMPLE 2.7.–

```Ada
generic
 type a_t is private ;
package L_generic is
  type list is private ;
  function cons (v: a_t; l: list) return list ;
  function empty return list ;
  function is_empty return boolean ;
...
private
  type link ;
```

```
   type list is access link ;
   type link is record value: a_t ; next: list ; end record ;
end L_generic ;
```

Definitions of the functions are not modified, the type `integer` is replaced by `a_t` in the module's body. As explained in Chapter 1, the type parameter `a_t` is universally quantified over all the components of the module.

In example 2.8, a specialization of the module `L_generic` implementing lists of integers is obtained by an instantiation of the module, i.e. by applying this module to the effective parameter `integer`. This is achieved by using the construct `new` of Ada.

EXAMPLE 2.8.–

```
Ada
package my_lists is new L_generic (integer) ;
```

The result of this instantiation is named `my_lists`, its type is that of the module `L_generic` in which the parameter `a_t` is replaced by `integer`, its value is that of the module `L_generic`, as explained in section 1.5.2. The remainder of the example performs two distinct instantiations of the module.

```
Ada
package my_lists is new L_generic (integer) ;
packages your_lists is new L_generic (character) ;
begin
  declare
  l: list := my_lists. vide ;
  c: list := your_lists.vide ;
  begin
  l := my_lists.cons (5, my_lists.cons (7, my_lists.cons (9, l))) ;
  c := your_lists.cons ('a', your_lists.cons ('b', your_lists.cons ('c', c))) ;
  end ;
end ;
```

Both instances `my_lists` and `your_lists` are modules sharing the same code.

2.1.6.3. *Module parameterized by a function*

A formal parameter for a generic can be a function or a procedure defined by its name and its type. The compiler verifies that the effective parameter has the same type as the formal one. It binds the formal parameter to the value (a closure) of the effective parameter in the environment contained in the closure representing the value of the generic.

2.1.6.4. *Module parameterized by a module, one step towards functors*

A generic may be parameterized by a module. Its type is declared by using the same syntax as that used to instantiate an existing generic. Example 2.9 defines the generic module G1, parameterized by the type t1 declared `private`.

EXAMPLE 2.9.–

```Ada
generic
  type t1 is private ;
package G1 is ... end G1 ;
```

Let us continue example 2.9. The module G2 has a module parameter FP2, declared as an instance of the module G1 applied to any discrete type (which is denoted by <>):

```Ada
generic
  with package FP2 is new G1 (<>) ;
package G2 is ... end G2 ;
```

The type of the parameter FP2 is obtained by substituting t1 with <> in the type of G1. FP2 may be instantiated by any module having the same field declarations as val_G1, their types being obtained by applying this substitution to the type of the corresponding field of G1. Thus, any module instantiating G1 with a discrete type, for instance integer, is a possible effective parameter for FP2 and has the same confinement as G1.

Typechecking and evaluation of the code of G2 can be performed since G2 can access the non-confined fields of FP2, hence those of G1. Let us continue example 2.9.

```Ada
with package FP3 is new G1 (integer) ;
package I2 is new G2 (FP3) ;
...
```

The type of FP3 is obtained by substituting t1 by integer in the type of G1. integer being a discrete type, the type of FP3 is compliant with that of the parameter FP2 (which is that of G1 with t1 substituted by any discrete type). Therefore, G2 can be instantiated by FP3 and its declaration is well-typed.

It is possible to establish dependencies between the parameters. For instance:

```Ada
generic
  type t2 is private ;
  with package FP2 is new G1 (t2) ;
package G2 is ... end G2 ;
```

Here, a type parameter t2 is introduced and FP2 is declared as an instance of G1, where t1 is substituted by t2. Thus, the type of FP2 is obtained by substituting t2 to t1 in the type of G1. This dependency between G1 and t2 will have to be satisfied by any instantiation of G2.

Declarations of formal parameters of generics may restrict the possible instantiations. We already used such a restriction with <>, which limits instantiations by only discrete types. This enables us to use operators and properties coming from types accepted by the restrictions in the body of the generic. The interested reader may consult the reference manual [AUT 19].

The Ada language does not allow auto-genericity, as shown by example 2.10.

EXAMPLE 2.10.–

```Ada
with A ;
generic
  with package P is new A (<>) ;
package A ; -- Illegal: A makes a reference to itself.
```

It is also impossible to create mutually recursive instantiations: if a generic module A includes an instantiation of another generic B, then the unit obtained by instantiating B cannot include an instantiation of A. However, module nesting allows us to nest generics and the formal parameters of the surrounding module can be used in the nested module.

2.1.7. *Modules and separate compilation*

In Ada, a module does not correspond to a file (as is the case in some other languages). The specification and the body of a module may be in different files: they form two compilation units that can be separately compiled. In this case, the specification must be compiled before the body since the latter uses information generated by the compilation of the specification.

The compilation result is bound to the module name and stored in a library. The linker combines the compiled modules that are required by a program to create the final executable.

2.2. Modules in OCaml

OCaml [INR 19] is a functional language of the ML family, distributed by Inria as *open source* since 1996. This language is used in this book to allow a better understanding of certain concepts by programming them. The reader has noticed that OCaml is a functional language which also offers imperative features, structured datatypes and a pattern-matching mechanism controlled by the compiler. OCaml uses static scope, is compiled into bytecode or native code and provides strong static typing with type inference, also called type synthesis (Ans. 1.1 and Ans. 1.4). It can be used in an interactive mode to enter an expression which is immediately compiled then executed on the fly. Several books are dedicated to OCaml programming [CON 14, DUB 04, WEI 99]. Interested readers may consult the document [ANS 11] which presents a complete study of the language in the realm of cybersecurity.

Most of the functional languages allow modular programming: Haskell [HAS 19], STANDARD ML [MIL 19], OCaml, etc. provide a syntactic construct to develop and manage modules. They implement all the features of *kits* introduced in Chapter 1, sometimes with slightly different semantics for some of them. This section presents the main features of OCaml modules. Objects will be presented in section 4.3.

2.2.1. *Module definition*

An OCaml module name is introduced by the keyword `module` and must begin with a capital letter. Its body, which is a list of fields, is enclosed between the keywords `struct` and `end`.

```
OCaml
module Module_name = struct
  (* List of fields. *)
end
```

Example 2.11 mimics the example implementing lists in Ada and defines an OCaml module.

EXAMPLE 2.11.–

```
OCaml
module MyList =
struct
  type 'a typl = Nil | Cons of 'a * 'a typl
  exception Error of string
  let empty = Nil
  let cons x nl = Cons (x, nl)
  let head nl =
    match nl with
    | Nil -> raise (Error "head empty list") | Cons (h, _) -> h
  let tail nl =
    match nl with
    | Nil -> raise (Error "tail empty list") | Cons (_, t) -> t
  let rec add nl1 nl2 =
    match (nl1, nl2) with
    | (Nil, _) -> nl2 | Cons (h, t), _ -> Cons (h, add t nl2)
  let rec lg nl =
    match nl with Nil -> 0 | Cons (_, t) -> 1 + lg t
end
```

An OCaml module is an implementation of a *kit* (Ans. 1.2). It can be explicitly defined via providing the list of its fields definitions or can be obtained by a functor application. These fields can be values, functions, types or exceptions, but can also be modules, module types, classes or objects. Field types are synthesized by the compiler. Modules are typed and their type is also synthesized. Such a type has the same name as the module and is defined by the list of the types of components (Ans. 1.5 and Ans. 1.6). This corresponds to the definition of the type of a *kit* given in Chapter 1. The type of the module MyList is synthesized by the typechecker and shown below.

```OCaml
module MyList :
  sig
    type 'a typl = Nil | Cons of 'a * 'a typl
    exception Error of string
    val empty : 'a typl
    val cons : 'a -> 'a typl -> 'a typl
    val head : 'a typl -> 'a
    val tail : 'a typl -> 'a typl
    val add : 'a typl -> 'a typl -> 'a typl
    val lg : 'a typl -> int
  end
```

OCaml calls the syntactical structure defining the type of a module the *signature*. The compiler infers the type of a module and thus generates its signature. An OCaml module M is made of a body and a signature.

A module defines its own namespace (Ans. 1.3). Identifiers of a module are accessible using the dot-notation. A module value is that of the related *kit*, fields being evaluated sequentially, following their order of introduction in the source code (Ans. 1.10). A module is a first-class value (Ans. 1.14).

2.2.2. *Export and confinement*

In OCaml, it is possible to define a signature independently from any module by using the following syntax:

```OCaml
module type ModuleTypeName = sig
  (* Declarations. *)
end
```

The confinement operation in OCaml is performed by associating a module P, a signature S and a name RP for the obtained module, which is different from P (Ans. 1.16 and Ans. 1.17). This operation directly corresponds to the operation $RP = \text{From}(P,S)$ in Chapter 1. The signature S provides the list of declarations of the exported fields, and thus defines the confinement mention S. Hence, it is possible to define several exports for a same module (Ans. 1.18). Any module field can be confined by removing its name from the export signature. As we saw while studying confinement in Chapter 1, fields representing type definitions can be exported either by providing their full definition, or by only giving their name (detailed later), or they can be omitted in S. Note that the signature automatically inferred by the OCaml compiler does not confine any type.

For instance, the signature ConfL of example 2.12 causes the export of the type 'a typl and of the operations allowing us to build and inspect values of this type.

EXAMPLE 2.12.–

```OCaml
module type ConfL =
  sig
    type 'a typl = Nil | Cons of 'a * 'a typl
    val empty : 'a typl
    val cons : 'a -> 'a typl -> 'a typl
    val head : 'a typl -> 'a
  end
```

Let us confine the module MyList of example 2.11 using the signature ConfL. In others words, we apply operation $M1 = \mathsf{From}(\text{MyList,ConfL})$.

```OCaml
module M1 : ConfL = MyList
```

Once M1 is created, its fields are usable using the dot-notation. As expected, exported components cons, empty or head can be used whereas add is not accessible from M1, as shown by the continuation of example 2.12.

```OCaml
# let l1 = M1.head (M1.cons (2, 3) M1.empty) ;;
val l1 : int * int = (2, 3)

# M1.add ;;
File "", line 1, characters 0-6:
Error: Unbound value M1.add
```

The semantics of confining a module P by a signature S is that of the operation $RP = \mathsf{From}(\text{P,S})$, where RP is the exported module. There is no code duplication for fields shared by P and RP. However, types of P and RP are different because their signatures are different (Ans. 1.21). Moreover, if P contains a field defining a type t, then the type P.t is different and incompatible with RP.t (if S exports t) (Ans. 1.23). For instance, the type typl of M1 is not the same as the type typl of MyList or of any other module defined by a confinement of MyList exporting this type: M1.typl is not MyList.typl. Example 2.13 illustrates this situation:

EXAMPLE 2.13.–

```
OCaml
# let l1 = M1.cons (2, 3) M1.empty ;;
val l1 : (int * int) M1.typl = M1.Cons ((2, 3), M1.Nil)
# let l2 = MyList.cons (2, 3) MyList.empty;;
val l2 : (int * int) MyList.typl = MyList.Cons ((2, 3), MyList.Nil)
# l1 = l2 ;;
File "", line 1, characters 5-7:
Error: This expression has type (int * int) MyList.typl
       but an expression was expected of type (int * int) M1.typl
```

2.2.2.1. *Signature matching*

A module M can be confined by a signature S if it satisfies, or, as we say, *matches*, this signature, i.e. if the three following conditions can be verified by the typechecker:

1) any field present in S is present in M;

2) for any field m in S which is not a type declaration, the type of m in M is more general (subtyping induced by parametric polymorphism) than its one in S;

3) type definitions in S and in M must be identical, hence have the same number of type parameters (same arity).

Signature matching defines a subtyping relation (see section 5.7.1 of Volume 1).

Example 2.14 illustrates conditions 1 and 2. Let S be a signature. The field f is not defined in M1, which leads to an error. The function f of M2 is the identity, but it is restricted to integers to satisfy S:

EXAMPLE 2.14.–

```
OCaml
# module type S = sig
  val f : int -> int
end ;;
module type S = sig val f : int -> int end

# module M1 : S = struct
   let g x = x + 1
end ;;
File "", line 1, characters 16-42:
Error: Signature mismatch:
       ...
       The field 'f' is required but not provided

# module M2 : S = struct
  let f x = x
end ;;
module M2 : S
```

```
# M2.f ;;
- : int -> int = <fun>
```

Example 2.15 illustrates condition 3: type typl of the signature LC does not define a valid confinement of MyList:

EXAMPLE 2.15.–

```
OCaml
# module type LC =
    sig
    type typl = Nil | Cons of (int * int) * typl
end ;;
module type LC = sig type typl = Nil | Cons of (int * int) * typl end
# module M : LC = MyList ;;
File "", line 1, characters 17-21:
Error: Signature mismatch:
        ...
        Type declarations do not match:
          type 'a typl = 'a MyList.typl = Nil | Cons of 'a * 'a typl
        is not included in
          type typl = Nil | Cons of (int * int) * typl
        They have different arities.
```

Type inference handles the dot-notation and typing ensures the consistency of uses of modules and of signatures which confine some of their fields.

Making the types of modules exported from a same module M different allows one to adapt confinement depending on the needs of different importers, by only exporting the components that these ones require. Typechecking verifies that the confinement is properly respected, which brings strong guaranties on the uses of fields of M, especially when the confinement is used to hide some "secret" values [ANS 11].

2.2.2.2. *Flattening a module*

As already seen, to access a non-confined field of a module, the dot-notation must be used. The construct open performs the flattening operation on the module. Example 2.16 flattens the module MyList of example 2.11.

EXAMPLE 2.16.–

```
OCaml
# open MyList ;;
# let list1 =   cons (2, 2) (cons (1, 1) empty) ;;
val list1 : (int * int) MyList.typl = Cons ((2, 2), Cons ((1, 1), Nil))
```

The semantics of open has been studied in Chapter 1. Bindings introduced by a flattening are put at the head of the current environment Env: if n is bound to v in Env and is also exported by M, the flattening of M in Env masks this binding (n, v) already present in Env.

Two modules can define different components that have the same name. In example 2.17, x is a field of both M and N. Modifications of the environments are written as comments in the example. env_P represents the environment defined by the namespace dedicated to modules, env_v is the environment defined by the namespace for values.

EXAMPLE 2.17.–

```OCaml
OCaml
       (* env_P, env_v *)
# module M = struct let x = 42 end
       (* env1_P = (M, (x = 42)) + env_P *) ;;
# module N = struct let x = "hello" end
       (* env2_P = (N, (x, "hello")) + env1_P *) ;;
# let x = true ;;
x : bool = true
       (* env1_v = (x, true) + env_v *)
# open M ;;
       (* env2_v = (x, 42) + env1_v = (x, 42) + (x, true) + env_v *) ;;
# open N ;;
       (* env3_v = (x, "hello") + env2_v *) ;;
# x ;;
- : string = "hello"
```

The semantics of OCaml indicates that the selected binding is the most recently introduced. The binding (x, true) is masked by (x, 42), which is itself masked by (x, "hello").

2.2.2.3. *Restriction on the scope of* open

The scope of open can be restricted to an expression. The construct open M in e reduces open M to the environment used to evaluate e.

Let ENV be an environment containing a binding of the module M to a value $\{ d_1 = e_1, d_2 = e_2 \}$. The construct let open M in e evaluates e in the environment $(d_2, e_2) \oplus (d_1, e_1) \oplus$ ENV. Example 2.18 illustrates this point.

EXAMPLE 2.18.–

```OCaml
OCaml
# let open M in x + 2 ;;
- : int = 44
# x ;;
- : string = "hello"
```

REMARK.– The module Pervasives of the standard library is automatically opened when writing an OCaml program. It defines the basic operations on the predefined types – booleans, strings, exceptions, numbers, etc. It is important to never mask the bindings of the identifiers of this module.

2.2.2.4. *Nested modules*

Modules can be nested. The usual rules to manage names apply, as shown by example 2.19.

EXAMPLE 2.19.–

```OCaml
# module M = struct
   let x = 5
   module M_nested = struct
     let x = 3
     let y = x * 2
   end
   module M1 = M_nested
end ;;
# let z = M.M1.y + M.x ;;
val z : int = 11
```

2.2.3. *Confinement of type definitions*

A signature may only mention the name of a type. Its definition is thus confined. Let us extend our example dealing with lists. In example 2.20, the module MyList of example 2.11 defines the type of lists 'a typl as a polymorphic type. This type abstracts the type of elements but makes visible the implementation choices made to represent the structure of the list. It is possible to hide these implementation choices by confining the definition of 'a typl and only by providing its name (and its arity if this type is polymorphic). The signature AbsL confines the definition of 'a typl.

EXAMPLE 2.20.–

```OCaml
module type AbsL =
  sig
     exception Error of string
     type 'a typl
     val empty : 'a typl
     val cons : 'a -> 'a typl -> 'a typl
     val head : 'a typl -> 'a
     ....
  end
```

Using values of type 'a typl can only be achieved through functions present in the signature, like empty, cons, head, tail, etc. Exporting only the name of a type forbids pattern matching on values of this type.

To implement a module M satisfying a signature only containing a type name t, it suffices that M provides a definition for t. Example 2.21 defines the structure MAbsL by confining the module MyList with the signature AbsL:

EXAMPLE 2.21.–

```OCaml
# module MAbsL = (MyList: AbsL) ;;
module MAbsL : AbsL
# let l = MAbsL.cons 'a' MAbsL.empty ;;
val l : char MAbsL.typl = <abstr>
```

The annotation `<abstr>` printed by OCaml means that the definition of the type `MAbsL.typl` is confined, its value cannot be displayed otherwise it would reveal the implementation of this type. However, the type of the elements of a list (here `char`), instantiating the type variable, is visible.

The developer may choose a different implementation for lists. In example 2.22, the module `NewL` uses the predefined type `'a list` as a definition for `typl` and gives new definitions for the other fields according to this choice.

EXAMPLE 2.22.–

```OCaml
module NewL : AbsL = struct
  type 'a typl = 'a list
  exception Error of string
  let empty = []
  let cons h t = h :: t
  ...
end
```

It is then possible to introduce a new version of the exported module `MAbsL` using `NewL`. Thanks to lexical scope, any code using its first version does not need to be modified.

```OCaml
# module MAbsL = (NewL: AbsL) ;;
module MAbsL : AbsL

# let l2 = MAbsL.cons 'a' MAbsL.empty ;;
val l2 : char MAbsL.typl = <abstr>
```

Let us continue example 2.22 by now confining the type of the elements of a list (we call it `elem`). Suppose that these elements are built from couples of type `(int*string)`. The following signature confines types `elem` and `typl`. It provides the function `hash` which returns a value of type `elem`.

```
OCaml
module type AbsL2 =
  sig
    type elem
    type typl
    exception Error of string
    val empty : typl
    val hash : int -> string -> elem
    val cons : elem -> typl -> typl
    val head : typl -> elem
  end
```

The module NewL2 provides a definition for both confined types and satisfies the signature AbsL2.

```
OCaml
module NewL2: AbsL2 = struct
  type elem = (int * string)
  type typl = Nil | Cons of (elem * typl)
  exception Error of string
  let empty = Nil
  let cons h t = Cons (h , t)
  let hash v s = (v , s)
  let head nl =   match nl with
    | Nil -> raise (Error "head empty list")
    | Cons (h, _) -> h
end
```

Let us compare the signatures AbsL and AbsL2. AbsL introduces the field type 'a typl and AbsL2 the field type elem.

The type variable 'a of type 'a typl can be instantiated by any type at any time when typing an expression using fields present in the signature AbsL. In contrast, the type elem can be replaced by any type but at the time a module satisfying AbsL2 is introduced, therefore giving a definition for elem.

Let us return to the discussion in section 1.5.1.1. Fields of the signature AbsL have parameterized polymorphic types. This means that each of these types is universally quantified over its own free type variables (if any) and the scope of the quantification is (only) the type of the corresponding field of AbsL. Any field such as cons present in AbsL can be used by importers just after the definition of MyAbsL to build lists of integers, of booleans, etc.

Considering AbsL2, elem is a type variable which is *free* inside this signature but the scope of its universal quantification is the whole signature. This explains why this type variable must be instantiated beforehand in a module, for example NewL2. After the definition of NewL2, importers can use cons but only to build lists of couples of type int * string. Building lists of integers requires the definition of another module matching AbsL2, defining type elem by integer.

2.2.3.1. *Sharing types between modules*

Example 2.13 shows that a type provided in a signature S corresponds to as many exported types as there are modules satisfying the signature, even if the definitions of these types are confined. The export strongly separates exported modules. Let M1 and M2 be two modules confined by S. It is impossible to use functions of M1 to manipulate both its values and those built from M2, even if these values, seen from S, have "the same type". While this feature is very useful for ensuring invariants, it sometimes requires the introduction of a new operation to manipulate together the values of both types. The construct with "opens a window" on the confinement by imposing a constraint in S on a type t whose definition is confined in S.

The modules M1 and M2 must then satisfy this constraint to be compliant with S. In return, M1.t and M2.t are considered identical by the typechecking algorithm.

Let us define a module NewL3, which has the same type as NewL2, by writing the same structure. As illustrated in example 2.23, elements built from functions of these two modules have different types.

EXAMPLE 2.23.–

```
OCaml
# module NewL3: AbsL2 = struct
  type elem = int * string
  type typl = elem list
  exception Error of string
  let empty = []
  let cons h t = h :: t
  let hash v s = (v , s)
  let head nl =
    match nl with
    | [] -> raise (Error "head empty list") | h :: _  -> h
end ;;
# let 12 = NewL2.cons (NewL2.hash 3 "a") NewL2.empty ;;
val 12 : NewL2.typl = <abstr>
# let 13 = NewL3.cons (NewL3.hash 3 "a") NewL3.empty ;;
val 13 : NewL3.typl = <abstr>
# let elem1 = NewL2.head 12 ;;
val elem1 : NewL2.elem = <abstr>
# let elem2 = NewL3.head 13 ;;
val elem2 : NewL3.elem = <abstr>
# elem1 = elem2 ;;
File "", line 1, characters 6-11:
Error: This expression has type NewL3.elem
       but an expression was expected of type NewL2.elem
```

Rewriting NewL2 and NewL3 below allows one to jointly manipulate elements built by the operations of these modules. The compiler is informed that the types elem of these two modules are equal. But the confinement has been partially altered.

```OCaml
module NewL2: AbsL2 with type elem = (int * string) = struct
  type elem = (int * string)
  ...
end

module NewL3: AbsL2 with type elem = (int * string) = struct
  type elem = (int * string)
  ...
end


# let 12 = NewL2.cons (NewL2.hash 3 "a") NewL2.empty ;;
val 12 : NewL2.typl = <abstr>
# let 13 = NewL3.cons (NewL3.hash 3 "a") NewL3.empty ;;
val 13 : NewL3.typl = <abstr>
# let elem1 = NewL2.head 12 ;;
val elem1 : NewL2.elem = (3, "a")
# let elem2 = NewL3.head 13 ;;
val elem2 : NewL3.elem = (3, "a")
# elem1 = elem2 ;;
- : bool = true
```

2.2.4. *Functors*

OCaml provides functors, presented in section 1.6. A reminder that a functor is a module parameterized by one or several modules.

Example 2.24 illustrates the notion of functor. We want to define a functor FOrdL, taking as the input a module describing some values and a function allowing a comparison of them. The result of this functor will be a module implementing ordered lists of these values. Thus FOrdL takes a formal parameter, which is a module whose signature, OrdType, characterizes comparable values. The result of applying this functor to a module satisfying the signature OrdType is a module satisfying the signature OrdL, which describes the ordered lists. Let us first define the signatures OrdType and OrdL.

EXAMPLE 2.24.–

```OCaml
type comparison = Inf | Equal | Sup
module type OrdType =
  sig type elem val compare : elem -> elem -> comparison end

module type OrdL = sig
  type element
  type ordlist
  val empty : ordlist
```

```
  val add : element -> ordlist -> ordlist
  val member : element -> ordlist -> bool
end
```

The signature OrdType specifies that values of type elem have a comparison operation. The type ordlist, introduced in the signature OrdL, is intended to be the type of ordered lists, element being the type of the elements of the list. Since certain values, like functions for instance, cannot be compared (see function equality in section 6.6 of Volume 1), ordlist cannot be declared by a polymorphic type.

Example 2.25 gives a first definition of the signature SOrdL of the functor FOrdL. Its type element is defined as the type elem of the formal parameter Elt and the other declarations are identical to those of the fields of OrdL.

EXAMPLE 2.25.–

```
OCaml
module type SOrdL =
  functor (Elt : OrdType) ->
    sig
      type element = Elt.elem
      type ordlist
      val empty : ordlist
      val add : element -> ordlist -> ordlist
      val member : element -> ordlist -> bool
    end
```

Constraints can be established between parameters of a functor. For instance, they can be used to force some equality between some types of the result module and some types of the functor's parameters. Thus, the signature SOrdL can also be written as follows:

EXAMPLE 2.26.–

```
OCaml
module type SOrdL =
  functor (Elt : OrdType) -> (OrdL with type element = Elt.elem) ;;
```

A definition of FOrdL can, for instance, rely on OCaml's lists, and provide an ordered list implemented by the predefined type list as a result. Such an implementation is given in example 2.27 below.

EXAMPLE 2.27.–

```
OCaml
module FOrdL: SOrdL = functor (Elt : OrdType) ->
  struct
    type element = Elt.elem
    type ordlist = element list
    let empty = []
    let rec add x s = match s with
```

```
     | [] -> [x]
      | hd :: tl ->
        match Elt.compare x hd with
          | Equal -> s | Inf -> x :: s | Sup -> hd :: add x tl
  let rec member x s =
    match s with
      | [] -> false
      | hd :: tl ->
         match Elt.compare x hd with
          | Equal -> true | Inf -> false | Sup -> member x tl
end

module FOrdL : SOrdL
```

In the general case, a functor can have any number of parameters, each one being specified by its name and its signature.

As seen in section 1.6, modules used as effective parameters of the functor must satisfy typing constraints between *kits*, i.e. the same field names and compatible component types. In example 2.28, the functor FOrdL is applied to OrdStr to build the module LOrdStr, providing ordered lists of strings. One can then build an ordered list list1, containing strings.

EXAMPLE 2.28.–

```
OCaml
module OrdStr = struct
  type elem = string
  let compare s1 s2 = if s1 = s2 then Equal else if s1 < s2 then Inf else Sup
end ;;
module OrdStr :
  sig type elem = string val compare : 'a -> 'a -> comparison end

# module LOrdStr = (FOrdL (OrdStr)) ;;
module LOrdStr :
  sig
    type element = OrdStr.elem
    type ordlist = FOrdL(OrdStr).ordl
    val empty : ordlist
    val add : element -> ordlist -> ordlist
    val member : element -> ordlist -> bool
  end

# let list1 = LOrdStr.add "z" (LOrdStr.add "a" LOrdStr.empty) ;;
val list1 : LOrdStr.ordlist = <abstr>
```

In OrdStr, the type elem is defined by string. When applying the functor FOrdL to the module OrdStr, its formal parameter Elt is substituted by OrdStr: Elt.elem is replaced by the definition of OrdStr.elem, that is, by string. Hence, in the body of the functor, the field element element whose definition is Elt.elem is replaced by the type OrdStr.elem, thus by string.

Now suppose that the definition of the type `elem` of `OrdStr` is confined, for instance by typing `OrdStr` with `OrdType`, as in example 2.29 that follows. Therefore, the field `element` can be only bound to the type `OrdStr.elem`. In the same way, the type of `add` in `LOrdStr` is `OrdStr.elem -> ...` and `add` cannot be applied to the value `"aa"` of type `string`: a type error is raised.

EXAMPLE 2.29.–

```
OCaml
module OrdStr : OrdType = struct
  type elem = string
  let compare s1 s2 = if s1 = s2 then Equal else if s1 < s2 then Inf else Sup
end ;;
module OrdStr : OrdType

# module LOrdStr = (FOrdL (OrdStr)) ;;
module LOrdStr :
  sig
    type element = OrdStr.elem
    type ordlist = FOrdL(OrdStr).ordlist
    val empty : ordlist
    val add : element -> ordlist -> ordlist
    val member : element -> ordlist -> bool
  end

# let list1 = LOrdStr.add "a" LOrdStr.empty ;;
File "", line 1, characters 28-31:
Error: This expression has type string but an expression was expected of type
        LOrdStr.element = OrdStr.elem
```

This situation can be solved as seen previously, by explicitly establishing, with the clause `with`, a constraint between the type `elem` and its definition.

2.3. Modularity, namespaces and *W-kit*

Section 2.1 demonstrated how the module language of Ada could be faithfully modeled by the notion of *kit*. Section 2.2 presented features of the OCaml module language corresponding to advanced features of *kit*. Some languages, for instance C, do not provide any syntactic construct for the notion of module. Some others, like Python, offer constructs to define a rather basic notion of module.

2.3.1. *Declaration interfaces*

Most languages allow a program to be split into several source files F_i which are compiled separately. The link edition briefly addressed in section 1.2.3.5 in Volume 1 builds the program's object code from the object codes of F_i, ensuring the consistency between declarations, interfaces, object codes of F_i and the choices made by the developer. A file F_1 may need to use an entity f declared in a file F_2 and f must be defined in one of the files F_i. The language must provide a syntactic construct, which we call the *declaration interface*, to ensure that each source file F_i "knows" the names of entities defined in these F_i. Now several F_i may define an entity with the same name f. Thus the system must determine which definition must be bound to the name f. This choice is made according to some indication given by the developer or by following a general rule specific to the language. The following question arises: Let g be an entity defined in a file F_1 but absent from any declaration interface of the F_i. Can one of the F_i, say F_2, which differs from F_1, use g? If the answer is yes, the relation between g and its definition is established by the linker. Otherwise, as g cannot be used outside of F_1, one may consider that g is confined in F_1. Therefore this family F_i of files, used to build a program, has a certain resemblance to a family of *kits* used for a program construction. Hence the introduction of the notion of weak *kit* in the following section.

2.3.2. W-kits

A source file may contain functions, variables, types, classes, etc. The declaration interfaces can be seen as an export mechanism, and their use as an import mechanism. They can more or less provide a kind of confinement. In a language providing declaration interfaces and separate compilation, a file can be considered as a weak notion of a *kit*, called here *W-kit*. These languages sometimes call such files *modules*. They do not offer any notion of type of module looking like the type of a *kit*. Controls performed by the system on uses of these *W-kits* remain relatively poor and are mostly done during the link edition. We do not describe these *W-kits* any further but we will refer to them when presenting different languages, the language C in this chapter and others in Chapter 4.

2.3.3. *Modularity and header files in C*

The C language only offers the file structure to implement *kits*. However, it is possible to rely on the header files mechanism and the preprocessor to recover certain properties of modularity and confinement. Here we study a way to proceed without going into all the subtleties and possible uses of the C preprocessor.

A source file name.c contains definitions of variables, functions, types, etc. It is possible to create a file name.h containing the declarations of identifiers that must be accessible from other source files. This file name.h can be seen as a *declaration interface* describing an export of name.c and is traditionally called a *header file*. The import of non-confined components of name.c is achieved by using the directive #include "name.h" (or #include <name.h> for predefined libraries) inside the importer source file, say fil.c. The directive #include imports, but also flattens, the namespace of the .h file in the current environment: the notion of qualified name does not exist in C. Indeed, the directive #include "name.h" textually includes the content of this file inside the content of fil.c where this directive is located.

A C source file can thus be modeled as a *W-kit*, with a confinement defined by the header files related to this source file, with an export operation and an import operation automatically performing a flattening. The compiler detects the use of an identifier not declared in any of the interfaces at two moments, depending on the role of this identifier. If this identifier represents a variable or a type, an error is raised while building the object code. If it represents a function, a warning is emitted while building the object code. If this function is not found in one of the object codes making the whole program, an error is finally raised during the link edition.

Fields of the file are evaluated sequentially, i.e. the scope of a field spans from its declaration (or its import) to the end of this file. Thus, there is a risk of masking due to an import (this point will be addressed later). Values of imported fields are not shared: the directive #include causes code duplication. For this reason, header files usually do not contain definitions, just declarations. Indeed, if several .c files of the program include the same .h containing definitions, these definitions will appear in the object code generated for each of these .c, leading to an error at link-time.

We now illustrate the confinement in C with example 2.30. The file test.c imports ftest.h. It uses the variable a and the function id defined in ftest.c. However, only id is declared in ftest.h.

EXAMPLE 2.30.–

```C
/* --- File ftest.h --- */
extern int id (int) ;

/* --- File ftest.c --- */
int a = 36 ;
int id (int y) { return (y) ; }

/* --- File test.c --- */
#include <stdio.h>
#include "ftest.h"
int main () {
  printf ("We can see %d\n", id (a)) ;
  return (0) ;
}
```

```
$ gcc ftest.c test.c -o test.out
test.c:6:21: error: use of undeclared identifier 'a'
  printf ("We can see %d\n", id (a)) ;
                                ^
1 error generated.
```

The variable a is not declared in `ftest.h` nor in `test.c`; trying to use it creates an error, a is confined in `ftest.c`.

Using a function *f* that is not declared in the current source file, and in declaration interfaces it includes, does not necessarily cause a compilation error. The developer can provide the file containing the definition of *f* on the command line used to compile the program. This is sufficient to allow the generation of an executable. The compiler, however, warns the programmer that the declaration of *f* is implicit. Example 2.31 illustrates this point. The function `id` is not declared. The file `ftest.c` is provided on the compilation command line and the executable can be produced.

EXAMPLE 2.31.–

```c
/* --- File test.c --- */
#include <stdio.h>
int main () {
  printf ("We can see %d\n", id (33)) ;
  return (0) ;
}
```

```
$ gcc ftest.c test.c -o test.out
test.c:9:15: warning: implicit declaration of function 'id' is invalid in C99
      [-Wimplicit-function-declaration]
  printf ("We can see %d\n", id (33)) ;
                             ^
$./test.out
We can see 33
```

With example 2.32, we add the directive `#include "ftest.h"`. When evaluated, the names a and `id` are added to the namespace of `test.c`.

EXAMPLE 2.32.–

```c
/* --- File ftest.h --- */
int a ;
int id (int) ;

/* --- File ftest.c --- */
int a = 40 ;
int id (int y) { return (y) ; }

/* --- File test.c --- */
#include <stdio.h>
#include "ftest.h"
int main () {
  printf ("We can see %d\n", id (a)) ;
  return (0) ;
}
```

```
$ gcc test.c ftest.c -o test.out
$ ./test.out
We can see 40
```

The compiler can verify the consistency between the names declared in an interface declaration `name.h` and the use of these names in a source file `name.c`. It suffices to place the directive `#include name.h` in the source code of `name.c` before any use of the names exported by `name.h`. We will follow this programming convention.

Several declaration interfaces can declare the same name and several files can give it different definitions. How is this redundancy handled? We provide an answer using example 2.33.

EXAMPLE 2.33.–

```c
C
/* --- File ftest.h --- */
int a ;
int id (int) ;

/* --- File ftest.c --- */
#include "ftest.h"
int a = 4 ;
int id (int y) { return (y) ; }

/* --- File gtest.h --- */
int a ;
int id (int) ;

/* --- File gtest.c --- */
#include "gtest.h"
int a = 10 ;
int id (int y) { return (y) ; }

/* --- File test.c --- */
#include <stdio.h>
#include "ftest.h"
#include "gtest.h"
int main () {
  printf ("We can see %d et %d\n", a, id (a)) ;
  return (0) ;
}
```

```
$ gcc ftest.c gtest.c test.c -o test.out
duplicate symbol _id in:
    /var/folders/mw/0w9p2fcj51z21hhd4469g29m0000gn/T/ftest-183cd4.o
    /var/folders/mw/0w9p2fcj51z21hhd4469g29m0000gn/T/gtest-47c960.o
duplicate symbol _a in:
    /var/folders/mw/0w9p2fcj51z21hhd4469g29m0000gn/T/ftest-183cd4.o
    /var/folders/mw/0w9p2fcj51z21hhd4469g29m0000gn/T/gtest-47c960.o
```

```
ld: 2 duplicate symbols for architecture x86_64
clang: error: linker command failed with exit code 1 (use -v to see invocation)
```

The compiler accepts the redundancy of declarations in the .h files as long as they are not conflicting (i.e. they do not have different types). However, it rejects redundancy in definitions. The choice between several definitions must be made by the developer, deciding which files they send to the compilation. But in any case, only one definition will be usable in the final executable.

```
$ gcc test.c ftest.c -o test.out
We can see 4 et 4
```

A variable var may need to be shared between several files F_i. This variable has to be defined once in one of the F_i. The declaration of var, starting with the keyword extern, must be present in all the files F_i needing to use var (for instance by using the #include directive). The keyword extern indicates to the compiler that the memory allocation for var must be done once, when the definition of var is given. Hence the sharing of (or, more accurately, the sharing of the binding of) var between all the files F_i using it. Let us show this mechanism with example 2.34.

EXAMPLE 2.34.–

```
C
/* --- File ftest.h --- */
extern int a ;

/* --- File ftest.c --- */
#include "ftest.h"
int a = 40 ;

/* --- File gtest.h --- */
extern  int a ;
int fgtest (int) ;

/* --- File gtest.c --- */
#include "gtest.h"
int fgtest (int y) {
  extern int a ;
  a = a + 1 ;
  return (a) ;
}

/* --- File test.c --- */
#include <stdio.h>
#include "ftest.h"
#include "gtest.h"
int main () {
  printf ("We can see %d et %d\n", a, fgtest (a)) ;
  return (0) ;
}
```

```
$ gcc ftest.c gtest.c test.c -o test.out
$ ./test.out
We can see 40 et 41
```

We suggest readers adopt the following discipline. A header file `file.h` should be associated with any file `file.c`, listing the entities exported by `file.c`. Moreover, the file `file.c` should contain the directive `#include "file.h"` in order that the compiler can verify the consistency between the fields of `file.h` and those of `file.c`. This directive `#include "file.h"` should also be present in any file containing a call to one of the functions of `file.c`. It is not recommended to import functions of `file.c` directly, even if it is possible to do so (see example 2.31). However, readability of the structure and control of the program correctness remain, essentially, the responsibility of the C developer.

3

Class and Object Features

A functional program executes a sequence of function calls to create the result of the program, an imperative program executes a sequence of state changes to create the result state of the program. The two points of view can be easily combined, since most programming languages offer both possibilities, facilitated by the use of modular features. Object-oriented programming is sometimes presented as belonging to the concurrent paradigm, which differs significantly from functional and imperative ones. Different entities, often called *objects*, contribute to the elaboration of the result by exchanging messages in parallel; the reception of a message triggering an action or an evaluation. This view has spread from the arrival of the first object-oriented languages such as Simula, introduced in the 1960s to create simulation programs, Smalltalk, created in the 1970s by Xerox, Eiffel, etc. However, we present object-oriented programming, staying within the framework of functional and imperative programming.

Section 3.1 includes a very classical *description* of the object features, which also serves to establish our vocabulary. Section 3.2 proposes a *model* of these features, using the *kits* studied in Chapter 1. This modeling remains rather informal but provides guidance for reading a reference manual. This section briefly explains why we cannot more formally describe the typing and evaluation of objects and classes.

3.1. Object-oriented features

An object-oriented language offers objects, often classes, but can also offer – as in C++, for example – purely imperative or functional constructs, features of concurrent programming, etc. Here we present only the most common object-oriented features.

3.1.1. *Objects*

Object programming puts the emphasis on the notion of *data*, whether it is concrete data (person, etc.), mathematical concepts (polynomials, etc.), and so on. Some languages even consider any data as an object, including integers, booleans, etc. This is the case with Python, for example.

Any object has two main parts. The first part, called the *internal state*, models the data encoded by the object by a set of components called *attributes* (or *instance variables*) which represent the different constituents of the data. The second part of an object gathers the functionalities, often referred to as *methods*, which define its interactions with other objects or with itself.

The creation of an object can only be done during the execution of the program. An object is a *first class* value, that is, a value that can be obtained as the result of an assignment, of an application of a function, a procedure, a method, a test, etc. In a typed language, the type of an object is deduced from its attributes and methods. But the definition of this type is not necessarily detailed in the language syntax.

A *message*, also called a *method call*, denoted here by $O_D\#m\,(v)$, is a request made to a recipient object O_D, to execute one of its methods m. Upon receipt of the message, O_D performs the required task defined by m. In other words, the method m of O_D is applied to the actual parameter(s) v provided by the message $O_D\#m\,(v)$ sent to O_D. The attributes and methods of O_D are all accessible during the evaluation of $O_D\#m$. The definition of a method m can therefore use the attributes and methods of an object O_D, the "future recipient" of the message m. This object O_D is denoted in the body of m either by a dedicated identifier, self or this, or is left implicit, with the convention that the attributes and methods used by m are those of the object receiving the message m. We will use this in our examples. The definition of m can contain messages to O_D itself (that is, calls to other methods of this or to m itself), messages to other objects, calls to known functions and can create new objects. Thus, an object can send itself a message to update one of its attributes. The message $O_D\#m$ can of course only be executed if the object recipient O_D has this method m. If O_D is statically known, its possession of m can be checked by the language compiler, which will raise an error if it is missing. Otherwise, the absence will only be discovered at runtime and will cause an execution error.

Example 3.1 is about clothing. A skirt is modeled by an object skirt having an internal state that consists of two attributes: an integer year (year of sale) and a float price. This object skirt has a method sale which compares its parameter (current_year) with its attribute year (to possibly put this skirt on sale), a method set_price which assigns its attribute price, according to the result of the comparison carried out by sending the message this#sale (current_year) to itself, represented by this. The syntax used here takes up the words introduced above. The indicated types are those used by most object languages. The functional types are written t -> s, t being the type of the arguments and s the type of the result.

EXAMPLE 3.1.–

```
Object skirt =
begin
  attribute year : int = 2019
  attribute price : float = 100.0
  method sale : int -> bool = fun current_year -> (current_year > this#year)
  method set_price : int * float -> unit = fun (current_year, y) ->
    if this#sale (current_year) then this#price := y * 0.7
    else this#price := y
end
...
skirt#set_price (2019, 99.0)
```

The evaluation of the message skirt#set_price(2019, 99.0) triggers dispatch of the message this#sale(current_year). The attribute year of skirt is read (this#year) and compared with current_year, then the attribute this#price is modified by assignment.

Example 3.1 raises some questions, which will be answered with the presentation of classes:

1) In the definition of set_price, this seems to be a free variable. What is its status in the expression this#price?

2) this is instantiated by the object skirt during the evaluation of skirt#set_price. What is the mechanism of such a replacement?

3) Is it possible to modify the code of set_price to create an "analog" object for skirt, named, for example, skirt_in_sale which would memorize the sale price in its attribute price? This would avoid having to change the internal state of skirt.

4) But what is the meaning of "analog" and how is this new object created?

From an operational point of view, the notion of object as a *first class value* is the primitive notion of object-oriented programming. An object can be used as a basis for defining a collection of similar objects if one determines, from its definition, a construct, often referred to as an *object generator*, that allows you to define objects in a collection. This is the case in JavaScript, for example. These objects all have the same type and the same methods but have different internal states.

3.1.2. *Classes*

The notion of class can also be considered as the primitive notion of object-oriented programming. A class is seen as a construct that generates objects with attributes of the same name and the same type; only the values of these attributes differ. A class also contains methods which are shared by all the objects generated by this class. The two views of the object paradigm are not antinomic but are presented differently in tutorials and in reference manuals. We adopt a class-based approach, within the framework of a typed language with type declaration (unless stated otherwise).

3.1.2.1. *Classes, objects and their types*

On the one hand, the definition of a class introduces the declarations of the *attributes* (also called *instance variables*), that is their names and their types, and on the other hand, the definitions (name, type, defining expression) of the methods of the future objects of the class. These are called *object methods* or simply *methods* if there is no ambiguity. The description of the objects in section 3.1.1 remains valid when objects are built from a class.

The majority of typed class languages consider that the type of a class is described by the list of the names and types of the components of the class, in a similar way to the typing we adopted for the *kits* in Chapter 1. The type often has the same name as the class. Objects are also typed and their type is often the same as that of the class. The typing is often nominal: two classes with different names have different types, even if they have exactly the same attributes and methods.

3.1.2.2. *Object constructors*

Every class definition comes with at least one function, called the *object constructor*, which serves to build an object of the class. This function can have several parameters and usually has the name of the class. Generating an object of class C is done by applying the object constructor C to effective parameters. The application operation is traditionally denoted by new. It can be done at any time during program execution and its result is a value called *object* (or *object value* when needed), which is therefore a *first class value*. This object value can be named, which requires the introduction of a variable, that is, an identifier (often referred to improperly as an *object*). The value of this variable is most often in the imperative framework, a pointer to the object value which is the result of the operation new. In a functional language, this variable can be directly bound to the result of new, and this result can even remain anonymous.

Object constructors are often placed directly in the class definition but can also be provided outside the class. The body of a constructor defines the values of the attributes of the object to be created, it can also contain other instructions, executed at the time of object creation. There can be several constructors for the same class. They must have the same name as the class and differ by their formal parameters. Object constructors are not really methods of the class, even though some languages present them as such. We will see in section 3.2 that these constructors do not have the same semantics as methods.

Note that choosing the class as a primitive notion leads to a rather different point of view on objects: an object comes from a class, it always has its own internal state but no longer really has its methods, it "borrows" them from its class and therefore it shares them with the other objects of its class and subclasses, built by inheritance of this class. Applying (with new) an object constructor allocates a memory zone in which the attributes of the created object are stored, and installs the sharing of methods with the other objects of the class.

We call *creation of an object O of class C* the application of an object constructor of class C and we will say that O is an object of C.

Example 3.2 reformulates example 3.1 using a class. Skirts are represented by objects of the class Skirts. This class declares the attributes year and price, and the methods sale and set_price. We also define the object constructor Skirts which takes two arguments.

EXAMPLE 3.2.–

```
Class Skirts =
begin
  attribut year : int
  attribut price : float
  Skirts (y : int, p : float) = this#year := y ; this#price := p
  method sale : int -> bool = fun current_year -> (current_year > this#year)
  method set_price : int * float -> unit = fun (current_year, y) ->
    if this#sale (current_year) then this#price := y * 0.7
    else this#price := y
end
my_skirt = new Skirts (2018, 75.5)
my_skirt#set_price (2019, 100.0)
```

The value of the variable my_skirt is the object value obtained by the application, denoted by new placed in prefix position, of the constructor Skirts to effective parameters. The variable my_skirt is often improperly said to be an object of the class Skirts.

We consider the message my_skirt#set_price(2019, 100.0), sent to the object my_skirt. During its evaluation, the message this#sale (2019) is sent and, here, this denotes the object my_skirt. The attribute year of my_skirt is then read (this#year) and then compared with 2019; the attribute this#price is then modified by an assignment. Note that this assignment cannot be made with the constructor Skirts: a new application of Skirts would create a different object from my_skirt that should be named for future use.

A class can also have its own fields: variables, called *class variables* (to encode shared constants by all of its objects, for example), methods called *class methods*, functions and instruction blocks. It can also contain classes called *internal classes*, as well as exceptions.

3.1.2.3. *Confinement*

The fields (attributes, methods, etc.) of the classes can be confined to prohibit their use by an importer. As already seen in Chapter 1, the confinement marks can also be used to manage the extension, known as *inheritance* in the object framework, which builds a *subclass* from a class.

In object-oriented languages, confinement is usually defined by tagging attributes or methods in the class source code. But it can also be implicit, if for example the confinement of the internal state is the general rule in the language considered. In this case, it is possible to define functions – thus methods in object terminology – to access and modify the confined attributes of an object (they are sometimes called *getters* and *setters*). The classes themselves can be confined by attaching a mark to them.

Most object-oriented languages offer at least three degrees of confinement that interact with inheritance. Here the marks are named `public-st`, `private-st`, `protected-st` to avoid any confusion with those of different object languages. We define their meaning as follows. The mark `public-st` indicates that the identifier (of the attribute, of the method, of the class) is in fact not confined. It can be imported into all definitions of all classes and used without restrictions to create subclasses by inheritance. The mark `private-st` prohibits the import of the identifier and makes it invisible from a subclass. According to languages, a field marked `private-st` can be reintroduced in a subclass and considered as a new field. The mark `protected-st` confines the identifier within its class and its subclasses, often provided that these subclasses belong to the same library as this class.

Confinement policies differ quite considerably between languages. These will be considered in Chapter 4. Recall that confining an identifier adjusts its scope by making it invisible from certain syntactic constructs, depending on where they are placed within the source code. This does not mean that a confined identifier is inaccessible to these constructs: *getters* and *setters* can be provided to manipulate the value of such an identifier.

3.1.2.4. *Simple inheritance*

A class can be extended by adding attributes and methods to get a new class, unless a dedicated mark (often `final`) prohibits it. This mechanism is called *simple inheritance*, the inherited class is sometimes called the *super-class* and the class that inherits is the *subclass*. The super-class can, depending on the language, be referred to by its name, by the keyword `super` or by an identifier chosen by the user.

A subclass has all the fields of its super-class, even if they are invisible because of confinement or other reasons. A method m (or an attribute) marked `private-st` in a class C is present in a subclass R of C even if the definitions added in R cannot use m. Object constructors, on the other hand, are not inherited. However, the process of creating an object of R begins with the creation of an object of C, then completing it with the fields added by R before returning this new object. Any object constructor of a subclass must therefore call an object constructor of the class. Some object languages require this call to be explicit but others add this call implicitly, if, for example, the class has a constructor with no formal parameters.

Example 3.3 builds a class using simple inheritance. We use the keyword extending to denote inheritance. The class Skirts of example 3.2 is extended to the class SkirtMadeOf by adding an attribute material of type string and a method get_made.

EXAMPLE 3.3.–

```
Class SkirtMadeOf extending Skirts =
begin
  attribut material : string
  method get_made : unit -> string = fun () -> this#material
end
```

Let us continue this example by introducing the object constructor of the class SkirtMadeOf which must call the constructor of the inherited class Skirts. This one is not inherited but it is visible in the subclass (unless it is confined): the subclass can use it.

```
SkirtMadeOf (y : int, p : float, s : string) =
  Skirts (y, p) ; this#material := s
```

The class SkirtMadeOf inherits the method sale from Skirts but as the silk skirts are not sold out, it is necessary to adapt this method sale in the subclass SkirtMadeOf, as follows:

```
method sale : int -> bool = fun current_year ->
  if this#get_made () = "silk" then false else (current_year > this#year)
```

The *reintroduction* of a field during inheritance is authorized by all object-oriented languages. Depending on the language, the attributes, methods, variables and class methods may or may not be reintroduced. This reintroduction can be considered either as an overloading of the field or as a redefinition of it. These two possibilities are discussed further in the following.

In example 3.3, the method sale has been reintroduced. We will elaborate a little on the effect on the method set_price of this reintroduction, which will be called a *redefinition* in this case. The redefinition not only allows the reintroduction of a method of the superclass by a method of the same name with a different body but also changes the behavior of the methods using the redefined method. It usually requires the type of the redefined method to be identical to the type of the original method. This is the case in example 3.3. In contrast, if a reintroduction is not a redefintion, it is an overloading, and the type of the overloading method may differ from that of the overloaded one.

Some languages can prevent the reintroduction of certain fields by tagging these fields with a dedicated mark (for example `final`). Such marks put on a whole class prohibit its inheritance without acting on the confinement of this class.

Some languages allow the reintroduction operation to modify confinement: a method marked `private-st` in the super-class (and therefore not visible in any subclass) can be reintroduced in a subclass with a `public-st` status that can remain implicit in the source code of this subclass if, for example, any unmarked field is considered to have the `public-st` status.

3.1.2.5. *Subclassing*

The objects of a subclass R of a class C do not have the same type as those of C: the names of the classes differ and the fields may differ. Inheriting a method does not change its type. A method m of C can use `this`, which designates an object of C. An object of the subclass R can receive m as a message. If m is not reintroduced in R, is this message ill-typed?

Object-oriented languages often (though not always) assume that inheritance defines a preorder between types of classes and subclasses, called *subclassing*; the type of the super-class being considered "greater" than the types of its subclasses. We can make the hypothesis that this subclassing preorder induces a subtyping preorder on object types: the type of an object of a subclass can be considered as a subtype of the type of an object of its super-class (see section 1.7.2.3). In short, an object of a subclass can be considered, during typing, as an object of its super-class: this property is sometimes called *object polymorphism*. Thus the receipt of a message defined in the super-class by an object of a subclass remains well-typed. In other words, a super-class method can be called by an object of a subclass without typing errors. We will return to this point in section 3.2.5.

Let us continue example 3.3 by giving an intuitive view of subclassing. Let `silk_skirt` be an object of the class `SkirtMadeOf` introduced by:

```
silk_skirt = new SkirtMadeOf (2019, 300, "silk")
```

– First, we type `silk_skirt#sale (2019)`. Under the hypothesis that the type of an object is that of its class and that this type has the name of its class, the type of `silk_skirt` is `SkirtMadeOf`. So, `silk_skirt#sale` is of type $int \rightarrow bool$ and the message `silk_skirt#sale(2019)` returns a value of type `bool`.

– Let us type the message silk_skirt#set_price (2019, 100.0). The method set_price of Skirts differs from that of SkirtMadeOf because sale has been redefined. Types Skirts and SkirtMadeOf are different. But SkirtMadeOf is a subclass of Skirts and, under the subclassing hypothesis, the type Skirts is more general than the type SkirtMadeOf. The expression silk_skirt#set_price is thus well-typed. So the message silk_skirt#set_price (2019, 100.0) is well-typed, of type unit.

3.1.2.6. *Late binding*

Let us now evaluate the message silk_skirt#set_price (1919, 100.0) from example 3.3. This is a call to the method set_price of Skirts. Its evaluation requires the evaluation of the sub-expression this#sale (current_year), thus the evaluation of the method sale, but which one? Two choices are possible: sale of class Skirts or sale of class SkirtMadeOf. The second possibility is most often the one chosen and corresponds to the strategy "extension with back-update", discussed in Chapter 1, and known as *late binding* in the context of objects. The method sale is then often said to be *redefined* or *overridden* in SkirtMadeOf. Thus, the evaluation of sale will trigger the evaluation of the message this#get_made () and the price of the skirt will not decrease. This point will be developed in the next section.

3.1.2.7. *Multiple inheritance*

A new class can be built by aggregating attributes and methods of several classes and possibly adding new attributes and methods. This mechanism is called *multiple inheritance*.

Example 3.4 introduces the class Hat with an attribute value and a method sale.

EXAMPLE 3.4.–

```
Class Hat =
begin
  attribute value : int
  Hat (z : int) = this#value := z
  method set_value : int -> unit = fun y -> this#value := y
  method sale : unit -> unit = fun () ->
    if this#value > 100 then this#set_value (100) else this#set_value (50)
end
```

In example 3.5, the class Formaldress is obtained by multiple inheritance of the classes Skirts of example 3.3 and Hat of example 3.4.

EXAMPLE 3.5.–

```
Class Formaldress extending  Skirts, Hat =
Formaldress (y, p, z) = Skirts (y, p) ; Hat (z)
...
```

The object constructor of `Formaldress` calls those of `Skirts` and `Hat`. The two inherited classes have the method `sale`. Which one will be chosen to build `Formaldress` and how?

Simultaneously inherited classes can include methods that have the same name, *in fine* the compiler or the interpreter must choose which of these methods will be inherited by the subclass being introduced. Several solutions are possible. The language can propose a syntactic rule stating, for example, that the inherited method is that of the last class mentioned in the declaration of multiple inheritance, or a mechanism of renaming of some of the inherited classes can be proposed in order to clarify the origin of the method to be inherited. Underlying this problem of multiple inheritance is the fact that a method of a class cannot be used outside of its class, like an ordinary function, which would then be easy to rename. In example 3.5, with the first choice of multiple inheritance rule, the class `Formaldress` will inherit `Hat#sale`.

All object-oriented languages propose a syntactic construct (a keyword like `extends` in Java or a simple sign : in C++) to use simple or multiple inheritance. Some languages assume that there is a class, sometimes called `Object`, from which all the inheritance chains are issued: all classes inherit from `Object`. It is not always necessary to explicitly mention the inheritance of this `Object` class, since the compiler systematically adds this inheritance to any class built without it.

3.1.2.8. *Abstract classes, parameterized classes*

A class is said to be *abstract* if the definition of at least one of its methods is deferred. The definition is, in general, given in a subclass. The declaration of such a method is preceded by a keyword which can be `abstract` or `virtual` depending on the language. This indication allows the compiler to endorse the fact that the method definition is voluntarily omitted. It is not possible to build objects of abstract classes.

Some object languages accept that the definition of a field is done outside the class body but in the same compilation unit. This is only a syntactic choice, which does not correspond to the choice to defer a definition, always announced by a keyword.

A class whose methods are all abstract is often called an *interface*. An interface therefore contains only fields introduced by their name, type and possibly a mark of confinement. Depending on the language, as soon as a class inherits from an interface, all the methods of this interface must or must not be defined in the subclass. Interfaces are often used as a kind of contract, requiring the class that inherits from them to implement all the functionalities declared in the interface. In Java, in combination with simple inheritance, this enables the retrieval of a kind of multiple inheritance.

Many languages offer a form of parametrization for classes, accepting at least type parameters. Parametrization was discussed in section 1.5. We will link this presentation of parameterized *kits* to the parameterized classes in the next section.

3.1.2.9. *Introspection and reflection*

Some object languages propose a mechanism, called *introspection*, to obtain information at runtime about manipulated objects such as their type, class, methods, and the classes they inherit. The *reflection* mechanism goes a step further by allowing attributes, functions, methods, etc. to be dynamically created and modified at runtime, possibly with the use of introspection. With this mechanism, it is even possible to interpret a character string (or another form of data) as a command to be executed at the moment of its interpretation. Reflection therefore allows the execution process to be dynamically modified. A language offering such a mechanism provides the developer with tools derived from those used by the compiler and/or interpreter to allocate memory, manage branches, etc. Many interpreted languages, which therefore have a dynamic evaluation, and also some compiled languages, offer these mechanisms. It is recommended to use reflection only after having properly measured all the consequences, which can be heavy.

3.1.2.10. *Object-oriented programs*

An object-oriented program is a set of declarations and definitions of variables, functions, classes, declarations and constructions of objects, interactions between objects defined by sending messages; all of these actions being possibly intertwined. As in functional or imperative programming, a set of interactions can be a composition and/or a sequence of elementary interactions, which constitutes the execution of the program. It starts in an initial state built by the import of classes, modules, objects, etc. already known according to the possibilities offered by the language. Bindings to classes, objects, etc. can be added to the current environment at runtime and the memory can be modified. The analysis of these evolutions of environments and memory can be done by following the execution rules already stated for functional and imperative programs in Chapters 3 and 4 of Volume 1. In other words, once the entire class structure has been completed, a program remains a sequence of computations of values, instructions, function (method) calls, and exception raising and handling. Some object-oriented languages, such as Java, adopt the point of view that "everything is an object" and therefore, the main program itself is a method (see section 4.1).

Finally, among the languages that implement objects as pointers, almost all of them use a *garbage collector* (see section 7.6.3 of Volume 1). Some languages also offer functions called *object destructors*, which are associated to classes in the same way as object constructors. They are called when an object is to be destroyed, either by an explicit instruction in the source code, or by the *garbage collector*, just before releasing the memory space allocated to this object. They are mainly used to carry out "service operations", such as closing channels and data files at a time specified by the program (and not when the garbage collector is running, which is not known in advance).

3.2. *kits* and object features

In this section, we model classes and objects using the *kits* studied in Chapter 1. This modeling *differs* from the traditional presentation of classes and objects given in section 3.1. Constructors are defined in a more formal way. Methods have an additional parameter, which helps to better explain late binding. Links between objects, attributes and methods are detailed.

3.2.1. *Modeling classes*

3.2.1.1. C-kits *and classes*

A class C is modeled by a parameterized *kit* called a *C-kit*, denoted by C_K, which is characterized by specific rules about parameters and components. The set of parameters is divided into three families playing different roles. The F_a family, possibly empty, is used to initialize the attributes of the objects of the class; it is thus a family of value parameters. Most object languages use F_a to define object constructors, without highlighting its status as a class parameter. As it is essential here to easily model the construction of an object, we introduce F_a. The F_p family, if it is not empty, introduces type or value parameters so as to build a *C-kit* parameterized by a type and/or a value. The F_k family, if it is not empty, introduces parameters which are *C-kits* (see the functors in section 1.6). For ease of reading, we limit the F_a family to only one parameter, denoted by d, and we do not always consider F_p and F_k, whose study in Chapter 1 also covers their use in *C-kits*.

The components of a *C-kit* C_K are partitioned into different (possibly empty) groups that perform or receive different sorts of treatment, as detailed below:

1) A group of components, called *attributes*, which are mutable or non-mutable variables, whose types are known (if the language is typed) and whose values are expressions that can use the formal parameters of F_a of C_K. The set of attributes is usually called the *internal state*. In the following, we use only one attribute a of type t_a and only one parameter d in F_a.

2) A group of components called *methods*. A method of field m is a function with one formal parameter, noted θ, called *var-obj*: $m = \lambda\theta.f$. The body f of this function m is (generally) a function of one (or more) parameter(s) z: $f = \texttt{fun}\ z \rightarrow b$. Our notation uses two abstraction operators $\texttt{fun}$ and λ because their semantics are not the same (as detailed in the following). The expression b is called the *body of the method*, it can use the attributes a, denoting them by $\theta\#a$ and the methods l of the *C-kit*, denoting them by $\theta\#l$. The expression b can also use those fields of C_K which are neither attributes nor methods, denoting them simply by their name. But b cannot use the formal parameters F_a of C_K. It can, on the other hand, use those of F_p and F_k. Most typed object languages require that the declaration of a method also introduces its "type". Under this denomination, the required type is that of the

function $f = \text{fun } z \rightarrow b$ and not that of $m = \lambda\theta.f$. We will conform to this usage, calling the type of $\text{fun } z \rightarrow b$ the *type of the method* m and, if necessary, referring to the type of $\lambda\theta.f$ as the *full type* of the method m.

3) A group of components that are *C-kits*, here called *internal* C-kits *with back-update*, whose definitions may use the methods and attributes of C_K and the parameters of F_p and F_k. Their attributes can use parameters of F_a.

4) A group of components, annotated here as static_in, including exceptions, functions called *class methods*, variables called *class variables* and *C-kits* called *internal* C-kits *without back-update*. Their definitions cannot use any parameter of the F_a family or the methods of C_K. They can use parameters of F_p and F_k. In a static scope language, these fields are evaluated at the creation of C_K if F_p and F_k are empty and otherwise at the moment of instantiation of F_p and F_k, as seen in Chapter 1. These fields, which have already been studied in Chapter 1, will only be mentioned if necessary.

5) The *C-kit* can have components that introduce types. We do not mention them in our model, to make its presentation lighter. It will suffice to refer to the general study of the *kits* to model these fields.

In a typed language, the type of fields is of course provided (unless they are inferred). Thus a *C-kit* C_K has the following form:

$$C_K(d) = \{\ a : t_a = r;\ m_1 : tm_1 = \lambda\theta.f_1;\ \ldots;\ m_p : tm_p = \lambda\theta.f_p\ ;\ s : t_s = exp\ \}$$

Field a is an attribute, t_a is its type and r its defining expression that may contain occurrences of the formal parameter d of F_a. The field m_j (for $j \in [1..p]$) is a method of type tm_j whose defining expression is $\lambda\theta.f_j$ where $f_j = \text{fun } z_j \rightarrow b_j$. The variable θ is a variable bound in the body b_j of f_j by the abstraction λ. To lighten the presentation, we omit F_p and F_k parameters and we do not explicitly include all possible class variables and methods, exceptions, or internal *C-kits* with or without back-updates. We represent them collectively by a single static_in component denoted by the field s of type t_s and defined by the expression exp.

In the examples, the abstraction $\lambda\theta$ is denoted V_this ->. The variable V_this is often noted this (or self) in object-oriented languages. Some of these languages do not require the methods to be explicitly functions of the variable V_this representing a object. In this case, any occurrence of V_this (so this or self) in the body of a method appears as a free variable, which does not reflect its semantics. The attributes used in the body of methods are not always preceded by V_this. We do this in example 3.6. It defines the *kit* Skirts set by $F_a = \{\ y, p\ \}$, omitting the type of methods to lighten description.

EXAMPLE 3.6.–

```
Kit Skirts (y : int, p : float) =
begin
  var year : int = y
  var price : float = p
  method sale =
    lambda V_this -> fun current_year -> (current_year > V_this.year)
  method set_price = lambda V_this -> fun (current_year, z) ->
    if V_this#sale (current_year) = true then V_this#price := z * 0.7
    else V_this#price := z
end
Skirts (a : int, b : float) = year := a ; price := b
```

The *C-kit* Skirts has two attributes, year and price, and two methods, sale and set_price. The class Skirts of example 3.1 is modeled by the *C-kit* Skirts.

3.2.1.2. C-kit *types*

As a *C-kit* is a *kit*, its type has already been defined in Chapter 1. Being parameterized by the three families F_k of type t_k, F_p of type t_p and F_a of type t_a, a *C-kit* does indeed have a functional type which takes the form $t_k \to t_p \to t_a \to T$, where T is the type of the body of the *C-kit*, thus the collection of the types of its fields. Most often, object languages name the type of a *C-kit* by its own name and do not detail the definition of this type, assimilated to the type T of its body. The parametrization of a *C-kit* by the family F_a is rarely explicit in the type of the *C-kit*. However we will give such an example in OCaml. The parametrization by the families F_p and F_k is always explicit; the inclusion of the types of these parameters in their declaration allows the functionality of the *C-kit* type to be retrieved.

3.2.1.3. *Instantiation of* F_p *and* F_k

Any instantiation of parameters of the families F_p and F_k must result in a *C-kit* remaining parameterized by F_a. These instantiations have been studied in Chapter 1. They must precede the instantiation of F_a.

3.2.1.4. *Instantiation of* F_a

Instantiation of parameters of the F_a family can only be done on a *C-kit* C_K, which has no other parameters. Moreover, all parameters of F_a must be instantiated at the same time in all attribute definitions. Therefore this instantiation builds a complete *kit*, called an *O-kit* (and called an *object* in object-oriented languages). Since the parameters of F_a can only be used by the attribute fields of C_K (or the attributes of its internal *kits* with back-update), the other fields of C_K are not modified by this instantiation. With the syntax used to describe the *C-kit* C_K in section 3.2.1.1, let us call $C_K(v)$ the *O-kit* obtained by applying C_K to the effective parameter v and let $w = r[d \leftarrow v]$. We have:

$$C_K(v) = \{\, a : t_a = w; \; ; m_1 : tm_1 = \lambda\theta.f_1; \; \ldots; \; m_p : tm_p = \lambda\theta.f_p \,; s : t_s = exp \,\}$$

Effective parameters instantiating F_a must have the same type as the corresponding formal ones in F_a. So the type of $C_K(v)$ is the type of the body of C_K, which was called T in the preceding paragraph. This is why, informally, *O-kits* are said to have the same type as the *C-kits* they come from.

3.2.2. *Modeling objects*

3.2.2.1. O-kit *and objects*

An *object* from the class C, modeled by a *C-kit* C_K and depending only on F_a, is itself modeled by an *O-kit* O_C created by instantiation of F_a in C_K. The attributes of O_C are obtained by instantiation of F_a. The other fields of O_C are those of the *C-kit* C_K. The fields of C_K which are not attributes can thus be shared with all the objects created from C_K.

With our modeling of objects, the type of an object O_C is the type of the *O-kit* modeling it, thus the type T of the body of the *C-kit* C_K, as explained in the previous section. This choice is in accordance with the typical uses of objects but does not reflect certain aspects of our modeling, such as the full types of methods. A more accurate modeling of typing requires too much development to be included in this book.

Object languages choose to consider the value of an *O-kit* as a first class value (Ans. 1.14). An object O_C can therefore be used in an expression, can be passed as an argument, can be the result of a computation, etc. Class languages do not offer any form of inheritance of *O-kits*: an object primarily represents given data. The development of data structures and of tools is done exclusively at the class level. This is why an *O-kit* can only be created from a *C-kit* with only parameters to define its attributes.

3.2.2.2. *Object constructors*

We did not need the additional notion of object constructors to talk about the instantiation of a *C-kit* parameterized by F_a, and thus about the creation of objects of a class. However, in section 3.1, we have described the notion of a constructor of objects of a class, or, to put it more succinctly, an *object constructor*. Let us put these object constructors back into the framework of our modeling.

An *object constructor* C_I of a class C modeled by a *C-kit* C_K is a function $\mathtt{fun}\, x \to C_K(x)$, which performs the instantiation of the F_a family of parameters of C_k. Its application to an effective parameter v results in the *O-kit* $C_K(v)$, described above. The application of this function C_I is often denoted by the identifier $\mathtt{new}$ in prefix notation (even though the exact meaning of $\mathtt{new}$ may differ from one language to another). So we have:

$$\mathtt{new}\, C_I(v) \rightsquigarrow C_K(v)$$

More precisely, the evaluation of new $C_I(v)$ in a state $E = (\text{Env}, \text{Mem})$ returns the value v_{obj} of the *O-kit* $C_K(v)$. Suppose now that the result of this application is named: $O = \text{new}\, C_I(v)$. In a functional view of objects, Env is extended with the binding (O, v_{obj}). In an imperative design, the evaluation (usually) makes an allocation $\uparrow v_{obj}$ which reserves a memory location to store v_{obj} and provides the reference $r \in \mathbf{R}$ of the allocated space, thus modifying Mem. Env is extended with the binding (O, r) (see Chapters 3 and 4 of Volume 1).

The implementation of objects can be more complicated in some languages and can be done by giving access to an object only through pointers. In this case, the identifier O is bound in Env to an address r_1 and in Mem, the value of r_1 is r.

Let us continue example 3.6 with the creation of an object my_skirt defined by my_skirt = new Skirts (2018, 75.5). The application of the constructor Skirts realized by new Skirts (2018, 75.5) is evaluated in a state $E = (\text{Env}, \text{Mem})$. The result is an *O-kit* whose attribute year has the value 2018 and the attribute price has the value 75.5. Let v_{obj} be its value, that is the value of the *O-kit* My_skirt. In a functional implementation of objects, Env is extended with the binding (my_skirt, v_{obj}). In an imperative implementation, Mem is extended with a couple (r, v_{obj}) and Env is extended with the binding (my_skirt, r). The *O-kit* my_skirt could have been defined directly as follows in Chapter 1:

```
Kit My_skirt =
begin
  var year : int = 2018
  var price : float = 75.5
  method sale (V_this) = fun current_year -> (current_year > V_this.year)
  method set_price (V_this) = fun (current_year, z) ->
    if V_this#sale (current_year) = true then V_this#price := z * 0.7 ...
end
```

Let us compare the description of the object constructors in section 3.1.2.2 and their modeling. The formal parameter d does not appear in syntax of classes, the link between the effective parameter of the constructor and the value of the corresponding attribute is done via the attribute name. Introducing this formal parameter d allows the dissociation of the attribute field, which is a non-modifiable constituent of the class, of its own value in each object. It also makes it possible to differentiate two evaluation times: the attributes of an object are determined by the application of the object constructor at the object creation, while the attributes a that appear in a method m of an object, thus in the form this#a in our model, will be instantiated only upon receipt of a message sent to m.

The concrete syntax of most object-oriented languages forces an object constructor to have the name of the class it instantiates and to be placed in the body of the class. Some languages allow *default values* to be given directly to attributes, this assignment can even be done systematically by the compiler (which may cause some surprises).

Most languages accept several object constructors that differ by the number of their parameters. They all have the same name as the class. The compiler uses the types of the effective parameters (a form of overload) to choose which constructor to apply. If there are less effective parameters than attributes, the values of the attributes are either their *default values* or are obtained later by instructions placed in the body of the constructor C_I. A constructor may have no parameters. In this case, only the allocation is performed by new $C_I()$ and the attributes are updated as we have just explained.

An object constructor, called *by default*, is often provided by the language, it is used especially if no object constructor is explicitly included in the class. Its definition and mode of use differ according to the language. The body of an object constructor may also contain other instructions, which may therefore perform side effects (a case to consider if undesirable side effects are feared, see [JAE 14]).

Most object languages (though not Python) do not allow modification of an object: no addition or deletion of any field. If we add (or remove) fields to a *kit*, its type changes. Now, this type, as we have defined it and even with just an intuitive notion of it, is a kind of runtime invariant, very useful when it comes to understanding and rereading source code. An object is, moreover, a first-class value that is intended to represent some data. Changing the type of this data during execution can have harmful effects. On the other hand, assigning a new value to an attribute is possible, it is not a modification of the *O-kit* but simply an update to the value designated by this attribute: the "global design" of the *O-kit* does not change.

We have modeled the construction of an object from of a *C-kit* by parameterizing the definition of this *C-kit* by F_a. We could also have modeled it by defining this *C-kit* as an incomplete *kit* whose attributes are only declared, the object constructor then being a function creating a complete *kit*. The two models would lead to the same result but the one chosen, with its more functional aspects, has the advantage of highlighting the functionality of attributes of classes.

3.2.3. *Inheritance, redefinition and late binding*

3.2.3.1. *Inheritance*

In section 3.1, we presented the general notion of inheritance in object-oriented languages. It is modeled by the *C-kit* extension, which is only one particular case of the *kit* extension studied in section 1.7. Any *C-kit* P can therefore be extended by adding attributes and methods to produce a *C-kit* R, of course with all the restrictions brought by P marks. An *O-kit* O_R created by instantiation of R has all the fields of P, even if these fields are made invisible to R by confinement operations and therefore cannot be read, modified or redefined in R (but they can be reintroduced by R). This is why any object constructor of R must call an object constructor of P, which is the only possibility for defining the attributes of R inherited from P but confined in P, thus out of the scope of R. The obligation for any constructor of a subclass to call a constructor of its super-class is thus justified.

O-kits cannot (in general) be extended (even if our model would allow it). This choice is justified by the fact that the notion retained as primitive for our model of object languages is that of class. The extension is at the level of classes and not at the level of objects. In a nutshell, an object only encodes a single data value.

3.2.3.2. *Redefinition*

Continuing with the notations of the previous section, and of section 1.7.1.5, we return to the modeling of a method given in section 3.2.1.1. As already seen in Chapter 1, reintroduction of a field in R can be done with or without back-update of the P fields. With back-update, this reintroduction is often called *redefinition* or *overriding* and the evaluation strategy is called *late binding*. It must take into account:

1) the fact that a method can only be called by sending a message to an object that has it;

2) the obligation to perform evaluation of these calls using late binding.

All object-oriented languages accept method redefinitions insofar as this redefinition complies with confinement. Extension with back-update is generally the chosen evaluation rule but some languages, such as C++ for example, offer both extension modes, with and without back-update.

3.2.3.3. *Late binding*

Let C be a *C-kit*, m be a method of C and O an *O-kit* from C defined by $O = C(v)$. The message $O\#m(w)$ is an application of method m of O, therefore the method m of C to the object O and to w, which is called the *effective parameter* of this message. The evaluation of this message, sent in a context without inheritance, is as follows:

1) method m was modeled by $m = \lambda\theta.f$ with $f = \texttt{fun } z \rightarrow b$. The expression $O\#m$ denotes the application of m to the object O, so the expression $(\lambda\theta.(\texttt{fun } z \rightarrow b))\,O$;

2) the evaluation of this application returns the value of the expression $f[\theta \leftarrow O]$, so the (value of the) function $\texttt{fun } z \rightarrow (b\,[\theta \leftarrow O])$;

3) it remains to evaluate the application of this function of the formal parameter z to the effective parameter provided by $O\#m(w)$. The result is $b[\theta \leftarrow O][z \leftarrow w]$.

Let us take example 3.6 once again and evaluate the message `my_skirt#sale (2019)`:

1) the formal parameter V_this is substituted by the value of my_skirt in the body of sale;

2) the so-obtained function fun current_year -> (current_year > my_skirt #year) is applied to 2019;

3) the value of the attribute my_skirt#year, that is 2018, is compared to the value of current_year, 2019, and this comparison returns the value true.

Let us now detail the message evaluation if inheritance is involved. Let R be a subclass of C, the extension of C being made with back-update. Let RO be an object of R and m a method of C, not reintroduced in R. Suppose that a method l of C is redefined in R and that the body b of the method m contains a sub-expression $\theta\#l$. To simplify the explanation, let us set $b \equiv \theta\#l$. We describe the evaluation of the expression $RO\#m$:

1) $RO\#m$ is an application of m to the object RO. Its evaluation returns the value v of the expression $f[\theta \leftarrow RO]$.

2) Since $f = \mathtt{fun}\ z \rightarrow b$, v is equal to $\mathtt{fun}\ z \rightarrow (b[\theta \leftarrow RO])$.

3) With the simplified version of b, v is equal to $\mathtt{fun}\ z \rightarrow \theta\#l[\theta \leftarrow RO]$, therefore to $\mathtt{fun}\ z \rightarrow RO\#l$.

We can see here that our modeling makes it possible to render late binding: θ is correctly substituted by the object RO which received the message, and not by O.

Example 3.7 corresponds to example 3.3. It extends the *C-kit* Skirts.

EXAMPLE 3.7.–

```
Kit SkirtMadeOf extending Skirts =
begin
  var material : string
  method get_made = V_this -> fun () -> this#material
  method sale = V_this -> fun current_year ->
    if V_this#get_made () = "silk" then false else (current_year > V_this#year)
  SkirtMadeOf (y : int, p : float, s : string) =
    Skirts (y, p) ; this#material := s
end

silk_skirt = new SkirtMadeOf (false, 300, "silk")
```

We followed the evaluation of the message silk_skirt#set_price (1919, 100.0) in section 3.1. We justify this evaluation here, keeping everything about typing:

1) silk_skirt is an *O-kit* created by application of the constructor SkirtMadeOf. The method set_price of the *O-kit* silk_skirt is that of the *C-kit* Skirts;

2) the expression `silk_skirt#set_price` denotes the application of `set_price` to `silk_skirt`. Recall that `set_price` is a function of the formal parameter `V_this`. The evaluation of `silk_skirt#set_price` substitutes `V_this` by `silk_skirt` in the body f of the method `set_price`. The result of this substitution is the following function:

```
fun (current_year, z) -> if silk_skirt#sale (current_year) = true
                    then silk_skirt#price := z * 0.7 else ...
```

3) the application of this function to (1919, 100.0) remains to be evaluated. This leads to evaluate `silk_skirt#sale (current_year)`;

4) the expression `silk_skirt#sale` denotes the application of `sale` to `silk_skirt`. This *O-kit* `silk_skirt` is an instantiation of `SkirtMadeOf`. Thus the method `sale` of this *O-kit* is the one redefined in `SkirtMadeOf`. The late binding strategy has been followed. Let us also note that `V_this` has been substituted in the expression `V_this#price` by `silk_skirt`.

This modeling can seem quite complicated. Let us comment on why it cannot be simplified. The only alternative would be to decide that the evaluation of $O = \text{new}\,C$ creating O substitutes all occurrences of θ in C by O. The method m of O would therefore be equal to $\text{fun}\ z \to (b[\theta \leftarrow O])$. So $\theta\#l$ would be replaced by $O\#l$ in m and it would be impossible to *make a back-update* replacing $O\#l$ by $RO\#l$ during the evaluation of $RO\#m$. Therefore, instantiating methods at the time of construction of an object, i.e. using an entirely lexical evaluation, is only appropriate to a language that does not use late binding. As we will see in section 4.2, the strategy of evaluation with back update is used for C++ methods that are tagged with `virtual`, those without this tag being evaluated without back-update.

Modeling of a method m by a function whose formal parameter is an *O-kit* and which will be applied only when receiving a message to m, was used to render late binding (late with respect to object creation). This also justifies prohibiting the use of formal parameters of F_a in method definitions, because their substitution by actual parameters would be made at object creation. Methods can also be parameterized by a value, say y, by including y in the F_p parameter family and resuming the modeling of *kit* parameters detailed in Chapter 1. A class modeled by such a parameterized *C-kit* cannot be used to create objects. It will be necessary to first instantiate y with an effective value to be able to do so.

Note that only the binding of the variable θ in a method m is delayed until a message is sent to an object O "possessing" m. In a lexically scoped language, any identifier occurring in the body b of m that is different from the formal parameters z and θ is evaluated in the environment ENV of the definition of the *C-kit* C. Once the substitution $[\theta \leftarrow O]$ is made, the evaluation of $(b[\theta \leftarrow O])\,(w)$ continues by extending ENV, as seen in the presentation of closures in Chapter 3 of Volume 1.

3.2.3.4. *Confinement and inheritance*

Confinement of a *C-kit* is exactly the same as confinement of a *kit*, which was studied in Chapter 1. The interaction between confinement and inheritance was presented in section 1.7.2. Its adaptation to confinement of classes made by marks was intuitively presented in section 3.1.2.3. Confining by marks does not change the name of the *C-kit* (Ans. 1.17) and it is not possible, with this confinement technique, to define several confinements for the same *C-kit* (Ans. 1.18). We will study a different confinement technique with OCaml classes.

O-kits keep the confinement marks of their *C-kits*. For example, any field l marked `private-st` in a *C-kit* C can only be used by C fields, it is not exported by C. It remains marked `private-st` in any *O-kit* instantiating C so cannot be used outside of C. It is present in all *C-kits* R that inherit from C, and therefore in all *O-kits* instantiating R, but it remains invisible in all of them.

We have seen that confinement of a *kit* P produces some restrictions on the type of the exported *kit* RP, in accordance with confinement. This difference between types of P and RP often remains implicit in object-oriented languages, confinement is not really considered as acting on types, especially if it is made by tagging fields of classes. Indeed, exported classes keep the name of the original class. Types of a class and of its objects have the same name, which is the name of the class: there is no room to distinguish between all these types.

We have also seen that confinement could restrict the possibilities of extension and thus influence the type of an extended *kit* R. The type of RP is often more restrictive than the type of R: in other words, export restrictions are often more constraining than inheritance restrictions.

3.2.4. *Incomplete* C-kits, *parameterized* C-kits

There are two forms of incompleteness for a *C-kit* called an *interface* and a *not fully defined C-kit*.

3.2.4.1. *Interfaces*

A *C-kit* C of which all fields are only declared is called an *interface* and is thus an incomplete *C-kit*. The definition of an interface C only introduces the names and the types of the fields, thus what we have called the type of C. In some languages, the expressions "class type" and "interface" are synonymous. Depending on the language, an interface can be defined directly or created automatically from the *C-kit*. Seen as class types, an interface created by an export of a *C-kit* often has fewer fields than the interface of this *C-kit*, which is designed for its inheritance. The automatically created interfaces are rarely explicited.

3.2.4.2. *"not-defined"* C-kits

In the second form of incompleteness, only certain methods or some (class) fields introduced by `static_in` are *not-defined* in the *C-kit*. These fields are tagged by a keyword such as `abstract`, `virtual`, etc. placed before the field declaration and/or at the level of the class itself. An abstract class is an incomplete *C-kit*.

The completion of an incomplete *C-kit* corresponds exactly to that of an incomplete *kit*, presented in section 1.4.2. The type of a method definition is identical to the one given by its declaration. It builds a new *C-kit*. This completion can be made in several steps, the marks remaining on the fields not yet defined. It is impossible to create *O-kits* from an incomplete *C-kit*. The compiler usually helps to detect such errors. Object-oriented languages do not generally offer two distinct syntactic constructs for the definition of a field *not-defined* and for inheritance.

3.2.4.3. *Parameterized C-kits and functors*

Parameters of the F_p family are used to define parameterized *C-kits* by a type or a value; these were studied in Chapter 1. The parametrization by a type variable T allows a *C-kit* to be constructed, which represents a data structure parameterized by T, even if the language does not handle parametric polymorphism.

Functors are usually not provided by object-oriented languages. We consider them briefly for the sake of completeness. The family F_k of parameters represents the formal parameters of a functor of a *C-kit*. The properties of *kit* functors were studied in section 1.6. Here, such a functor takes one (or more) *C-kit* as a formal parameter and its application to an actual *C-kit* returns a new *C-kit*. The body of the functor thus defines a class, all fields of which can use the fields of the *C-kit* parameter. The main problem with such functors is brought by typing.

The word "functor" is sometimes used improperly in the presentation of languages, in terms of its definition here. The parametrization of a class C by the name of a class P, without providing a way for C definitions to use P fields, corresponds to the parametrization of C by the single type P and not by the value of C.

We recall that it is not possible to create *O-kits* from parameterized *C-kits* by F_p or F_k. These two families must first be instantiated to obtain a *C-kit* which remains parameterized only by F_a before any object creation.

In general, languages do not offer all of these parametrization possibilities. For example, successive versions of C++ have progressively enriched the parametrization possibilities with types and values, but do not yet offer functors (as we have defined them).

3.2.5. *Subclassing, subtyping*

The subclassing preorder was introduced in section 3.1.2.5, this is an example of nominal subtyping (see section 1.7.2.3). Let us develop our study of it a little further.

3.2.5.1. *Subclassing*

Simple inheritance defines a "more general" order between classes and their subclasses, the inherited class being considered more general than its subclasses: the ancestor is the most general. One can thus build inheritance chains $C_0 > C_1 > \ldots C_{n-1} > C_n$, where C_0 is an existing class, C_1 inheriting from C_0 and, more generally, C_{i+1} inheriting from C_i. This order can be used by some compilers to process a message $O \# m$. If m is not defined in the class of O, say C_n, then m is searched for in the super-class C_{n-1} then throughout the whole inheritance chain, if necessary. If m is not found in C_0, there is a typing error, an execution error or an exception raising, depending on the language.

Similarly, multiple inheritance defines an order between classes and subclasses, but a succession of inheritance steps does not only build a chain but also a tree whose root is the last subclass to be built and the leaves are the classes – known in advance – used to "start" the multiple inheritance steps. This tree becomes a graph, often called an *inheritance graph* if we regroup all occurrences of a given class into a single node. The two forms of inheritance thus make it possible to construct a class that manipulates complex entities, piece by piece.

Some languages start all inheritance chains or graphs from a class often called Object, which is greater than any other class and thus allows the search for a method receiving a message to be limited.

3.2.5.2. *Subtyping*

The subclassing relationship defines some base cases of a subtyping relation. The extension of such an order to other families of types was studied in section 5.7.1 of Volume 1; this highlighted the difficulty of obtaining compatibility with some operations, for example with assignment.

Subtyping and assignment

Let C_K be a *C-kit* and D_K be an extension of C_K, O_C be an *O-kit* from C_K and O_D be an *O-kit* from D_K. If there exists an operation in the language to assign an *O-kit*, is the assignment $O_D := O_C$ legal? Such an assignment can be rejected immediately because O_D could have more fields than O_C; the fields not already present in O_C would not be modified by such an assignment but the fact remains that they have a value, perhaps not expected by the developer as any non-initialized mutable variable.

It is also possible to accept this assignment at compile-time and to insert in the object code a check of the type of the object value, assigned to O_D at runtime.

Subtyping and structured data

The extension of subtyping to structured data (lists, arrays, etc.) also poses a problem of consistency. A list is usually specified in algorithmics as a grouping of *homogeneous values*, i.e. values that can be treated in a uniform way. This is what makes it possible to iterate the same treatment on all the elements of the list. The type, say t_list, of a list is determined from the type, say t, of its elements. But how do we determine this type t if the language accepts subtypes, as is the case for most object-oriented languages? Let us call t_e the type of an element of the list. In the context of the inheritance, t_e is a subtype (at least of itself) and there exists a chain $t_e \leq t^1 \ldots \leq t^n$, where the t^j are the types of the ancestors of t_e. For the type t, one can decide to choose a common majorant of all the types t_e of the elements, so the type of a common ancestor of all the subclasses used to create the elements of the list. If this common majorant does not exist and if it is accepted by the system, then the lists will be deliberately heterogeneous and therefore will no longer correspond to the usual specification of lists in algorithmics.

If the existence of a common majorant is required then two problems remain. First, the common majorant may not be unique. Either the developer chooses this majorant, therefore the ancestor class, leaving the possibility of defining subclasses later, or this choice relies on the system, using the class `Object` introduced in section 3.1. This class, present in some languages like Java, is the origin of all inheritance graphs and thus plays the role of the greatest ancestor: its type is the *greatest element* of the family of subtypes and allows for typing any list, in particular.

This choice does not ensure complete consistency with the specification of lists. Let us see the problem within an example. Let us decide that the types `int` and `bool` are subtypes of the type `float`, then [1.5; true; 3] is of type `float list`. Adding 1 to all elements of this list cannot be done in a uniform way since the addition of integers is not the addition of floats and never will be (see Chapter 6 of Volume 1). We thus lose the consistency with the specification of a uniform treatment of list elements. Certainly, this adaptation of treatments is often very convenient but it also hides the complexity of iteration on lists in the presence of subtypes. As soon as there is an execution error, this complexity must be explored in order to eliminate errors.

Subtyping and methods

The extension of the subclassing relationship into a relationship of subtyping on functions was studied in section 1.7.2.3. The choice made by object-oriented languages is quite often the one described in the abovementioned section: contravariance for effective parameter types and covariance of the result type reduced to equality. In other words, if the declaration of a method m introduces it with the type $t_a \rightarrow t_r$, then any expression whose type is a subtype of t_a can be accepted as an effective parameter of m, but the type of the result must be t_r.

In languages where the formal parameter V_this of any method remains implicit, the acceptance of contravariance remains implicit. Let C_K be a *C-kit* and D_K an extension of C_K. Let m be a method of C_K: $m = \lambda\theta.f$ with $f = $ fun $z \rightarrow b$. Let $t_1 \rightarrow t_r$ be the type of f. So, the full type t of m is $C_K \rightarrow (t_1 \rightarrow t_r)$, C_K being used here to denote the type of objects of the class C_K. Let O_D be an *O-kit* from D_K. The full type of D_K is a subtype of the full type of C_K. The method m can therefore be applied to O_D during the evaluation of the message $O_D\#m(w)$, without any typing error, and this is justified by the choice of contravariance on the implicit argument V_this of m.

The choice to keep the type of the method result during inheritance, analyzed below, is also consistent with subtyping on functional types. Let us continue our example. Suppose that m returns its effective parameter (one of the attributes could, for example, be modified), so an *O-kit* of type C_K. Thus the type of $O_D\#m(w)$ is C_K but the value of $O_D\#m(w)$ is O_D itself. As the result of the application of m, O_D is an *O-kit* from C_K, thus of type C_K, however, it was created from D_K. This choice of covariance on the result types ensures consistency of the extension of subclassing to subtyping; but it does not always satisfy the developer, because some information on O_D is lost, just as in our example, by modifying only one of its attributes. Let us look at a possible solution, widely used by developers.

3.2.5.3. Coercions

The conversion of the type of an object according to some needs of the typing algorithm is generally called *coercion*. This does not mean that the value of the object is physically modified. A coercion can be explicit and is then called a *cast*. A first form of cast allows the object O_D to be considered as an *O-kit* of type C_K by "forgetting" its fields added or redefined in D_K. This form of coercion can be checked by the compiler, thanks to the declaration of O_D.

A second form of *cast* allows the fields of D_K, which are not present in C_K, to "reappear". It solves the problem raised above. The developer, knowing that O_D is of type D_K and knowing that m only modifies an attribute of O_D, can convert the result of the evaluation of $O_D\#m(w)$ (of type C_K) into a value of type D_K. This second form of *cast* makes it possible to consider a value of a type t as a value of type t_s, a subtype of t. It is a dangerous operation if the value is not of type t_s. The error will often only be detected at runtime because verification requires that the value to be converted is known.

Coercion can be implicit: it is done silently by the compiler or interpreter. It can lead to unexpected results, the origin of which will not always be easy to find.

3.2.5.4. *Inheritance and binary methods*

A *binary method* is a method m of C_K which has a formal parameter z of the same type as θ. A binary method raises a typing problem if its body contains an expression of the form $op\,(\theta, z)$, where op is a binary operator. The code of a binary operator, such as equality, comparison, addition, etc., often assumes that the two operands have the same memory representation, this one being defined by their type itself. Let us demonstrate the problem using the following example.

Suppose that the operation `compare` compares the values of two *O-kits* from C_K. Let m be a method defined by $m{:}C_K \rightarrow \texttt{bool} = \lambda\theta.\texttt{fun } z \rightarrow (z\,\texttt{compare}\,\theta)$. The type provided by the declaration of m does not include the type of θ, as is usual in object languages. The full type of m is $C_K \rightarrow C_K \rightarrow \texttt{bool}$. The type of θ and z is C_K. Let O_D be an *O-kit* from D_K and O be an *O-kit* from C_K. The message $O_D\#m$ can be accepted because D_K is a subtype of C_K. But the expression $O_D\#m(O)$ is ill-typed: in the sub-expression $(z\,\texttt{compare }\theta)$, the variable θ substituted by O_D of type D_K and z is substituted by O of type C_K. The function `compare` is not necessarily adapted to the comparison of O_D and O, whose values do not have the same memory representation.

The solutions to this problem are often only workarounds. The typing algorithm usually cannot recognize that m is a binary method and, therefore, cannot impose an equality constraint between the types of θ and z. This solution can trigger an error, as we have just seen. It is possible to redefine the method m in D_K or to use coercion. It would also be possible to use a syntactic marker to indicate that a method is binary.

3.2.5.5. *Overloading*

Overloading was introduced in section 5.7.2 of Volume 1. Overloading a method, if allowed, is in no way a redefinition of that method. If methods of the same name do not have the same type, and if the language accepts method overloading, these methods may be accepted by typing if the compiler is able to resolve overloading. The resolution algorithm depends on the language.

Determination at runtime of the method receiving a message and resolving overloading are two different processes. Let O_C be an object from class C receiving the message $O_C\#m$, which may have been overloaded and also redefined. The resolution of overloading chooses the version of m, say m^1, appropriate for typing this message at typing time, thus at compile-time if the language is statically typed. The choice of the executed m, say m^2, is made at runtime by searching in the hierarchy of classes inherited by C. The only requirement is that the type of m^2 is compatible with that of m^1, so as to continue to guarantee typing correction.

Two mechanisms may be combined in the presence of overloading: overloading itself and implicit type conversions. As a general rule, the compiler determines the type of effective parameter(s) and searches, among the different definitions bound to the same name, for one whose parameter type is exactly that of the effective parameter. If this is not the case, the compiler may attempt to make an implicit conversion on the type of effective parameter in order to retrieve the type of one of the definitions, according to a criterion of "best transformation". The exact definition of this criterion varies depending on the language.

Overloading resolution rules can be quite complex because of their interference with confinement, inheritance, subtyping, functions with a non-fixed number of arguments or optional arguments, or when the language has elaborate syntactic constructs such as *templates* of C++. Chapter 4 provides an overview of overloading handling in the languages studied.

3.2.6. *Type languages, classes and objects*

In Chapter 1, we defined the type of a *kit* as the collection of the names and types of its components and we chose nominal typing, parametrization being considered as introducing functional or quantified types. This definition has been adopted to define class types in section 3.1.2.2. We have determined that the type of an object is the type of the body of its class and is named by its class name, therefore we chose nominal typing. This very simple approach to types allows us to very intuitively check the correctness of typing: if the parameter z of a method m is of type int, then the effective parameter for z in the message cannot be of type bool (except in a language like Python where bool is a subtype of int). But these chosen type definitions are far too simple to construct a true type theory, say $\mathcal{T}$, that models all class and object features.

Let us look at some difficulties in trying to define such a theory $\mathcal{T}$ which should guarantee that, whichever syntactic construct (confinement, extension, instantiation, etc.) is used in a program, if the typing algorithm proves that the program is well-typed, then it returns a value of the expected type or loop forever (partial correction theorem).

– Are the types of the same method m in a class C and in an object of C the same? Yes, as in the description in section 3.1, under the assumption that the type t_c of a class and the type t_{obj} of its objects are identical. However, modeling a method m as a function of θ gives to m the type $t_{obj} \rightarrow t_f$, where $\theta{:}t_{obj}$ and $f{:}t_f$. Therefore, we have here a first form of recursion between t_c and t_{obj} which should be taken into account. In addition, a method m can return an object of the class or the value of a sub-expression of the form $\theta\#l$. To type m, it is necessary to know the type t_{obj} of θ, and to type θ it is necessary to know the type of m. So there is also a second form of recursion between the type of the class, the type of an object and the collection of method types.

– A class is modeled by a *C-kit* parameterized by a family F_a, whose instantiation creates an *O-kit*. This parametrization of a *C-kit* C gives it a functional type $C_{Type} = t_a \to \{l_1 : t_1; \ldots; l_n : t_n\}$, where t_a is the type of the formal parameter corresponding to the attribute a. How is this dependency of the C type on the attribute types, say t_d, managed? We stated that t_a be equal to t_d, however we mentioned that this constraint may be relaxed. For example, F_a may contain a parameter, say O_a, to be instantiated by an object, say O. Should the types of O_a and O be strictly equal or can the type of O be a subtype of the type of O_a? How do we model this last choice within the theory $\mathcal{T}$?

– Some fields of a *C-kit* P can be confined and the type of the so obtained confined *C-kit* RP is not that of P. If the *C-kits* do not have fields introducing type definitions, the type of RP is the one given in section 1.3.5: $RP_{Type} = \{ c_{i_1} l_{i_1} : t_{i_1} ; \ldots; c_{i_m} l_{i_m} : t_{i_m} \}$. What is the interaction between the export modeling and the theory $\mathcal{T}$?

– The type of an object can, depending on the language, be either totally deduced from the source text of the program, thus *statically determined*, or it can be obtained only at runtime, so *dynamically determined*, if for example the object is the result of evaluating an expression. This does not mean that typing is performed statically or dynamically. The typing algorithm can be run at compile-time and it can insert typing queries in the object code of the program to be checked at the time of object creation. How do we integrate this two-step typing process within the theory $\mathcal{T}$?

– A *C-kit* P can contain an internal *C-kit* PI, with or without back-update. This leads to an additional form of recursion between the type of P and the type of PI, since PI can use fields of P and vice versa.

– Typing should also allow some form of subtyping, consistent (or not) with subclassing. It would also be useful to render casts and coercions as type conversion functions.

The hypothetical type theory $\mathcal{T}$ should therefore deal with all these points. Unfortunately, to our knowledge, any type theory developed so far becomes logically inconsistent as soon as some of these points are modeled together. Therefore, there is very little hope for discovering a theory such as $\mathcal{T}$. However, there exist several type theories that are able to successfully model several aspects of object-oriented languages. Moreover, research into type theories is very active because such theories are needed as a firm basis for automatic program verification tools. Readers interested in type theories can consult the books and articles [ABA 96, BRU 96, BRU 99, CAS 19, PIE 05].

Important advances have been made recently with the definition and the study of the so-called second-order type systems, introduced in [RÉM 14], a new approach to tools for data structures [WIL 18] and a different conception of adding some object-oriented features to a given type theory [CAU 15].

Classes in Selected Languages

This chapter presents classes and objects provided by various languages, based on the model studied in Chapter 3. Java's classes are examined in section 4.1, providing an instantiation of the model presented in section 3.2. Section 4.2 depicts the object mechanism of C++, which is a slightly more complex implementation of the model examined in section 3.2. Object-oriented features of OCaml are presented in section 4.3 and they provide an interpretation of the model, which is pretty different from those of Java and C++. This chapter ends with a presentation of classes and objects of Python, also examining some other features in order to say a little more about this language used in this book, to implement semantics of functional and imperative features in Volume 1.

4.1. Classes in Java

4.1.1. *General presentation*

The programming language Java was created in 1995 by Sun Microsystems and is now distributed by Oracle Corporation. The version used here is Java SE (Standard Edition) 10.0.2. Elements of concrete syntax and terms used here come from the reference manual [GOS 19] and the documentation provided by *Oracle*.

Java is a language based on classes (class) (Ans. 1.2). It is statically typed (Ans. 1.1), allows explicit type conversions (cast) but also implicit ones: adding a value of type String to a value of type int converts this integer into a String and returns a String. Hence, the language is not strongly typed, an expression possibly having several types during the execution. The compiler can add type checks during the execution, which allows one to assume that the typechecking is (relatively) safe. Overloading, presented in section 5.7.2 of Volume 1, is available in Java and is described in section 4.1.5.7 (Ans. 1.26).

The source code of any class or interface is placed in a file which can only contain one class F tagged as public. This file must then be named F.java. Moreover, if F owns a class method forcibly named main and declared as

```
public static void main (String args []) { body-of-main }
```

then F.java is a Java program that can be executed.

A Java source file is compiled into an intermediate lower level language, specific to Java, called a *bytecode language* (Ans. 1.1). Java provides a bytecode interpreter, known as the Java *virtual machine* (or *JVM*). Hence, the compiler does not directly produce native code for the microprocessor. There exist several variants of such a compilation–interpretation mechanism, already presented in section 1.2.3.6 of Volume 1.

REMARK.– The examples provided in Java only aim to illustrate certain points, they are designed to be as short as possible, they do not respect any specific naming convention in order to do not hide difficulties. You can only mimic these examples if you ask yourselves a question while reading the reference manual of the language.

4.1.2. *Modules and packages*

A Java package is a group of compilation units (classes and interfaces) and sub-packages accessible to the Java system, which can be stored in a directory of the operating system, in a database, etc. All the development environments for Java provide a mechanism to manage these modules and packages. A Java module is a collection of packages. Modules do not have any structure. The package or a module that they belong to is indicated at the head of the compilation unit.

Java modules and packages define their own namespaces, hence they can be considered as *W-kits*, introduced in section 2.3.2 (Ans. 1.2 and Ans. 1.3). Note that these *W-kits* contain some classes, hence some *C-kits*, which manipulate objects, i.e. *O-kits*, thus creating a hierarchy of namespaces. For instance, let M be a module and P a package of M containing a compilation unit C.java hosting the class C. The full name of the class is M.P.C and the field l of the class C has the qualified name M.P.C.l. Let N be another module also containing a package P, this latter is referenced as N.P, thus without ambiguity. However, a package cannot contain two compilation units with the same name.

Java modules and packages allow us to manage imports and exports of their compilation units thanks to dedicated usage directives. The export of a package P only requires P to be accessible via the system and is achieved in accordance with the confinement tags set on the classes and their fields, which we will study later. The imports of a class (or of a component) are achieved by using the qualified name of the class in the package. Any component of a package accessible from the Java system may be imported, with respect to the confinement restrictions (Ans. 1.15 and Ans. 1.24). For instance, a class C tagged public can be used in any compilation unit by naming it with its qualified name M.P.C if its source file is located in the package P of the package M.

The flattening of a component name of a package is performed with the directive imports name. For example, the declaration imports M.P.C allows us to access the components of the class C, denoting them by their fields in C. Obviously, these accesses are only authorized according to the confinement marks present on the class or fields (see section 4.1.4).

Java handles the visibility rules of flattened names in a very precise manner and raises a compilation error or a definitive masking in case of flattening a component whose name is already used in the importer compilation unit or whose name has already been flattened. For instance, flattening a class M.C in a compilation unit containing the definition of another class named C causes the masking of the imported definition. Flattening two classes C coming from two different files raises a compilation error (Ans. 1.25).

4.1.3. *Classes*

Let us have a quick look at classes before going deeper in to the study of certain points. A Java class is a *C-kit* (Ans. 1.2) possibly owning some attributes (variables introduced without a keyword), some methods (functions introduced without a keyword), some class variables and class methods (introduced by the mark static), some internal *C-kit* (introduced by class) called *nested classes* if they are tagged by static and *inner classes* if they are not. The definitions of these various fields may use the other fields according to the description given in section 3.2.1.1: no definition of static field can use methods and attributes, method definitions (including those of the *inner classes*) can use any field.

To denote an object of their class or of a subclass, the methods use the keyword this. The attributes can be used without prefixing them by this. A Java class may also contain code placed in a block, which can be seen as an anonymous field of the *C-kit* (Ans. 1.12). If this block is marked static, it represents an initialization block of the class and is executed when the class is created. Otherwise, it is executed at each call to one of the object constructors of this class. Java proposes class parametrization by type variables, in accordance with the description given in section 1.5 (Ans. 1.32).

4.1.3.1. *Values, types and genericity*

Values manipulated in Java are basic values (numbers, booleans), strings, arrays and objects, the latter three being references. Let us remind ourselves that the word "reference" denotes a pointer (that cannot be directly handled) on the memory area allocated for the value (see section 7.5 of Volume 1). Java provides only the notion of a method to implement functions and a method is not a first-class value (Ans. 1.13). The language has a static (lexical) scope (Ans. 1.4) except for message sending, evaluated with late-binding strategy (Ans. 1.39).

A class C, as well as an interface, defines a type also named C, which is also the type of the objects of this class (Ans. 1.5). The order of the fields is important (Ans. 1.10), as shown by example 1.10 of Chapter 1, where the attribute x is defined by int x = y + 1 before the declaration of the attribute y. Giving first a constructor in a class body declares *ipso facto* the attributes, as shown by example 4.2. All the fields of a class must be explicitly typed in the definition of the class (Ans. 1.6). As it is the case for a class, the introduction of an interface also creates a type taking the name of the interface. Types defined by classes or arrays (denoted by type_element[]) are called *reference types*. Note that character strings are implemented by the class String and are not mutable. This point has been addressed in section 7.5.2 of Volume 1.

A class C<T> parameterized by the type variable T defines a family of types C<T_i>, obtained by substituting T by the type T_i. Such types C<T> are called *parameterized types*.

Thus, Java provides three families of types: primitive types like int, parameterized types and reference types. A class C is well-typed if:

1) all attributes, class variables and internal classes of C have different names and are well-typed (no overloading for these fields);

2) all methods of C are well-typed, given that any occurrence of this in a field of C has type C;

3) if two methods of C have the same name, then the types of their arguments are different (overloading) (Ans. 1.9);

4) any redefinition of a method preserves the type and the order of the redefined method's parameters, as well as its result type, even if the result is an object of the superclass (Ans. 1.38 and Ans. 1.40) (consider however, the possible relaxation of this rule with example 4.10);

5) the type of the superclass of C is not a subtype of C (no cyclic inheritance);

6) the assignment x = exp is well-typed if the type of exp is a subtype of the type declared for x (see example 4.11);

7) a message C.m(exp) is well-typed if the method m, not overloaded, is declared by A m (B x) in C (or in the inheritance graph of C, presented in section 4.1.5.4). The type of exp must be a subtype of B and the type of the message's result is A;

8) if m is overloaded, the compiler attempts to resolve overloading (see section 5.7.2 of Volume 1). A successful resolution ensures that the inheritance graph of C contains at least one definition of m, which allows us to correctly typecheck C.m(exp).

Two classes with the same fields, which have the same types, define two different class types, as shown by example 4.1 (Ans. 1.7). This example defines two classes C and D that have the same fields: an attribute name and a method set. The class classesequality only owns one field, which is the class method main. This defines an object from each class and attempts to test their equality. However the equality used in this context is a binary method which requires its operands to have the same types. Hence, an error message is issued.

EXAMPLE 4.1.–

```Java
import java.util.Date ;
class C {
  String name ;
  void set (String s) { name = s ; }
}
class D {
  String name ;
  void set (String s) { name = s ; } ;
}
public class classesequality {
  public static void main (String args[]) {
    C lucie = new C () ;
    D lucie1 = new D () ;
    lucie.set ("Lucie") ;
    lucie1.set ("Lucie") ;
    System.out.println (lucie == lucie1) ;
    }
}
```

The error message is :

```
$ javac classesequality.java
classesequality.java:17: error: incomparable types: C and D
  System.out.println (lucie == lucie1) ;
                            ^1 error
```

Let us add the instruction (lucie1 = (D) lucie) in the body of main. The compiler emits the following error message (Ans. 1.8):

```
error:  incompatible types:  C cannot be converted to D
```

4.1.3.2. *Object constructors*

The object constructors of a class must appear in the definition of the class and take the name of the class. They must differ by the number and the types of their arguments. If no constructor is defined, the compiler provides a default constructor, without arguments. This is the case in example 4.1. The first instruction of a constructor is either a call to another constructor of the class or the call to the constructor of the class super. If this is not the case, the compiler inserts a call to super () which is the default constructor of the parent class. As any class inherits implicitly (or explicitly if the developer stated it) from Object, there is an automatic insertion of all the constructors without arguments present in the inheritance path up to its end which is Object. An object constructor may be confined in order to control the creation of objects from the class.

Example 4.2 illustrates some points already addressed. The class C contains two attributes: x with a primitive type int and next with a reference type on C. Thus, we have here a kind of recursivity allowing us to implement, for instance, linked lists. The field z is a class variable and get_z is a class method. The method get_C is recursive (Ans. 1.11).

EXAMPLE 4.2.–

```Java
class C {
  /* Constructors */
  C (int a) { x = a ; next = null ; z = z + 1 ; }
  C (int a, C nxt) { x = a ; next = nxt ; z = z + 1 ; }
  /* Methods */
  void get_x () { System.out.print ("attribute x = " + this.x) ; }
  void get_C () {
    this.get_x () ; C.get_z () ;
    System.out.println ("  the next") ;
    if (this.next != null) this.next.get_C () ;
    else System.out.println ("  end") ;
  }
  /* Attributes */
  int x ;  /* Of primitive type */
  C next ; /* Of reference type */
  /* Class variable */
  static int z = 0 ;
  /* Class method */
  static void get_z () { System.out.println (" and field z = " + z) ; }
}

public class Test {
  public static void main (String[] args) {
    C anchor = new C (25) ;
    System.out.println ("the anchor") ;
    System.out.print ("anchor.get_C () : ") ;
    anchor.get_C () ;
```

```
    C link = new C (36, anchor) ;
    System.out.println ("the link") ;
    System.out.print ("link.get_C () : ") ;
    link.get_C () ;
    }
}
```

The execution produces the following display:

```
the anchor
anchor.get_C () : attribute x = 25 and field z = 1
  the next
  end
the link
link.get_C () : attribute x = 36 and field z = 2
  the next
attribute x = 25 and field z = 2
  the next
  end
```

The class C owns two object constructors, both of them modifying z. This explains why the call anchor.get_C (anchor) prints field z = 1 and the recursive call performed on the cell following link (which is thus anchor) prints field z = 2.

4.1.3.3. *Binary methods*

In Java, a binary method is typechecked by giving to this the type of the class in which the method is defined. The obligation to keep identical types for its argument and for this is ignored. In example 4.3, the class C has an attribute attr of type int, two binary methods, a method test and a constructor performing a side effect. The class D inherits from C, introduces an attribute attr of type C, hence masking the one of C (which is not recommended but is useful here for the explanation). D redefines the method binary_m. The function main creates an object a_C of type C then an object b_D and assigns a_C to its attribute attr.

EXAMPLE 4.3.–

```
Java
class C {
  int attr ;
  public void binary_m (C o) { System.out.println (this == o) ; }
  public void binary_add (C o) { System.out.println (this.attr + o.attr) ; }
  public void test (C o) { System.out.println (this.attr) ; }
  public C () { System.out.println ("New C") ; }
}

class D extends C {
    C attr ;
    public void binary_m (D o) { System.out.println (this == o) ; }
}
```

```
class TestBinary {
  public static void main (String[] args) {
    C a_C = new C () ;
    a_C.attr = 25 ;
    a_C.test (a_C) ;

    D b_D = new D () ;
    b_D.attr = a_C ;
    b_D.attr.attr = 4 ;
    a_C.test (a_C) ;

    a_C.binary_m (a_C) ;
    a_C.binary_m (b_D) ;
    a_C.binary_add (a_C) ;
    b_D.binary_add (a_C) ;
    a_C.binary_add (b_D) ;

    b_D.test (a_C) ;
    a_C.test (b_D) ;
  }
}
```

The execution displays the following results, with comments directly inserted in this output:

```
$ java TestB
New C       -- call to the constructor C () for the creation of a_C
25          -- call to a_C.test (a_C)
New C       -- implicit call to the constructor C () for the creation of b_D
4           -- call to a_C.test (a_C) after the assignment b_D.attr.attr = 4 ;
true        -- a_C.binary_m (a_C) ;
false       -- a_C.binary_m (b_D) ;
8           -- a_C.binary_add (a_C) ;
4           -- b_D.binary_add (a_C) ;
4           -- a_C.binary_add (b_D) ;
4           -- b_D.test (a_C) ;
0           -- a_C.test (b_D) ;
```

Note that the assignment of the field b_D.attr.attr with 4 performs a side effect on the field attr of C: a reference is a kind of pointer. This explains the value 8 returned by the evaluation of a_C.binary_add (a_C). The execution of the last message sending a_C.test (b_D) first shows that the method test can be applied to an object belonging to a subclass of C. It also reveals the default value given by the compiler to b_D.attr, which is 0 and can be unexpected.

4.1.4. *Marks*

4.1.4.1. *Confinement*

Java uses a number of marks, either to confine, or to specify more precisely the access rules to a definition. These marks may be set on the classes themselves or on their fields. The confinement does not change the type of the class (Ans. 1.19).

Let C be a class hosted by a package P. The class C and one of its fields 1 are accessible according to their confinement mark as follows (Ans. 1.16):

– public: any class of any package can access C and 1;

– with no mark: any class of P can access C and 1;

– protected: any class of P as well as those inheriting from C, hosted by other packages, can access C and 1;

– private: 1 is only visible in C but is inherited by the subclasses of C. The mark private cannot be set on C except if C is a subclass. A field tagged private can be reintroduced in a subclass with another mark.

In example 4.4, the method see of A is tagged private. It has an argument of type int. It is called by the method f. The class B inherits from A and introduces a method see taking no arguments. Its constructor calls the one of A.

EXAMPLE 4.4.–

```Java
class A {
  private int num ;
  A (int x) { num = x ; }
  private void see () { System.out.println (this.num) ; }
  void f () { System.out.print ("In A : ") ; see () ; }
}

class B extends A {
  public void see () { System.out.println ("Not visible") ; }
  B (int x) { super (x) ; }
  /* Line 12  public void foo () { A.see () ; } */
}

public class Confine {
  public static void main (String[] args) {
    A three = new A (3) ;
    B four = new B (4) ;
    /* three.see () ; */
    three.f () ;
    four.see () ;
    four.f () ;
  }
}
```

```
}
```

```
In A : 3
Not visible
In A : 4
```

The evaluation of the message `three.f ()` calls the method `see` of A, which explains the display `In A : 3`. The evaluation of `four.see ()` calls `B.see ()`. The execution of `four.f ()` calls the method `see` of A and not the one of B, which would be the case with an evaluation using late-binding. The definition of `see` in B is thus not considered as a redefinition of the method `A.see`. The name of this method `A.see`, marked `private` in A, is not visible in B and cannot then be redefined in it but only introduced again.

The attempt to define `foo` (which is commented to avoid a compilation error) is not accepted by the compiler. The same happens for the message sending `three.see ()` in `main` since the method `see` of A is not visible from `main`.

```
test3.java:12: error: see() has private access in A
    public void foo () { A.see () ; }
```

Example 4.5 illustrates the role of marks while using `packages`. The use of `y` in `f` of B is not possible since the visibility of `y` (not marked) is restricted, in the inheritance steps, to its `package PP`.

Conversely, the visibility of `x` is extended to all the classes inheriting from A. It is possible to call the default constructor of A in C since the name A is exported without any restriction. However, fields of A are more strongly confined, which forbids their "direct" import in C: they are not visible in C because C does not inherit from A and does not belong to PP. Hence, it is impossible to perform any assignment on the attributes of `o`.

EXAMPLE 4.5.–

```Java
// File PP/A.java
package PP ;
public class A { protected int x ; int y ; }

// File RP/B.java
package RP ;
import PP.* ;
public class B extends A {
  public void f () { x = 2 ; y = 3 ; } /* Does not compile. */
}
```

```
// File RP/C.java
package RP ;
import PP.* ;
public class C {
  public void f () {
    A o = new A () ;
    o.x = 2 ; o.y = 3 ;
  }
}
```

```
$ javac PP/A.java
$ javac RP/B.java
RP/B.java:5: error y is not public in A cannot be accessed from outside package
  public void f () { x = 2 ; y = 3 ; } /* Does not compile. */
                     ^
1 error
$ javac RP/C.java
RP/C.java:7: error x has protected access in A
    o.x = 2 ; o.y = 3 ;
    ^
RP/C.java:7: error y is not public in A cannot be accessed from outside package
    o.x = 2 ; o.y = 3 ;
              ^
2 errors
```

4.1.4.2. *Other marks*

Let C be a class included in a package P. A field l of C and C itself are accessible according to *usage marks* as follows:

- abstract: l is only declared, C and l are said to be *abstract*. This point will be addressed later;

- static: a field l tagged static is a class field. Its evaluation is totally performed with a static (lexical) scope and therefore cannot be redefined. If l is a reference type, the value pointed by l can be modified;

- final C: the class cannot be inherited. Once defined, the field l cannot be masked or redefined;

- static final: l is defined as a constant field.

In example 4.6, num is an object of the class FinalTest, its attribute cl marked final is an object, let's say O, of the class A, whose attribute y has been modified by num.cl.inc (). There is no contradiction: the value of cl is a reference to the object O, it was not modified. However, the referenced value was modified. If the declaration of the attribute int y is marked private final then the compilation fails.

EXAMPLE 4.6.–

```Java
class A {
  int y ;
  void inc () { this.y = y + 1 ; }
  A (int v) { y = v ; }
}
public class FinalTest {
  private final A cl = new A (0) ;
  public FinalTest (int w) { this.cl.y = w ; }

public static void main (String[] args) {
  FinalTest num = new FinalTest (25) ;
  System.out.println (num.cl.y) ;     // Prints 25.
  num.cl.inc () ;
  System.out.println (num.cl.y) ;     // Prints 26.
  }
}
```

4.1.5. *Developing classes*

4.1.5.1. *Abstract classes*

An abstract class is an incomplete *C-kit* (Ans. 1.27). A method l which is *not defined* must be marked, as well as its class C, by abstract. Method l will be defined in a class inheriting from C (Ans. 1.37). The types of arguments and the type of the result of the definition are those of the declaration. In the following example, f can be applied to oD because D is a subclass of C. However, the attempt to replace the f definition in B by void f (D x) ... is rejected.

EXAMPLE 4.7.–

```Java
class C { int cc ; C (int a) { cc = a ; } }
class D extends C { D (int a) {super (a) ; } }

abstract class A extends C {
  A (int a) { super (a) ; }
  abstract void f (C x) ;
  }

class B extends A {
  B (int a) { super (a) ; }
  void f (C x) { System.out.println (x.cc) ; }
}

class testabstract {
  public static void main (String[] args) {
    C oC = new C (1) ;
    D oD = new D (10) ;
    B oB = new B (5) ;
```

```
   oB.f (oC) ; /* Returns 1. */
   oB.f (oD) ; /* Returns 10. */
  }
}
```

Any class owning, directly or by inheritance, an abstract method that is not yet defined must also be tagged `abstract` and cannot be instantiated to create objects.

4.1.5.2. *Parameterized classes*

Class parametrization has been studied in Chapter 1 and in section 3.2.4.3. Java only allows a parametrization by types (Ans. 1.32, Ans. 1.33 and Ans. 1.34). For instance, a class whose header is `C<T,S>` is parameterized by the type variables `S` and `T`. Such a class is also referred to as *generic*. A type variable cannot be instantiated by a primitive type. However, primitive types can be converted to reference types (by a conversion called *boxing conversion*). For example, an `int` can be converted to an object of type `Integer`, this class wrapping integers of type `int` and their operations. Hence, a wrapped primitive type can instantiate a type variable. A class method (thus marked `static`) of a parameterized class cannot use the type variable `T` since the body of this method could not be typechecked (`T` is not yet instantiated). Confinement marks can be used without any restriction for parameterized classes (Ans. 1.36).

A method can also be parameterized and must be instantiated before being used. The type parameters can be used in the declaration of both the arguments and result types.

Example 4.8 illustrates several points. Several elements are parameterized: the abstract class `Pair` (by `T` and `S`), the method `fgen` (by `U`) and the abstract method `f` (by `T`). `f` uses `T` to declare its argument's type and `g` only uses `Pair`, without specifying the type variables. The class `Complex` instantiates the type parameters `S` and `T`, inherits from the fields of the class `Pair` and defines `f`, whose argument must have the type instantiating `T` (hence `Integer`). The definition of `proj1` explicitly converts the `Integer` type of its result into `float`. It directly uses the attribute `fst` (thus without using `this`).

EXAMPLE 4.8.–

```Java
abstract class Pair <T, S> {
  T fst; S snd;
  <U> void fgen (U[] tab) {
    for (U elt:tab) { System.out.print (elt + " ") ; }
    System.out.println (" result of fgen") ;
  }
  abstract void f (T elt) ;
  void g (Pair elt) { System.out.println (elt.fst + " " + this.snd) ; }
}

public class Complex extends Pair <Integer, Integer> {
```

```
Complex (Integer a, Integer b) { fst = a ; snd = b ; }
float proj1 () { return fst ; }
void f (Integer elt) {
  System.out.println (" elt + this.fst = " + (elt + this.fst)) ; }

public static void main (String[] args) {
  Complex i = new Complex (6, 8) ;
  System.out.println (i.proj1 ()) ;
  Integer mytab [] = { 1, 2 } ;
  i.fgen (mytab) ;
  i.f (100) ;
  Complex j = new Complex (24, 36) ;
  i.g (j) ;
  }
}
```

The obtained output follows:

```
6.0
1 2  result of fgen
 elt + this.fst = 106
24 8
```

The evaluation of i.g (j), displaying the last line of the output, confirms that the instantiation of the type Pair of g's argument elt is performed even if there is no mention of S and T in the source code of g.

4.1.5.3. *Interfaces*

A Java interface I is an incomplete *C-kit* (Ans. 1.27), without attributes, object constructors or any other definition. All the methods declarations are public and class variables are marked static final, in other words they are constants (Ans. 1.30). An interface defines a type with the same name. This *C-kit* may be completed by a class C, this completion being denoted by the keyword implements. Usually, all the fields of I are defined in C. However, if some methods of I remain *not defined* in C, then C must be declared as abstract. An interface may also be parameterized with type variables (Ans. 1.28).

Example 4.9 uses the class C introduced in example 4.2. The generic interface LowerThan<T> is implemented in the subclass R of C, the type variable T is replaced by the type Integer. This class Integer wraps the type int and the compiler handles the required conversions between these two types (Ans. 1.29).

EXAMPLE 4.9.–

```Java
interface LowerThan<T> {
  public boolean less_than (T x, T y) ;
}

class R extends C implements LowerThan<Integer> {
  public boolean less_than (Integer x, Integer y) { return x < y ; }
  void compare (C o) {
    System.out.println ("this.x < o.x : " + less_than (this.x, o.x)) ; }
  R (int a, C n) { super (a, n) ; }
}

public class InterC {
  public static void main(String[] args) {
    C anchor = new C (25);
    System.out.println ("the anchor") ; anchor.get_C () ;
    R foo = new R (5, anchor) ;
    foo.compare (anchor) ;
  }
}
```

The execution of this example produces the following output:

```
the anchor
attribute x = 25 and field z = 1
  the next
  end
this.x < o.x : true
```

4.1.5.4. *Inheritance*

Java provides simple inheritance, which we already used in the previous examples, and implementation of interfaces. We now take a moment to review these notions in more detail.

Subclassing

Inheritance and interfaces implementation define a subclassing relation between classes and interfaces. As both of them can be used together by a same class C, this latter has an inheritance graph whose nodes are the classes transitively inherited by C and the interfaces transitively implemented in C. Any Java class inherits from a class called Object which is the root of the inheritance graph. Inheritance is extended to internal classes: an internal class can inherit from another one that has already been introduced.

Reintroduction

Let C be a class and R a subclass of C.

Any attribute a of C can be reintroduced in R. The field C.a remains present in R but is masked by R.a. This may introduce some ambiguities, leading to unexpected results. Since an attribute is used to represent data that must be visible to be processed, using the same name twice for an attribute is useless and not recommended.

A method m of C reintroduced in R overloads C.m if the type of R.m is different from that of C.m. Otherwise, R.m is a *redefinition* of C.m, which remains visible via the qualified name super.m. However, it is not possible to go back earlier in the inheritance steps: no super.super.m is available. The redefinition may be annotated by @override to ask the compiler for consistency checks.

A class method (hence marked static) f can be reintroduced in R. If C.f and R.f have the same type then R.f masks C.f, otherwise R.f overloads C.f (as for methods).

Method lookup

Let o be an object of a class C. If the message o.m is well-typed, then the method m with the expected type exists in one of the classes of C's inheritance graph. There can even be several suitable versions if m has been redefined several times. Let us call D the subclass of the value pointed by o when o.m is executed. This execution starts by looking for the method m in D, then goes back in the inheritance steps to C, then in C's graph. This lookup may continue if needed up to the class Object and if m is not found, an exception is raised. This means that the method m, used during the typechecking of the message, is not forcibly the m used at execution-time (see example 4.14).

Multiple inheritance

Java does not propose multiple inheritance. Implementing an interface I (or several interfaces) by a class C is close to an inheritance from I by C. This avoids the usual problem of selecting an inherited method in the presence of multiple inheritance.

4.1.5.5. *Subtyping*

Java proposes a subtyping relation denoted here by $\leq_T$, induced by the subclassing (declarations C2 extends C1 and C implements I) but also by some predefined relations between some primitive types (for instance float is a subtype of double). Moreover, whatever the type T, one has $T \leq_T$ Object. For example, the declaration class C extends C1 implements I induces $C \leq_T$ C1 and $C \leq_T$ I.

A method m whose formal parameter has type C_1 can be applied to any value of type C_2 if C_2 is a subtype of C_1 (contravariance of the argument). But the type of the result R_1 cannot be "super-classed": the covariance of the result is reduced to type equality. However, since version 1.5, Java accepts that the result type R_2 of a redefinition is a subtype of R_1 (which is sometimes called the *covariance of the result* but does not correspond to our definition of covariance). Let us examine this point with example 4.10.

EXAMPLE 4.10.–

```Java
class C {
  int x ;
  C (int a) { x = a ;}
  C get_C () { System.out.println ("of type C") ; return this ; }
}

class R extends C {
  R (int x) { super (x) ; }
  @Override
  R get_C () { System.out.println ("of type R") ; return this ; }
}

public class covariance {
  public static void main (String[] args) {
    C o1 = new C (25) ;
    C o2 = o1.get_C () ;
    R o3 = new R (5) ;
    R o4 = o3.get_C () ;
  }
}
```

```
of type C
of type R
```

The redefinition of get_C, modifying the type of the result, is accepted as shown in the above execution. However, if the definition of get_C and its redefinition are respectively replaced by:

```Java
C get_C (C o) { System.out.println ("of type C") ; return o ; }
R get_C (C o) { System.out.println ("of type R") ; return o ; }
```

then the compiler raises an error (which is fully satisfactory):

```
covariance.java:14: error: incompatible types: C cannot be converted to R
    R get_C (C o) { System.out.println ("of type R") ; return o ; }
                                                              ^
1 error
```

The extension to assignment, as studied in section 3.2.5.2, is only accepted if the type of the left-side value is a subtype of the type of the right-side value, as shown in example 4.11.

EXAMPLE 4.11.–

```Java
class C { int attr ; }
interface I { void set_d (int x) ; }
class D extends C implements I {
  int d ;
  public void set_d (int x) { this.d = x ; }
}

class Affectation {
  public static void main (String[] args) {
    C a_C = new C () ;
    D b_D = new D () ;
    a_C = b_D ;        // 1
    I h_I = b_D ;      // 2
    b_D = a_C ;        // 3
    h_I = a_C ;        // 4
  }
}
```

```
$ javac Test.java
Test.java:14: error: incompatible types: C cannot be converted to D
    b_D = a_C ;        // 3
          ^
Test.java:15: error: incompatible types: C cannot be converted to I
    h_I = a_C ;        // 4
          ^
2 errors
```

The assignments at lines 1 and 2 in the body of main are legal. The next lines, 3 and 4, are ill-typed. However, it is sufficient to apply the explicit conversions (*cast*) b_D = (D) a_C and h_I = (I) a_C to get these lines accepted.

The subtyping relation is extended, as studied in section 5.7.1 of Volume 1, by induction on the array types: if $T \leq_T S$, then $T[] \leq_T S[]$. The subtyping relation is not extended on the parameterized types: $T \leq_T S$ does not imply $C<T> \leq_T C<S>$. This impossibility may raise difficulties when using parameterized types, which oblige us to make explicit conversions. The following program in example 4.12 illustrates this point. It has indeed been compiled and executed without any issue.

EXAMPLE 4.12.–

```Java
class Pair <T, S> {
  T fst ; S snd ;
  Pair (T x, S y) { this.fst = x ; this.snd = y ; }
}

public class PB {
  public static void main (String[] args) {
    Pair <Integer, Integer> d1 = new Pair <Integer, Integer> (1, 2) ;
```

```
    Pair <Object, Object> d2 = new Pair <Object, Object> (3, 4) ;
  }
}
```

However, if we add the instruction d1 = d2 we obtain the following error message:

```
error: incompatible types: Pair<Object,Object>
cannot be converted to Pair<Integer,Integer>
   d1 = d2 ;
```

and if we replace it by d2 = d1, we obtain a similar message:

```
error: incompatible types: Pair<Integer,Integer>
cannot be converted to Pair<Object,Object>
   d2 = d1 ;
```

4.1.5.6. *Explicit type conversion*

Let C be a class and D one of its subclasses. The coercion of an object a of D to C, denoted by (C) a, is accepted by the typing algorithm. The coercion of an object o of C to an object of type D, denoted by (D) o, is also accepted after typechecking. However, it will not modify the value pointed by the object o and may lead to an error during the execution if the value of o cannot be interpreted as a value of type D.

In example 4.13, o1, whose value has type D, can be converted into an object of type C. The execution also shows the default value used for o2.b.

EXAMPLE 4.13.–

```
Java
class C { int a ;}

class D extends C { String  b ; }

public class Coercion {
  public static void main (String[] args) {
    C o1 = new D () ;
    D o2 = (D) o1 ;
    C o3 = new C () ;
    /* D o4 = (D) o3 ;   --- Not accepted */
    System.out.println
      ("o1.a = " + o1.a + ", o2.a = " + o2.a + ", O2.b = " + o2.b) ;
  }
}
$ java Coercion
o1.a = 0, o2.a = 0, O2.b = null
```

Conversely, the definition of o4 is not accepted since the type of its value is not a subtype of D. To prevent such a runtime error, it is possible to perform an *instance test*: the boolean expression o `instanceof` C is true if o has a value that is an instance of the class C, otherwise if it is false.

4.1.5.7. *Overloading*

Java only allows methods overloading. Operators are predefined and their semantics cannot be changed.

Suppose that m is an overloaded method of the class C, having two arguments. The overloading resolution is statically performed while typing the message o.m (v, w), where o has type C. The resolution algorithm searches the methods m in C, then if needed, in the ancestor classes of C. Suppose that two methods m are suitable. One of the versions of m, let us say m1, is a method of the class C_1 and the types of its arguments are t_1 and s_1. The other version of m, let us say m2, belongs to the class C_2 with arguments of types t_2 and s_2.

The resolution mechanism relies on couples whose first component is the class, the second one being the product of the arguments types and the result type. It defines an ordering $\leq_{Over}$ on the couples as follows:

(C_1, t_1 $\times$ s_1) $\leq_{Over}$ (C_2, t_2 $\times$ s_2) if and only if C_1 $\leq_T$ C_2 and: t_1 $\leq_T$ t_2 and s_1 $\leq_T$ s_2.

Then, this mechanism selects the method whose type is the smallest according to the ordering $\leq_{Over}$. This selected method, statically determined, is the one that will be executed. The following example 4.14 illustrates subtyping and overloading.

EXAMPLE 4.14.–

```Java
class C {
  void m1 (C x) { System.out.println ("C.m1") ; }
  void m2 (C x) { System.out.println ("C.m2") ; }
}
class D extends C {
  void m1 (C x) { System.out.println ("D.m1") ; }
  void m2 (D x) { System.out.println ("D.m2") ; }
}
public class DiffSurDef {
  public static void main (String [] argv) {
    /*1*/    C o_C = new D () ;
    /*2*/    D o_D = new D () ;
    /*3*/    o_C.m1 (o_D) ;
    /*4*/    o_C.m2 (o_D) ;
    /*5*/    o_D.m2 (o_C) ;
  }
}
```

```
/*3*/ D.m1
/*4*/ C.m2
/*5*/ D.m2
```

Class D redefines m1. The object o_C having been declared of type C, is assigned with a value of type D. This is correct since D is a subtype of C (line /*1*/). Typing the occurrence m1 in the message o_C.m1 (o_D) line /*3*/ is achieved by searching in class D (the type of the value of o_C) the method m1. Its application to o_D is well-typed because D is a subtype of C. This explains the obtained output.

Class D overloads method m2. The resolution is statically done, in contrast with the handling of the redefinition. Through typechecking, we notice that C.m2 is suitable to type o_C.m2 (o_D) and that D.m2 does not fit because the type of o_C, at compile-time, is not D. Thus, C.m2 is bound to the occurrence of m2 in this message.

To typecheck o_D.m2 (o_D), both methods m2 are suitable. Because (D, D × void) $\leq_{Over}$ (C, C × void), the method D.m2 is chosen.

The compiler may insert legal type conversions to resolve overloading. However, it will never apply transforms, possibly causing an information leak in the sense defined in sections 6.1.2.4 and 6.1.4.1 of Volume 1. The program in example 4.15 shows various usages of the overloading and the raised issues.

EXAMPLE 4.15.–

```Java
class Test {
/*a*/  public void f (int a, int b) { System.out.println ("int, int") ; }
/*b*/  public void f (long a, int b) { System.out.println ("long, int") ; }
/*c*/  public void f (long a, short b) { System.out.println ("long, short") ; }
}

public class Resolution {
  public static void main (String[] args) {
    short i_short = 0 ;
    int i_int = 1 ;
    long i_long = 2 ;
    Test o = new Test () ;

    /*1*/   o.f (i_int, i_int) ;    // int, int
    /*2*/   o.f (i_short, i_int) ;  // Conversion short to int -> (int, int)
    /*3*/   o.f (i_int, i_short) ;  // Ambiguous: (int, int) or (long, short)?
    /*4*/   o.f (i_int, i_long) ;   // Impossible
  }
}
```

The resolution of the call to f /*1*/ is done with version /*a*/ of f.

Call /*2*/ requires a conversion of the argument short into int, which enables us to call version /*a*/ of f: short is a subtype of int. The conversion of short into long could have been possible, leading to the use of version /*b*/ but the couple (C, short × int × void) is smaller in the ordering $\leq_{Over}$ than the couple (C, long × int × void).

Call /*3*/ is ambiguous and the compiler raises an error. Indeed, two conversions are possible. Version /*a*/ can be used but version /*c*/ of f can also be selected because int is a subtype of long. The couples (C, long × short × void) and (C, int × int × void) are not comparable and the resolution fails.

Call /*4*/ cannot be resolved and leads to an error at compile-time. The type long of the second argument of f is neither a subtype of int nor of short. Presented in another way, converting a value of type long into a value of type int or short would lead to an information leak because types int and short are both encoded with a number of bits lower than the number of bits required for a long (see section 6.1.2 of Volume 1).

4.1.5.8. *Other features*

Java provides a garbage collection mechanism, studied in section 7.6.3 of Volume 1, allowing us to destroy objects that are no longer accessible in the program. The class Object contains a finalize method (with an empty body by default) that can be redefined and is executed when an object is collected, hence before the deallocated memory zone can possibly be reallocated. This method thus plays the role of an object destructor.

The exceptions mechanism of Java has been presented in section 8.3.3 of Volume 1. Here, we did not address introspection as it was already introduced in section 3.1. Many other Javafeatures are not described due to a lack of space, for instance the use of <? extends C> instead of <T> in parameterized classes to restrict instanciations of T to all the subclasses of C. After the overview of Java provided here, the reader may consult the reference manual [GOS 19] to address the advanced features of this language. The reader may also be interested in the article [IGA 01] which presents a mathematical model of a Java kernel.

4.2. Classes in C++

C++ is in essence an imperative language, borrowing many characteristics from C, hence providing low-level features. Several of these features have already been studied in Chapters 6, 7 and 8 of Volume 1.

C++ also provides high-level constructs, in particular object-oriented features which played an important role in the conception of some languages such as Java and

Python. C++ is statically typed. Implicit type conversions are performed by the compiler (Ans. 1.8) and the user may also write such conversions. Hence, the language is not strongly typed (Ans. 1.1). C++ is compiled into native code, it uses the mechanism of static scope except for methods redefinitions (Ans. 1.4). There exist several compilers for C++ and they do not all accept the same syntax but semantical differences are not essential.

In this section, we only present the main object-oriented features of C++, without always giving all the declinations of the studied syntactic construct. We attempt to provide the simplest possible examples, even if they are not always realistic. In particular, we do not use pointers and arrays when they are not really needed, in order to emphasize the studied point.

4.2.1. *Header files, namespaces, confinement*

As in C, the structure of C++ files allows us to implement *W-kits* (Ans. 1.2). A source file name.cpp (or .cp) contains definitions of functions, variables, classes, etc. It may be associated with a *declaration interface* name.h, also called a *header file*, which defines a form of confinement (Ans. 1.15) already studied for C (see section 2.3.3). The management of source files and declaration interfaces by the compiler and the linker in C++ is different from the one of C. The language adds some constraints on declarations to prevent the ambiguities presented in section 2.3.3.

Variables declarations in P.h not defined in the file P.cpp must be introduced by the keyword extern. Several declarations (hence marked extern) for a same variable are allowed in the .h or .cpp files but only one definition is authorized among the files sent to the linker (otherwise an error is raised). Let us remind ourselves that the expression extern int a is only a declaration of the global variable a and int a is only its definition without explicit initialization. The compiler only initializes global variables with the default value 0. However, relying on this default behavior is not recommended.

In C++, any function must be declared in a header file before being used in another source file. The declaration extern void f () means, in C++, that the function does not have any arguments, whereas in C it provides no information about possible arguments.

The most important difference between C and C++ from the point of view of *W-kit* implementation is that C++ provides a real management system of namespaces (Ans. 1.3). Chapter 1 presented the notion of a namespace using three spaces (type names, names of variables, functions, exceptions defined in the current program and *kit* names). In C++, a namespace *myname* can be introduced without relation to a predefined category of names, using the keyword namespace followed by *myname* and a block containing at least the declarations of the names belonging to this namespace. Definitions can be provided in a separate file. A namespace may be extended by adding new names. The scoping operator denoted by :: allows us to specify which namespace an identifier belongs to. For instance, the namespace std refers to the standard library, std::cout is a name of this namespace representing the standard output (the terminal or the screen) and std::cout << exp prints the value of exp. Example 4.16 shows the creation and the use of a namespace.

EXAMPLE 4.16.–

```C++
/* --- File namespace.cpp */
#include <iostream>
namespace K {
  void f () { std::cout << "K :: f" << std::endl ; }
}
namespace P {
  void f () { std::cout << "P :: f" << std::endl ; }
}
int main () {
  K::f () ;
  P::f () ;
  return (0) ;
}
```

This file named namespace.cpp is compiled then executed, leading to the following display.

```
$ g++ -o namespace.out namespace.cpp
$ ./namespace.out
K :: f
P :: f
```

Let us define a header file for this program, only exporting the namespace K:

```C++
/* namespace.h */
namespace K { void f (void) ; }
```

and consider example 4.17.

EXAMPLE 4.17.–

```
C++
/* --- File test0.h */
void print_X (void) ;
extern int my_x ;

/* --- File test0.cpp */
#include <iostream>
#include "namespace.h"
#include "test0.h"

int my_x = 0 ;
int y = 33 ;
void print_X () { std::cout << "my_x = " << my_x << std::endl ; }
void print_Y () { std::cout << "y = " << y << std::endl ; }

int main () {
  print_X () ;
  print_Y () ;
  K::f () ;
  /* P::f () ; */
  return (0) ;
}
```

Then, let us compile and execute this program test0.

```
$ g++ -o test0.out namespace.cpp test0.cpp
$ ./test0.out
my_x = 0
y = 33
K :: f
```

In example 4.17, the directive #include <iostream> allows us to use the tools iostream of the standard library related to input/output. This use of the directive #include does not cause a flattening. If std is removed from std::cout a compilation error occurs. Likewise, the directive #include "namespace.h" does not allow us to directly use f. As the namespace P is not exported in namespace.h, the compiler rejects the commented line P::f (). The header file declares my_x (extern int my_x) and #include "test0.h" provides the visibility of the name my_x.

The difference in behavior between the different uses of #include is due to the namespaces. The file test0.cpp does not introduce a new namespace: its names belong to the global namespace and are directly accessible.

Flattening a namespace name is achieved with the directive using namespace name in a file P.cpp. For instance, if the directive using namespace std is used, we can use `cout << exp` to print exp's value. Let us modify the file `test0.cpp` of example 4.17 by flattening `std` and `K`. We can now cease using the qualified names to rewrite example 4.18.

EXAMPLE 4.18.–

```c++
/* --- File test0flat.cpp */
#include <iostream>
#include "namespace.h"
#include "test0.h"
using namespace std ;
using namespace K ;

int my_x ;
int y = 33 ;
void print_X () { cout << "my_x = " << my_x <<  :endl ; }
void print_Y () { cout << "y = " << y << endl ; }

int main () {
  print_X () ;
  print_Y () ;
  f () ;
  return (0) ;
}
```

The execution of example 4.18 is the same as the one of example 4.17:

```
$ g++ -o test0flat.out namespace.cpp test0flat.cpp
$ ./test0flat.out
my_x = 0
y = 33
K :: f
```

Flattening should only be done with full knowledge of the risks of masking or overloading (Ans. 1.26). It cannot be done in a header file, say P.h, because it could mask names already present in some importer files, with developers having no way of modifying the header P.h if they are not the owners of it. The directive `using namespace name::f` only flattens the name f.

4.2.2. *Classes*

A C++ class is a *C-kit* whose fields can be attributes, methods, class methods, class variables (introduced by `static`) and internal classes (Ans. 1.2). A class declaration introduces a type wearing the same name (Ans. 1.5), fields must be introduced with their types (Ans. 1.6). A class cannot contain instruction blocks that are not related to a field (Ans. 1.12). Objects are first-class values (Ans. 1.14).

Typechecking is nominal (Ans. 1.7). A class also defines a namespace (Ans. 1.3) that cannot be extended nor flattened (Ans. 1.25).

Let us examine a minimal example, made of one unique file `easy.cpp` and containing the declaration/definition of a class and the function `main` required by any program. This function has to return a value of type `int`. Directives `#include` enable us to use the tools related to input/output and strings, the `using` directive avoids the need to prefix `cout` and `endl` by `std::` (like in example 4.16). The class owns an attribute x, an object constructor `C (int a)` and a method `print` directly using x.

The function `main ()` creates an object o of `C` by calling the object constructor. It then calls the method `print` "of" o and terminates, returning 0.

EXAMPLE 4.19.–

```C++
/* --- File easy.cpp */
#include <iostream>
#include <string>
using namespace std ;

class C {
  int  x ;
public :
  C (int a) { x = a ; }
  void print () { cout << "value of x :" << x << endl ; }
};

int main () {
  C o = C (4) ;
  o.print () ;
  return (0) ;
}
```

The output obtained after compilation and execution of example 4.19 follows:

```
$ g++ -o easy.out easy.cpp
$ ./easy.out
value of x :4
```

Example 4.19 provides a first and very simple approach of the notion of class. With example 4.20, more in line with usual practices in C++, we review how to build a class P. We first start with the file P.h.

EXAMPLE 4.20.–

```
C++
/* --- File P.h */
#include <iostream>
#include <string>

class P {
  int age ;

 public:
  P () ;
  P (int a, std::string n) ;
  ~P () ;
  void set_age (int a) ;
  void print_age () ;
  void set_name (std::string n) { name = n ; } ;
  void still_young (int x) ;
  bool is_young () ;
  static void warning (std::string n) ;
  static int max_age ;

  /* protected : */
  std::string get_name () const ;

 private:
  int get_age () ;
  std::string name ;
};
```

The file P.h begins with some directives and the import of some functions of the standard library using declaration interfaces. As previously stated, no namespace flattening can be done in a header file. Then, the class P is declared. The attributes (here age) located at the beginning of the file, before any mark, are implicitly marked private and may (depending on the compiler) get default values (it is the case for age). However, if a class is introduced using struct instead of class, declarations that are not explicitly marked are implicitly tagged as public. The marks (more detailed further) private, public or protected can be set on any field. All the fields declared after a mark p and before another one (or the end of the file) are tagged p. Here, public marks all the declarations from P () to get_name included since protected is commented. The fields get_age and name are marked private. The header file contains the declarations of the object constructors (here P () and P (int a, std::string n)) and the object destructor ~P (detailed later). It also contains declarations of methods and possibly their definitions (in the case of set_name). Defined this way, a method has the default status inline: the compiler may replace a call to this method with a direct expansion of the instructions present in its body, for the sake of optimizations. Class variables (max_age) and class methods (warning) are declared using the keyword static. The annotation const on a method (get_name), seen in section 7.4 of Volume 1, means that this method does not modify its arguments, and in particular its implicit argument V_this. The order in which fields are introduced does not matter (Ans. 1.10).

Example 4.21 continues the previous one. The file P.cpp defines the class P. The order of the field definitions is again not important (Ans. 1.10) and a field may be recursive without any specific keyword (Ans. 1.11). Types in definitions must be identical to those in declarations (Ans. 1.29).

EXAMPLE 4.21.–

```cpp
C++
/* --- File P.cpp */
#include "P.h"
using namespace std ;

P::P () { age = 0 ; name = "X" ; }
P::P (int a, string n) { age = a ; name = n ; }
P::~P () { cout << "Cleaning " << name << endl ; }

int P::get_age () { return (age) ; }
void P::set_age (int a) { age = age + a ; }
void P::print_age () { cout << this -> get_age () << endl ; }
string P::get_name () const { return (name) ; }
int P::max_age = 122 ;
void P::still_young (int x) { age = age - x ; }
bool P::is_young () { this->still_young (10) ; return (age < max_age) ; }
void P::warning (string n) { cout << n << " age <= " << max_age << endl ; }
```

One may notice the flattening of the namespace std, whose scope is restricted to the file P.cpp. The directive #include "P.h" allows us to "see" the declaration of P in P.cpp. However, the definition of a field of P is done by using the full name of the field (P::P (), for instance) because the namespace P defined by the class cannot be flattened. Only the annotation const has to be repeated, confinement marks do not.

The two object constructors, having different numbers of parameters, are distinguished by the overloading mechanism. The constructor P() directly initializes the attributes. The object destructor performs a side effect to highlight its call.

The class variable max_age is initialized with 122. As seen in section 3.2, any method is a function taking the variable V_this as parameter, denoted if needed in the method's body by the keyword this. In C++, this is a constant pointer (implicitly declared P *const this), whose pointed value is the object that is the effective parameter of V_this (hence the object receiving the message of the method). This explains why the message is sent using an arrow, this->get_age () in print_age. The method set_age modifies the value of the attribute age, without using this. Class attributes and class methods can be used without any restriction in method definitions. The method name, tagged private, is used by get_name.

Note that a method defined outside the declaration of its class cannot be implicitly *inlined*. To allow inlining, it must be annotated by `inline`.

Example 4.22 uses class P. The definition of f and the way it is used will be commented on later.

REMARK.– In some of the coming examples, messages displayed during the executions will be set as comments at the "best possible" locations in the source codes.

EXAMPLE 4.22.–

```cpp
C++
/* --- File mainP.cpp */
#include "P.h"
using namespace std ;

int f () {
  P* ploc = new P (20,"A") ;
  P oloc = P (12, "B") ;
  ploc->print_age () ;
  oloc.print_age () ;
  cout << "End running f" << endl ;
  return 0 ;
}

int main () {
  P old = P () ;
  old.print_age () ; /* 0 */
  old.set_age (90) ;
  old.print_age () ; /* 90 */
  old.set_name ("T") ;
  cout << old.get_name () << endl ; /* T */

  P *p ;
  p = new P (14, "Pierre") ;
  cout << (p->get_name ()) << endl ;    /* Pierre */
  p->print_age () ;   /* 14 */

  old.still_young (25) ;
  old.print_age () ; /* 65 */
  p->still_young (0) ;
  p->print_age () ;    /* 14 */

  P::warning (old.get_name ()) ; /* T age <= 122 */
  old.max_age = 300 ;
  P::warning (old.get_name ()) ;    /* T age <= 300 */

  cout << "old young? " << old.is_young ()    /* old young? 1; p young ? 1 */
       << "; p young ? " << p ->is_young () << endl ;
  f () ; /* See below. */
  cout << (p->get_name ()) << endl ;    /* Pierre */
                                        /* Cleaning T*/
```

```
    return 0 ;
}

/* Execution of f ()
... Skipped messages ...
20
12
End running f
Cleaning B
*/
```

The variable old denotes the object created by the call P () of the constructor, the call new P (14, "Pierre") returns a pointer on the created object which is stored in p. The attributes of these objects being marked private, the function main cannot access them directly. Calling a method is done using the dot-notation (like in old.set_age (90)) if the object is a variable of type P. Calling a method from an object stored via a pointer p is done with the arrow-notation (like in p->get_age ()). To call a class method, the scoping operator must be used (like in P::warning). A modification of a method or a variable declared static has an impact on all the objects of the class: this can be seen through the results of P::warning (old.get_name ()) before and after the assignment old.max_age = 300. The execution of f() creates two objects ploc and oloc. The scope of oloc is f and it gets freed at the end of the f execution. So, the destructor ~P is called, causing the display of Cleaning B. Conversely, being dynamically allocated, ploc survives to the end of f. The output of the f() execution is provided at the end of the example. After the f execution, the message p->get_name is executed, printing Pierre. The end of the execution is reached, ploc is freed and cleaning T is printed.

We note that, if the mark protected were not commented on in P.h, the following error would be raised:

```
mainP.cpp:19:15: error: 'get_name' is a protected member of 'P'
    cout << old.get_name () << endl ;
```

A method marked const cannot modify the object calling it. For instance, the method declared by std::string get_name () const; in the P class can modify none of P's attributes. If an object is marked const, it cannot be modified and thus can only call methods tagged const. It is also possible to mark an attribute as mutable. This allows us to define objects marked const, with some attributes that can be modified. We will not deepen this point, whose use requires a bit of prudence.

4.2.2.1. *Object constructors and destructors*

Object constructors take the name of the class. Their semantics complies with the description given in section 3.2. If no constructor is defined in the source code, the compiler adds a default constructor, without arguments, that does not initialize attributes with default values. This constructor becomes inaccessible as soon as a constructor is provided in the source code (this is the case in example 4.21). The definition of an object constructor may use default values (see P () in example 4.21).

Creating an object of the class P is done through the evaluation of an application P (v) of a constructor P, where v are the effective parameters of the application. The choice of the constructor to call is determined from the number and the types of the effective parameters (see section 3.2). The created value, which is thus an object, can be directly bound to a variable o using the declaration P o = P (v) (which may be shortened in P o (v)). The name o hence denotes a local variable of main (which is the case of old in example 4.22) or of the function that declared this variable (which is the case of oloc in the function f). Such a variable is sometimes called *automatic* since it will be automatically destroyed once the function's execution ends.

The value created by the evaluation of P(v) can also be accessible through a pointer with the definition P *p = new P (v). This is the case for ploc in the function f or p in example 4.22. Using the operator new performs a dynamic memory allocation. In example 4.22, the pointer p is created in the stack (or a register) by the declaration P *p. The evaluation of new P (14, "Pierre") creates the object, stores it in the memory zone allocated in the *heap* and assigns p with the address of this zone. In C++, applying an object constructor is denoted by a call to it (and not by the keyword new, introduced in section 3.2). new is not reserved in C++ for object creation but is used for dynamic memory allocation, whatever the type of the allocated value (see section 7.6.1 of Volume 1).

Any C++ class must contain a *destructor*, which is defined by default if none is explicitly provided. It gets called when an object is destroyed, i.e. when its memory zone is freed. Example 4.21 explicitly defines the destructor ~P, which performs a side effect. A destructor can be redefined in a subclass and can invoke any instruction, including "dangerous" ones. Hence, it must be carefully controlled during a code review. The instruction delete can be used to free the memory occupied by an object (see section 7.6.2 of Volume 1).

C++ also proposes a copy constructor, creating an object by copying an existing one. If none is defined in the class, one is implicitly added by the compiler. The definition P o = old (or in an equivalent manner P o (old)) introduces an object from the class P and initializes its attributes with the values of those of old.

NOTE.– Example 4.22 was built by first defining a file P.h containing the declaration of the class, then with a file P.cpp containing the definition of the class and finally, the file mainP.cpp. From this point on, examples will directly be given in one unique .cpp file (for reasons to do with space) and will generally contain the execution results in comments.

4.2.3. *Inheritance and confinement*

4.2.3.1. *Confinement*

C++ uses the following confinement marks: `public`, `private` and `protected`. Their effects are roughly those described in section 3.2 (Ans. 1.16). However, it is possible to tune the confinement of fields of a class C to provide a wider visibility on these fields to functions or classes outside class C. These functions or classes must be declared `friend` in C.

Let us examine in detail the effects of the confinement mode on the export and the inheritance. There exist several kinds of inheritance which will be presented later. In this paragraph, we use the `public` version of inheritance.

A field marked `private` in a class C is not exported, it is only visible by C's methods and by functions and classes declared `friend` in C. It is inherited by subclasses of C but is not visible inside them. However, it may be accessible through tools provided by C. This is the case for `age`, accessible via `get_age` in example 4.21. A field of C marked `protected` is not exported, it is only visible by the subclasses of C and by the `friend` classes of these subclasses. A field of C marked `public` can be exported without restriction to any function or class. Table 4.1 presents the various cases.

Mark	Public	Protected	Private
C	yes	yes	yes
Subclass of C	yes	yes	no
Without relation with C	yes	no	no

Table 4.1. *Effects of marks*

Example 4.23 illustrates the effect of confinement marks on the export. Error messages obtained during its compilation show that fields marked `private` or `protected` cannot be exported.

EXAMPLE 4.23.–

```
C++
/* --- File marks.cpp */
#include <iostream>
using namespace std ;

class C {
  int x ;
protected :
  int z ;
  int get_z () { return (this->z) ; }

public :
```

```
    C (int v_x, int v_z, int v_w) { x = v_x ; z = v_z ; w = v_w ; }
    int w ;
    int get_w () { return (this->w) ; }
    void print () {
        cout << "x=" << get_x () << " z=" << get_z () << " w=" << get_w ()
            << endl ; }
private :
    int get_x () { return (this->x) ; }
};

int main () {
    C o = C (1, 2, 3) ;
    o.get_x () ;   /*1*/ /* Because private */
    o.get_z () ;   /*2*/ /* Because protected */
    o.get_w () ;
    o.print () ;
    return (0) ;
}
```

```
$ g++ marks.cpp
marks.cpp:22:5: error: 'get_x' is a private member of 'C'
    o.get_x () ;   /*1*/ /* Because private */
      ^
marks.cpp:17:7: note: declared private here
    int get_x (){ return (this->x) ; }
        ^
marks.cpp:23:5: error: 'get_z' is a protected member of 'C'
    o.get_z () ;   /*2*/ /* Because protected */
      ^
marks.cpp:8:7: note: declared protected here
    int get_z () { return (this->z) ; }
        ^
2 errors generated.
```

If lines /*1*/ and /*2*/ get commented on, the source file compiles correctly
and the execution prints x = 1 z = 2 w = 3. The method print of class C uses the
methods get_x and get_z, which are accessible but not visible from the function main.

Confinement indications must be respected by internal classes and, reciprocally, a
class has to respect the marks of its internal classes. However, it may depend on the
used compiler. To circumvent this issue, it suffices to declare the class friend of its
internal classes if needed.

4.2.3.2. Inheritance

C++ proposes several kinds of multiple inheritance. There is no keyword to make
inheritance explicit (Ans. 1.37). The names of inherited classes are simply introduced
after the ":" separator placed after the name of the inheriting class, and separated by
commas. Hence, the declaration of a class R inheriting from P1, P2 and P3 starts with
R:P1,P2,P3. The extension operation presented in section 3.2 is available in three

versions. They allow handling, for each inherited class C, the visibility on C's fields required by the created class. The kind of extension is indicated in the inheritance clause by one of the keywords `private`, `protected` or `public` placed in front of the inherited class name. For instance, a class R inheriting with a version `public` from a class C is declared by `R : public C` and recovers all fields of C (see details below). If the inheritance clause does not state the kind of extension, then the compiler selects `public` by default for all the inherited classes introduced by `struct` and `private` for those declared by `class`.

It is possible to change the confinement of a method with a reintroduction (see example 4.24). Declarations tagged `friend` in C are never inherited in R. The object constructors of C are not inherited but can be called explicitly by any object constructor of R. If this last one does not call one of the object constructors of C, then the default constructor of C is automatically called. The destructor of C is not inherited but the destructor of R can call it and if it does not, then the C destructor is automatically called. Not explicitly defining object constructors of inherited classes can lead to unexpected results. Explicit calls to them may be achieved through several syntactic constructs. For example, `R (Rparam) : C (Cparam) { ... }` is a constructor of R, which calls a C constructor, whose actual parameters *Cparam* are defined from the formal ones in *Rparam*.

EXAMPLE 4.24.–

```
C++
#include <iostream>
using namespace std ;

class C { /* The one of the previous example. */};
class R : public C {
public :
  int a ;
  string x ;
  string get_x () { return (this->x) ; }
  R (int v_x, int v_z, int v_w, int v_a) : C (v_x,  v_z, v_w) {
    a = v_a + z + w ; x = "A string" ; }
  void show () {
    cout << "x = " << get_x () << " z = " << get_z () << " w = " << get_w ()
         << " a = " << this->a << endl ; }
};

int main () {
  C o_C = C (1,2,3) ;
  R o_R = R (10, 20, 30, 40) ;
  o_C.print () ; /* x = 1 z = 2 w = 3 */
  o_R.print () ; /* x = 10 z = 20 w = 30 */
  o_R.show () ;  /* x = A string z = 20 w = 30 a = 90 */
  return (0) ;
}
```

In this example, class R reintroduces the attribute x with another type and the method get_x. Both of them were `private` in C, and they become `public` in R. It then defines the method show. The main function defines the objects o_C from C and o_R from R. The values of attributes of these objects are printed. Then comes the result of show (output is given in comments). Note the result of o_R.print(): this method is not redefined in R and this call actually executes C's method print. The occurrence x in C::print designates the attribute x of the object o_R of type C created by C (v_x, v_z, v_w). This attribute, whose value is 10, is private to o_R and accessible in o_R through print. The method show cannot access it. The message o_R.show () sends the message get_x() to o_R, which instantiates this and whose attribute x is of type string.

Consider a class R inheriting from a class C. Table 4.2 presents the status, in R, of a field from C depending on the kind of inheritance from C used by R.

Version	In C	Public	Protected	Private
Public	In R	Public	Protected	Private
Protected	In R	Protected	Protected	Private
Private	In R	Private	Private	Private

Table 4.2. *Semantics of marks depending on the inheritance kind*

Let us comment on this table. Suppose that the class R inherits from C1 in the public version. This requires that any field of C1 tagged as private remains marked as private in R. The fields of C1 tagged as public remain public in R and those marked as protected in C1 remain so. If R inherits from C3 in the private version, all the fields of C3 are *ipso facto* marked as private in R, hence, for example, they cannot appear in the header file of R. If R inherits from C2 in the protected version, the fields of C2 that are not marked private are tagged as protected in R. Note that there is no explicit indication in the R definition that the inherited marks on fields changed, except the extension mark on the inherited class.

4.2.3.3. *Reintroduction and redefinition*

In section 1.7.1.5 we saw that during extension (named inheritance in the object-oriented context), reintroduction can be done with or without back-update. C++ provides both strategies (Ans. 1.39). The reintroduction of a method g is done with back-update if g is marked virtual and is often called *redefinition*. Without the virtual mark the reintroduction of g is done without back-update. Class methods cannot be marked virtual, which is consistent with their status.

Let us put the two extension strategies into the inheritance framework of C++. Let C be a class inherited (public to simplify) by another class D. Let h be a method of C whose body contains an occurrence of a method k, not marked virtual. Values of h and k are determined when compiling C (i.e. statically). Any future reintroduction of k will have no impact on h.

Let f be a method of C whose body contains an occurrence of a method g and suppose that the declaration of g is marked virtual and that g is redefined. Let us recall that typechecking a message obj.f (...) checks that the declared type of obj is compatible with that of f. This implies that the type of the redefinition of g has to be compatible with that of g in C. The annotation virtual on g forces the compiler to set a late binding evaluation mechanism for g. The evaluation of a message obj.f (...) must determine which method g is to be used, according to the class of obj. This value of g is the one present in the value bound to obj in the current environment. This choice is sometimes called "C++ dynamic typing".

If the keyword override is set after the formal parameters of the redefinition of g, the compiler can check that g was indeed tagged virtual in the inherited class (Ans. 1.38).

Example 4.25 illustrates these explanations and uses the notations that have already been introduced. Execution results are given in comments and are numbered next to instructions.

EXAMPLE 4.25.–

```
C++
/* --- File virtual.cpp */
#include <iostream>
using namespace std ;
class C {
public:
  int a;
  C (int v) { a = v ; }
  void f (int x) { cout << g (x + a) << " ; " ; }
  void h (int z) { cout << k (z + 100) << endl ; }
  virtual int g (int y) { return (y + 10) ; }
  int k (int w) { return (w + 9) ; }
};

class D : public C {
public:
  int b ;
  D (int v, int w) : C (v) { b = w ; }
  int k (int w) { return (w + 1000) ; }
  int g (int y) override { return (y + b) ; }
};

int main() {
  C o1 = C (2) ; o1.f (0) ; o1. h (0) ;           /*1-  12   ; 109 */

  D o2 = D (4,7) ; o2.f (0) ; o2.h (0) ;          /*2-  11   ; 109 */
  cout << o2.k (13) << " ; " << o2.g (4) << endl ; /*3-  1013 ; 11  */

  C o3 = o2 ; o3.f (0) ; o3.h (0) ;               /*4-  14   ; 109 */
  cout << o3.k (4) << " ; " << o3.g (4) << endl ; /*5-  13   ; 14  */
```

```
o1 = o2 ; o1.f (0) ; o1.h (0) ;                         /*6-   14   ; 109*/
cout << o1.k (4) << " ; " << o1.g (4) << endl ;         /*7-   13   ; 14 */

C *p1 = &o2 ; p1->f (0) ; p1->h (0) ;                   /*8-   11   ; 109 */
cout << p1->k (4) << " ; " << p1->g (4) << endl ;       /*9-   13   ; 11 */

C &o4 = o2 ; o4.f (0) ; o4.h (0) ;                      /*10-  11   ; 109*/
cout << o4.k (4) << " ; " << o4.g (4) << endl ;         /*11-  13   ; 11*/
return (0) ;
}
```

Comparing lines 1, 2 and 3 illustrates the evaluation modes. The method g being virtual and redefined in D, the call o2.f (0) is evaluated by late binding using D::g. The evaluation of the message o2.h (0) uses the value of h present in C since h is not redefined in D. Because k is not declared virtual, its reintroduction in D is evaluated without back-update. The evaluation of the sub-expression h (0) in o2.h (0) calls the method k of C.

The next lines show another point related to interactions between ways to declare a variable that is an object and the uses of its type and value. Line 4 declares a variable o3 of class C and initializes it with a value of the subclass D. The value of o3 is obtained by "truncating" that of o2 and cannot be interpreted as a value of type D. Similarly, the assignment o1 = o2 only copies the fields of o2 figuring in C in o1. The type of o1 is not modified by this assignment, as shown by lines 6 and 7.

Defining a variable of type pointer or reference introduces the type of the pointer, here C* at line 8. The type of the pointed value must be compatible with the pointer's type. This is the case here for the type D of the pointed value o2. Note that the assignment of p1 with the address of o2 does not modify o2. Lines 8, 9, 10 and 11 illustrate this point.

If a class R inherits a field m defined in several inherited classes, calling m is ambiguous. The number and the types of the arguments of the method m cannot be used to disambiguate: this would be an overloading resolution question, which does not take the inheritance hierarchy into account. An easy way to solve this issue is to use the qualified name of m, using the name of the inherited class (Ans. 1.39). In example 4.26, the class C is inherited by D1 and D2 and the class R inherits from D1 and D2. The object constructor of R calls those of D1 and D2, all of them calling that of C. This causes a compilation error: the field x of R cannot be defined. In the interest of saving space, classes' bodies are not given here but can be found in example 4.27 (which corrects this one).

EXAMPLE 4.26.–

```
C++
class C { int x ; ...  };
class D1 : public C { ... };
class D2 : public C { ... };
class R : public D1, public D2 { ... };
int main () { ... }
```

```
g++ diamond.cpp
diamond.cpp:23:23: error: non-static member 'x' found in multiple base-class
  subobjects of type 'C':
    class R -> class D1 -> class C
    class R -> class D2 -> class C
```

To fix these ambiguities, in any subclass inheriting from a common class C, it is possible to tag this inheritance declaration using `virtual` (as in the case of D1 and D2 in the continuation of the example). This use of `virtual` requires that the object constructor of R calls the constructor of the class C only once. Also note the use of the class namespace to disambiguate the reference to y.

EXAMPLE 4.27.–

```
C++
/* --- File diamond.cpp */
#include <iostream>
using namespace std ;

class C {
public:
  C (int v_x) { x = v_x ; }
  int x ;
};

class D1 : public virtual C {
public:
  int y ;
  D1 (int v_x, int v_y) : C (v_x) { y = v_y ; }
};

class D2 : public virtual C {
public:
  int y ;
  D2 (int v_x, int v_y) : C (v_x) { y = v_y ; }
};

class R: public D1, public D2 {
public :
  R (int w) : C (w), D1 (w + 1, w + 2), D2 (w + 3, w + 4) {} ;
  int z1 = D1::y ;
  int z2 = D2::y ;
};
```

```
int main () {
  R o = R (4) ;
  cout << "o.x = " << o.x << " o.z1 = " << o.z1 << " o.z2 = " << o.z2
       << endl ;
  return (0) ;
}

/* o.x = 4 o.z1 = 6 o.z2 = 8 */
```

4.2.3.4. *Inheritance and type conversion*

Let D be a class declared by D : public C. Any object of D can receive a message which calls a method of C (except if there is a confinement). If this object is accessible through a pointer, the compiler implicitly applies a conversion of this pointer of type D* into C* (Ans. 1.8 and Ans. 1.40). The opposite conversion, from C* to D* is rejected by the compiler. Example 4.28 contains two rejected instructions: p2 = &o1 and p2 = (C*) &o1.

EXAMPLE 4.28.–

```
C++
class C {
public :
  C (int v_x) { x = v_x ; }
  int x ;
};
class D : public C {
public :
  int y ;
  D (int v_x, int v_y) : C (v_x) { y = v_y ; }
};

int main () {
  C o1 = C (1) ;
  C *p1 = &o1 ;
  D o2 = D (10, 20) ;
  D *p2 = &o2 ;
  p1 = &o2 ;
  p2 = &o1 ;
  p2 = (C*) &o1 ;
  return (0) ;
}
```

```
$ g++ cast.cpp
cast.cpp:18:6: error: assigning to 'D *' from incompatible type 'C *'
  p2 = &o1 ;
     ^ ~~~
cast.cpp:19:6: error: assigning to 'D *' from incompatible type 'C *'
  p2 = (C*) &o1 ;
     ^~~~~~~~
```

The inheritance version used prevents certain conversions: it is not possible to convert a pointer of a subclass into a pointer of the class if the inheritance is not public. The errors obtained while compiling example 4.29 show the different cases, with very clear error messages.

EXAMPLE 4.29.–

```
C++
/* --- File conversion.cpp */
#include <iostream>
using namespace std ;

class C { public: int a ; } ;
class R1 : public C {} ;
class R2 : protected C {} ;
class R3 : private C {} ;

int main () {
  R1* p1 = new R1 () ;
  R2* p2 = new R2 () ;
  R3* p3 = new R3 () ;
  C* p = p1 ;
  p1->a = 5 ;
  p2->a = 1 ;
  p = p3 ;
  p3->a = 0 ;
  return (0) ;
}
```

```
$ g++ conversion.cpp
conversion.cpp:16:3: error: cannot cast 'R2' to its protected base class
  'C' p2->a = 1 ;

conversion.cpp:7:12: note: declared protected here  class R2 : protected C {} ;

conversion.cpp:16:7: error: 'a' is a protected member of 'C' p2->a = 1 ;

conversion.cpp:7:12: note: constrained by protected inheritance
hereclass R2 : protected C {};

conversion.cpp:5:23: note: member is declared here class C { public: int a ; } ;

conversion.cpp:17:7: error: cannot cast 'R3' to its private base class 'C'
  p = p3 ;

conversion.cpp:8:12: note: declared private here class R3 : private C {} ;

conversion.cpp:18:3: error: cannot cast 'R3' to its private base class 'C'
  p3->a = 0 ;

conversion.cpp:8:12: note: declared private here class R3 : private C {} ;

conversion.cpp:18:7: error: 'a' is a private member of 'C' p3->a = 0 ;
```

```
conversion.cpp:8:12: note: constrained by private inheritance here
  class R3 : private C {} ;

conversion.cpp:5:23: note: member is declared here class C { public: int a ; } ;
```

4.2.3.5. *Inheritance and subtyping*

The subclassing relation of C++ is considered to be a base case of a subtyping relation only if the super-class is inherited with the `public` annotation. It is extended to functions and accepts that the type of an effective parameter is a subtype of the type of the formal one (contravariance on the argument's type).

4.2.3.6. *Incomplete C-kits, abstract classes*

C++ calls an incomplete *C-kit* an *abstract class* (Ans. 1.27) but does not provide any particular syntax to state that the class is abstract. A class is abstract as soon as it contains a method that is not defined, introduced by prefixing its declaration with the keyword `virtual` and ending it with = 0. Such a declared method is said to be *pure virtual*. It has to be defined in a subclass. Any subclass of an abstract class still containing a pure virtual function is considered abstract (Ans. 1.31). An abstract class cannot be instantiated to create objects.

Example 4.30 defines an abstract class C, containing two *pure virtual* methods f and g. They are defined with different confinement marks in classes D1, D2 and D3, which all inherit from C using different inheritance versions (Ans. 1.30).

EXAMPLE 4.30.–

```c++
C++
#include <iostream>
using namespace std ;

class C {
public :
  virtual void f () = 0 ;
private :
  virtual string g () = 0 ;
};

class D1: public C {
public :
  void f () { cout << "f is defined in D1 " << endl ; }
public : /* To make explicit the mark on g */
  string g () { return ("g is defined in D1") ; }
};

class D2 : protected C {
public:
  void f () { cout << "f is defined in D2 " << g () << endl ; }
protected :
```

```
  string g () { return ("g is defined in D2") ; }
};

class D3: private C {
public :
  void f () { cout << "f is defined in D3 " << g () << endl ; }
private :
  string g () { return ("g is defined in D3") ; }
};

int main () {
  D1 o1 = D1 () ;
  o1.f () ;
  o1.g () ;
  D2 o2 = D2 () ;
  o2.f () ;
  /* o2.g () ;  g is protected */
  D3 o3 = D3 () ;
  o3.f () ;
  /* o3.g () ;  g is private */
  return (0) ;
}
```

```
f is defined in D1
f is defined in D2 g is defined in D2
f is defined in D3 g is defined in D3
```

WARNING.– A method marked `virtual` can be redefined in an inheriting class. A pure virtual method *must* be redefined in an inheriting class.

C++ does not provide syntax to declare a class completely undefined like Java's interfaces. They can be simulated by using only pure virtual methods in the definition of the class.

4.2.4. *Overloading in C++*

C++ allows overloading of both operators and methods (Ans. 1.9). However, class methods cannot be overloaded. The overloading resolution is performed at compile-time.

Example 4.31 defines a class `Interval` representing intervals of floating-point numbers, and implements a version of the + operator to use when it is called with (at least) one argument of type `Interval`.

EXAMPLE 4.31.–

```
C++
#include <iostream>
class Interval {
public:
  float min ;
  float max ;
  Interval (float min, float max) { this->min = min ; this->max = max ; }

  Interval operator+ (Interval i) {
    Interval res (0, 0) ;
    res.min = this->min + i.min ;
    res.max = this->max + i.max ;
    return (res) ;
  }
};

int main () {
  Interval i1 = Interval (1.0 + 2.0, 10.0) ;
  Interval i2 = Interval (5.0, 15.0) ;
  Interval res = i1 + i2 ;
  printf ("Result: [%f, %f]\n", res.min, res.max) ;
  /* Interval x = i1 + 3.0 ; */
  return (0) ;
}
```

```
Result : [8.000000, 25.000000]
```

The method operator+ introduces a new definition of +, which can still be used in infix position: i1 + i2 + i3 means i_plus (i1, i_plus (i2, i3)). Also note the use of + in the expression (1.0 + 2.0, 10.0). The overloading resolution removed the ambiguity in terms of which definition of + must be used in these contexts. The commented instruction Interval x = i1 + 3.0, which has been mentioned, clearly causes a type error at compile-time. To fix it, it suffices to add a new definition of +, using float as an argument.

EXAMPLE 4.32.–

```
C++
#include <iostream>
class Interval {
public:
...
  Interval operator+ (float v) {
    Interval res (0, 0) ;
    res.min = this->min + v ;
    res.max = this->max + v ;
    return (res) ;
  }
};

int main () {
```

```
Interval i1 = Interval (1.0, 10.0) ;
Interval i2 = Interval (5.0, 15.0) ;
Interval res = i1 + i2 ;
printf ("Result: [%f, %f]\n", res.min, res.max) ;
res = i1 + 3.14;
printf ("Result2: [%f, %f]\n", res.min, res.max) ;
return (0) ;
}
```

The compiler selects the new definition of + for the call res = i1 + 3.14159, on the basis of the type float of the effective parameter. The obtained output is now:

```
Result: [8.000000, 25.000000]
Result2: [6.140000, 13.140000]
```

These two implementations of + have operands of different types, one of these types (that of V_this) remains implicit. This is not very satisfactory if one considers the usual semantics of the addition, for which + takes two operands of the same type (numeric). To make the types of both operands explicit, one can "lift" the definition of the method + outside the class Interval, changing it into a function.

EXAMPLE 4.33.–

```
C++
#include <iostream>
class Interval { ... };

Interval operator+ (float v, Interval i) { return (i + v) ; }

int main () {
  Interval i1 = Interval (1.0, 10.0) ;
  res = 4.14159 + i1 ;
  printf ("Result3: [%f, %f]\n", res.min, res.max) ;
  return (0) ;
}
```

The function +, defined at global level, enables one to explicitly specify the types of both parameters, the first one being a float. Note that this function simply calls the version of the operator taking an interval and a float, by swapping the operands.

4.2.4.1. *Overloading and type conversion*

Example 4.34 is a translation in C++ of the program found in example 4.15, which was written in Java.

EXAMPLE 4.34.–

```
C++
#include <iostream>
class Test {
public:
  void f (int a, int b) { printf ("int, int\n") ; }
  void f (long a, int b) { printf ("long, int\n") ; }
  void f (long a, short b) { printf ("long, short\n") ; }
};

int main () {
  short i_short = 0 ;
  int i_int = 1 ;
  long i_long = 2 ;
  Test o;
  o.f (i_int, i_int) ;   /* int, int */
  o.f (i_short, i_int) ; /* Conversion  short to int: int, int*/
  o.f (i_int, i_short) ; /* Ambiguous: (int, int) or (long, short)?
  o.f (i_int, i_long) ;  /* Choice: int, int */
  return (0) ;
}
```

The first two calls are resolved as in the Java program, selecting the version of f taking two ints, with a conversion of the short into int in the second call. The third one is again ambiguous. The difference with Java is that three versions of f (there were only two in Java) can be used because C++ does not refuse information leaks. The compiler can convert the types of the arguments to use any of these three versions but there is no constraint to select a particular one. Unlike in Java, the fourth call is not rejected and uses the version of f taking two ints. The compiler accepts a possible information leak which allows for the conversion of the long into int.

4.2.5. *Parameterized classes*

The C++ language calls a parameterized *C-kit* a template. It is introduced by a keyword template followed by the list of the parameters between < and >, followed by the keyword class and the name of the class. This section presents some aspects of template, however an exhaustive presentation of this wide topic is outside the scope of this book. Examples are deliberately very simple and target the definition and instantiation of the parameters. The notion of functor does not exist in C++, even if this term is sometimes used in some presentations of the language (Ans. 1.34).

In order to be used, a template must be exported, it therefore has to be declared in a header file. Unlike a non-parameterized class, some compilers require that the public definitions of the template are provided in the header file. However, we will not follow this practice in the interest of saving space. It is understood that the code of the examples must be partially reproduced to create the corresponding .h files.

As we saw in Chapter 1, the semantics of a parameterized class is that of a function taking these parameters. This function must be applied to some effective parameters to get a fully defined class which would allow for object creation. Thus, a `template` cannot be compiled once and for all into executable code. The compiler has to produce as many object codes as there are different instantiations of the `template`.

4.2.5.1. *Type parameters*

A `template` can be parameterized by type variables (Ans. 1.32). A type variable `T` must be introduced with the keywords `typename` or `class` (`classname` is also accepted in the syntax). Fields of the parameterized class can use the type parameter in their definition. The instantiation of `T` by a type `my_type` creates a class named `P<my_type>`. In example 4.35, the class `TC1` is parameterized by the type variable `T`, which is used to typecheck the arguments of the constructor `TC1` and the results of methods `fst` and `snd`. The `main` function creates an object of class `TC1<int>`.

EXAMPLE 4.35.–

```
C++
#include <iostream>
using namespace std ;

template <typename T>
class TC1 {
public:
  T a ;
  T b ;
  TC1 (T x, T y) { a = x ; b = y ; }
  T fst () { return (a) ; }
  T snd () { return (this->b) ; }
};

int main () {
  TC1<int> o_P = TC1<int> (5, 6) ;
  cout << "o_P: " << o_P.fst () << " ; " << o_P.snd () << endl ;
  return (0) ;
}
/* o_P: 5 ; 6 */
```

Hence, the class `TC1` defines pairs of values with the same type. To define couples whose values have different types it suffices to introduce an additional type parameter, which is done in example 4.36.

EXAMPLE 4.36.–

```
C++
#include <iostream>
using namespace std ;

template <class T1, typename T2>
class TC2 {
public:
  T1 a ;
  T2 *b ;
  TC2 (T1 x, T2 *y) { a = x ; b = y ; }
  T1 fst () { return (this->a) ; }
  T2 snd (void) ;
};

template <class T1, typename T2> T2 TC2<T1, T2>::snd () { return *(this->b) ; }

class C {
public :
  int x ; int y ;
  C (int vx , int vy) { x = vx ; y = vy ; }
};

int main () {
  C *o_C = new C (1, 2) ;
  cout << "o_C: " << o_C->x << " ; " << o_C->y << endl ;
  /* o_C: 1 ; 2 */
  TC2<int, C> o_P = TC2<int, C> (5, o_C) ;
  cout << "o_P.fst (): " << o_P.fst () << endl ;
  /* o_P.fst (): 5 */
  cout << "o_P.snd (): " << o_P.snd ().x << " ; " << o_P.snd ().y << endl ;
  /* o_P.snd (): 1 ; 2 */
  return (0) ;
}
```

The method snd is defined outside the class TC2. It must be repeated that TC2 is a template (template <class T1, typename T2>), it is then necessary to give the type of the result of the method (T2) and then the qualified name of the method. The real name of the template class is TC2<T1, T2>; it defines the namespace in which snd has been declared (in other words, the class TC2).

The type variable T2 is instantiated by the type C and not by the class C: a class parameterized by a type is not a functor, there is no way to use the fields of the parameter T2 in the definition of TC2. Moreover, T2 could be instantiated by int, which is a type and not a class in C++. The attribute b is a pointer on a value of type T2, hence on an object of C in the class TC2<int, C>.

From the context, depending on the use of a template, the compiler may sometimes infer the required type instantiations to guarantee the consistency of the typechecking, and apply them implicitly. However, it is better to explicitly write them, first to aid the reading of the code, second to get better error messages in cases where the implicit instantiation led to an error.

4.2.5.2. *Value parameters*

A `template` may also be parameterized by variables that can only be instantiated by values representing integers (Ans. 1.33). The type of these values can be `int`, `char`, `long`, etc., an enum or a pointer or reference type. Example 4.37 uses a value parameter of type `int`.

EXAMPLE 4.37.–

```
C++
#include <iostream>
using namespace std ;

template <typename T, int min> class TC {
public :
  T a ;
  int p;
  TC (T x, int y) { a = x ; p = y ; }
  void warning () {
    cout << "Your offer must be greater than " << min << endl ; }
  bool OK () { return ((this->p) > min) ; }
};

int main () {
  TC<string, 10> o = TC<string, 10> ("flower", 25) ;
  o.warning () ;
  cout << "Is your offer " << o.a << " OK? " << o.OK () << endl ;
  return (0) ;
}
    /* Your offer must be greater than 10 */
    /* Is your offer flower  OK? 1 */
```

The value parameter `min` is used in the methods `warning` and `OK`. Creating the object o requires the instantiation of `T` by `string` and `min` by 10.

Example 4.38 adds a pointer on function `*f` as a parameter, `f` having type $T2 \rightarrow T1$. Hence C++ allows dependencies between types paramaterizing `templates` (Ans. 1.33). The class `TC` uses the parameter `f` to define the method `tf`.

EXAMPLE 4.38.–

```
C++
#include <iostream>
using namespace std;

template <typename T1, class T2, T1 (*f)(T2) >
class TC {
public :
  T1 a ;
```

```
    T2 *o ;
    TC (T1 x , T2 *y) { a = x ; o = y ; }
    T1 fst () { return (this->a) ; }
    T2 snd () { return (*this->o) ; }
    T1 tf (T2 o) { return (f (o)) ; }
};

class C {
public :
    int x ;
    int y ;
    C (int vx, int vy) { x = vx ; y = vy ; }
};

int g (C o) { return (o.x + 100) ; }

int main () {
    C *o_C = new C (1, 2) ;
    TC<int, C, &g> o_P = TC<int, C, &g> (5, o_C) ;
    cout << "o_P.fst () : "<< o_P.fst () << endl ;
    cout << "o_P.snd () : "<< (o_P.snd ()).x << " " ; "<< (o_P.snd ()).y << endl ;
    cout << "call to g instantiating f: " << o_P.tf (*o_C) ;
    return (0) ;
}
/*o_P.fst () : 5
o_P.snd () : 1 ; 2
call to g instantiating f: 101*/
```

The type of o_P is denoted by an expression which uses the instantiation of the template parameters: int for T1, C for T2 and &g for *f. The compiler itself instantiates the type of f by C → int, hence also the type of tf. Once the object o_P is created, messages can be sent to it using the typical syntax. The evaluation of the message o_P.tf (*o_C) requires the computation of the expression f (o) knowing that f is replaced by g and o by *o_C; hence it returns 101.

4.2.5.3. *Inheritance from parameterized classes*

It is possible to inherit from parameterized classes, or even to create new parameterized classes. This simply requires indication that the subclass is also a template and to establish links between the parameters of the inherited class and those of the subclass. Example 4.39 builds the subclass R of C as a struct in order to have its fields marked public by default, in order that they can be used directly by the function main. Note that the call to the constructor of C by that of R is performed using the name C<T>, as seen previously.

EXAMPLE 4.39.–

```
C++
#include <iostream>
using namespace std ;

template <typename T>
class C {
public :
  T a ;
  T b ;
  C (T x, T y) { a = x ; b = y ; }
  T fst () { return (a) ; }
  T snd () { return (this->b) ; }
};

template <typename T>
struct R: public C <T> {
  T d ;
  R (T x,T y, T z) : C<T>(x, y) { d = z ; }
  T third () { return (d) ; }
};

int main () {
  C<int> o_P = C <int> (5, 6) ;
  cout << "o_P : " << o_P.fst () << " ; " << o_P.snd () << endl ;
  R <int> o_R = R<int> (7, 8, 9) ;
  cout << "o_R : " << o_R.fst () << " ; " << o_R.snd () << " ; "
       << o_R.third () << endl ;
  return (0) ;
}
/* o_P : 5 ; 6
   o_R : 7 ; 8 ; 9 */
```

The ability to parameterize by values that can be pointers on any data structure makes the `template` very expressive. Note however that the use of these advanced features is dependent on version of the language used and may be pretty tricky. Once again, we encourage interested readers to consult the relevant books as well as the reference manual of the language.

4.2.5.4. *Other features*

Combining very low-level features with those that are high-level brings a wide range of possibilities for software development in C++. They satisfy the need to separate, reuse, confine, but also to finely manage the memory layout of data, and to control the execution time. For instance, in C++ a function is not a first-class value since it cannot be returned as a result but, because its code is stored in memory, it is possible to call it through a pointer on this code (Ans. 1.13). Combining features of all levels makes writing code more complex but also complicates code reading and maintenance. The need to control the allocated memory and execution time may be less important in some domains, which may enable a higher level C++ programming style to be adopted, avoiding the use of pointers and thus expressing the intention of the developer more directly.

4.3. Classes in OCaml

4.3.1. *Presentation*

The OCaml language was built by adding object-oriented features to the Caml language. The notion of object types used in OCaml enables the complete integration of functional, imperative, modular and object paradigms in the type language of OCaml. Thus, OCaml provides strong and static typing with inference, subtyping, parametric polymorphism and inclusion polymorphism. This ensures the global consistency of a development using these four paradigms (Ans. 1.1). The language does not accept overloading (Ans. 1.9). All constructs of OCaml have been the subject of semantic studies prior to their introduction into the language. This makes it possible to assume that this language satisfies the hypotheses of the partial correctness theorem 5.1 given in Volume 1.

The semantics of object-oriented features of OCaml may be studied by choosing classes or objects as the primitive notion and, often, objects are retained to do that. This semantics allows type inference to extend to objects and guarantees the partial correctness property. In order to relate this presentation of these features to the model of section 3.2, we start by describing classes. We give some examples, each time trying to only show the point being illustrated. Examples are executed in the interactive loop ("toplevel") of the language: instructions entered after the prompt # are compiled and then executed, and added to the current program. The execution result (or the compilation error if one occurs) is then displayed in the next lines.

4.3.2. *An overview of classes*

An OCaml class can be modeled by a *C-kit* (Ans. 1.2) whose fields can be attributes (called *instance variables*), introduced by val and methods, introduced by, method. Attributes and methods may have any type (according to the needs and obligations of type inference). They must all have different names in the same class (Ans. 1.8). The type of the class is inferred and built from the names of attributes and methods, along with their types and marks – virtual or private – (detailed later).

OCaml does not provide class variables or class methods. However they can be mimicked without difficulty, either by variables and functions defined outside the class or, if necessary, by a method that does not use the object receiving the message.

The definition of the body of the *C-kit* is enclosed between the keywords object (or object (s)) and end, s being the name chosen for the variable V_this, introduced in the presentation of (*C-kits*). Attributes are never exported by a class, they are either constant or mutable fields (mutable annotation). The definition of a method in a class c can use the attributes of c denoting them by their names, the object itself by the name s and the other methods by s#m. The order of the fields is important: a definition can only use attributes and methods already introduced (Ans. 1.10). Any method can be recursively defined with the keyword rec. Example 4.40 illustrates these points. The attribute x cannot be used before it is introduced. The type of the method fact is inferred and is displayed in the type of the class c.

EXAMPLE 4.40.–

```
OCaml
# class c = object val y = x + 1 val x = 2 end ;;
Error: Unbound value x
# class c = object
    method fact = let rec f (n) = if n <= 0 then 1 else n * f (n - 1) in f
end ;;
class c : object method fact : int -> int end
# let o = new c ;;
val o : c = <obj>
# o#fact (3) ;;
- : int = 6
```

A call to a method m, giving the object o as its (implicit) actual parameter and v as its (explicit) actual parameter, is performed with the syntactic construct o#m (v), which sends the message m to the object o. Example 4.41 relies on a syntactic construct to define a class, highlighting the fact that, as a *C-kit*, this class is a function that takes parameters of the family F_a to create the *O-kit*. This functional aspect appears in the inferred type of the class since it is a functional type. The example also shows the use of a variable, intro, being local to the body of the class. The method get_name is not a function, as indicated by its type. The method print uses get_name by "sending the message" to this and makes direct reference to the attribute age (without the help of get_age).

EXAMPLE 4.41.–

```
OCaml
# class person = fun whichname ->
  let intro = "Madam or Sir: " in
  object (this)
    val mutable age = 0
    val name = intro ^ whichname
    method much_more x = age <- age + x
    method get_name = name
    method get_age = age
    method print () =
      print_string (this#get_name ^ " age = ") ;
      print_int age ;
      print_newline ()
end ;;
class person :
  string ->
  object
```

```
val mutable age : int
val name : string
method get_age : int
method get_name : string
method much_more : int -> unit
method print : unit -> unit
```

4.3.2.1. *Types of classes and type inference*

As shown by example 4.41, the type of the class person has the same name as the class (Ans. 1.5 and Ans. 1.6). It is a functional type. The value of person is a function, its parameter belonging to the family F_a, defined here by whichname. Let us now use this class in example 4.42.

EXAMPLE 4.42.–

```
OCaml
# let dupont = new person "dupont" ;;
val dupont : person = <obj>
# (dupont#get_name , dupont#get_age) ;;
- : string * int = ("Madam or Sir: dupont", 0)
# dupont#much_more 80 ;;
- : unit = ()
# dupont#print () ;;
Madam or Sir : dupont age = 80
- : unit = ()
```

The object dupont is obtained by applying (with new) the object constructor person defined by the class person to the actual parameter "dupont". We will consider this point in more detail when we come to look at object constructors.

If the parameter family F_a is empty, the class is no longer a function, as indicated by the type of person1 in example 4.43.

EXAMPLE 4.43.–

```
OCaml
# class person1 =
  object (this)
    val mutable age = 0
    method much_more x = age <- age + x
    method get_age = age
end ;;
class person1 :
object val mutable age:int method get_age:int method much_more:int -> unit end
# let o = new person1 ;;
val o : person1 = <obj>
# o#much_more 40 ;;
- : unit = ()
# o#get_age ;;
- : int = 40
o#age := 25 ;;
```

```
Error: This expression has type person1
       It has no method age
```

The type of `person1` is not functional. The evaluation of `new person1` builds an object bound to o. Its attribute `age` is set to 0. It is impossible to create o with another value for `age`. This attribute can be updated by sending the message `o#much_more`. Also note the impossibility of directly assigning the mutable attribute `age`. While analyzing the expression `o#age`, the OCaml compiler only searches for a method called `age`, as an attribute is not visible outside its class.

Type inference may fail if not enough information is available in the context, as shown by example 4.44.

EXAMPLE 4.44.–

```
OCaml
# class person2 = fun (whichname, val_foo) ->
    object (this)
      val name = whichname
      method get_name = name
      val mutable foo = val_foo
end ;;
Error: Some type variables are unbound in this type:
class person2 : 'a * 'b -> object val mutable foo : 'b
    val name : 'a method get_name : 'a end
    The method get_name has type 'a where 'a is unbound
```

The OCaml printer displays the result of typechecking: `name`, `get_name` and `whichname` have the same type, which is a free type variable, denoted by `'a`. It is the same for `valfoo` and `foo` with `'b`. The typing algorithm could universally quantify these type variables at the head of the definition of `person2`, considering they are type parameters of the class. But the developer did not use the appropriate syntax to state it (see example 4.47); or, else the user did not provide enough information to have constraints added on these type variables. Let us see how to add them with example 4.45.

EXAMPLE 4.45.–

```
OCaml
# class person3 ((whichname : string), val_foo) =
    object (this)
      val name = whichname
      method get_name = name
      val mutable foo = (val_foo : 'b)
end ;;
class person3 :
  string * 'b ->
  object val mutable foo : 'b val name : string method get_name : string end
# let o = new person3 ("Pierre", 70) ;;
val o : person3 = <obj>
```

```
# o#get_name ;;
- : string = "Pierre"
```

In this example, the types of the formal parameters `whichname` and `val_foo` are made explicit. This provides a first solution to the problem of example 4.44. But, this is not a true solution as there is no way to use foo. The current example also shows that type annotations can be set at various places. One may also note a slightly different syntax for defining classes.

EXAMPLE 4.46.–

```
OCaml
# class person33 ((whichname : string), val_foo) =
  object (this)
    val name = whichname
    method get_name = name
    val mutable foo = (val_foo : 'b)
    method get_foo = foo
end ;;
Error: Some type variables are unbound in this type:
         class person33 :
           string * 'b ->
           object
             val mutable foo : 'b
             val name : string
             method get_foo : 'b
             method get_name : string
           end
       The method get_foo has type 'b where 'b is unbound
```

Let us solve the issue of example 4.44 more efficiently with example 4.47. We now use the appropriate syntax to create a parameterized class (parametrization will be presented a bit later).

EXAMPLE 4.47.–

```
OCaml
# class ['a,'b] person4 ((whichname : 'a), val_foo) =
  object (this)
    val name = whichname
    val mutable foo = (val_foo : 'b)
    method get_name = name
    method get_foo = foo
end ;;
class ['a, 'b] person4 :
  'a * 'b ->
  object
    val mutable foo : 'b
    val name : 'a
    method get_foo : 'b
    method get_name : 'a
  end
# let o = new person4 ("Pierre", 70) ;;
```

```
val o : (string, int) person4 = <obj>
# o#get_name, o#get_foo;;
- : string * int = ("Pierre", 70)
```

The type `person4` is now a parameterized type. Note the difference between the types of o in examples 4.45 and 4.47.

4.3.2.2. *Values of classes*

A class definition is statically evaluated, as seen for *C-kits*. The value of a class is a closure containing the body of the class, the family F_a if it is not empty and the definition environment Env of the class. The body of a class is evaluated at each application of this class, the formal parameters of F_a being bound to actual parameters to extend Env (as is the case for the application of an "ordinary" function – see Chapter 3 of Volume 1). If this body uses a global mutable variable, then the value referenced by this mutable variable may change between two object creations. We can illustrate this point with example 4.48.

EXAMPLE 4.48.–

```
OCaml
# let one_name = ref "Bob" ;;
 val one_name : string ref = {contents = "Bob"}
# let hello = "Hello! " ;;
val hello : string = "Hello! "
# class person5 =
   object (this)
     val mutable name = hello ^ (!one_name)
     method get_name = name
end ;;
class person5 : object val mutable name : string method get_name : string end
# let bob = new person5 ;;
val bob : person5 = <obj>
# bob#get_name ;;
- : string = "Hello! Bob"
# one_name := "Madam " ;;
- : unit = ()
# let hello = true ;;           (*1*)
val hello : bool = true
# bob#get_name ;;
- : string = "Hello! Bob"
# let alice = new person5 in alice#get_name ;;
- : string = "Hello! Madam "
```

The global variables `one_name` and `hello` are used in the definition of the class `person5`. The value of `person5` is a closure whose environment contains the binding of `one_name` to its address in memory and the binding of `hello` to its value "Hello! ". The value referenced by `one_name` is modified during the execution. Then the binding (`hello`, "Hello! ") gets masked in the current environment (line (*1*)) by the new definition of `hello`, which creates the binding (`hello`, `true`). As shown by the second evaluation of `bob#get_name`, the assignment of `one_name` and the masking of `hello` have no influence on objects that have already been created.

The object `alice` is built in an environment where `hello` is bound to `true` and this binding is not used to create `alice`: the evaluation of the class is performed using static scope. On the other hand, the new value referenced by `one_name` is used to define the value of the attribute `name` of `alice`. The new assignment of `one_name` will impact all the following applications of the object constructor `person`. Using a mutable global variable in this way is not recommended since it can lead to errors that are difficult to locate.

4.3.2.3. Object constructors and initializers

In section 3.2, we mentioned the fact that our model does not really require the notion of object constructor. This is confirmed by OCaml, which does not really need such constructors. This can be seen in the previous examples. Applying a class as a function of F_a is performed by `new`. The value returned by such an application is an object which can be bound to a name with `let` or be used directly as any other value.

However, it is possible to define a kind of object constructor for a class `C` by defining a function returning an object of `C`. In example 4.49, the function `my_construct` is defined outside the class and is *de facto* an object constructor of the class `person6`.

EXAMPLE 4.49.–

```OCaml
# class person6 = fun (whichname : string) ->
  object
    val mutable name = whichname
    method get_name = name
    initializer print_string ("one object of class person6 : " ^ name ^ "\n")
end ;;
class person6 :
  string -> object val mutable name : string method get_name : string end
# let my_construct x = new person6 ("My dear " ^ x) ;;
val my_construct : string -> person6 = <fun>
# let obj = my_construct "Paul" ;;
one object of class person6 : My dear Paul    (*1*)
val obj : person6 = <obj>
# obj#get_name ;;
- : string = "My dear Paul"
```

This example also shows how to define and use a particular anonymous function called *initializer*. It is introduced in the body of a class by the keyword `initializer` and is executed just after the creation of the object (Ans. 1.12). The definition of an initializer can thus use fields of the object just created. Line (*1*) of the example highlights the execution of the initializer after the object `obj` is created.

4.3.3. *Marks, incomplete classes, parametrization*

4.3.3.1. *Marks*

The *private* mark

A method m of a class c can be marked `private` but beware: this mark does not have the same meaning as in Java or C++. The method m appears in the type of the class c with its mark but this mark is not present in the type of objects of c (we will come back to this point later). This tag forbids the use of the name m outside c. The only possible occurrences of an expression s#m are in the bodies of methods of c, hence s is necessarily the name chosen for V_this. Example 4.50 illustrates these points. The method m cannot be used to build a message outside the definition of c. The message o#m causes an error, but s#m in the body of the method is accepted.

EXAMPLE 4.50.–

```
OCaml
# class c =
  object (s)
    method private m = 1
    method p y = s#m + y
end ;;
class c : object method p : int -> int method private m : int end
# let o = new c ;;
o : c = <obj>
# o#p 100 ;;
- : int = 101
# o#m ;;
Error: This expression has type c  It has no method m
```

A method marked `private` can be inherited. It loses its mark if it is redefined or tagged with `virtual` in order to prepare a later redefinition. In example 4.51, the mark on m1 disappeared from the type of the class c2 and the message o2#m1 can be evaluated, while o1#m1 is rejected. The error at line /*1*/ shows that m2 is not visible outside c1. Method m2 remains `private` in the inherited class, as shown by the type of c2. This explains the rejection of o2#m2.

EXAMPLE 4.51.–

```
OCaml
# class c1 =
  object
    method private m1 = 1
    method private m2 = 5
end ;;
class c1 : object method private m1 : int method private m2 : int end
# class c2 =
  object
    inherit c1
    method m1 = 4 * m2
end ;;
```

```
Error: Unbound value m2 /*1*/
# class c2 =
  object
    inherit c1
    method m1 = 4
end ;;
class c2 : object method m1 : int method private m2 : int end
# let o1 = new c1 and o2 = new c2 ;;
val o1 : c1 = <obj>
val o2 : c2 = <obj>
# o1#m1 ;;
Error: This expression has type c1 It has no method m1
# o2#m1 ;;
- : int = 4
# o2#m2 ;;
Error: This expression has type c2 It has no method m2
```

4.3.3.2. Virtual classes

The virtual mark

OCaml allows the definition of incomplete (*C-kits*) by marking the *not defined* fields with `virtual`. The class must then be tagged with `virtual` and cannot be instantiated. Completion has to be performed in the inheritance steps. Example 4.52 illustrates these points.

EXAMPLE 4.52.–

```
OCaml
# class virtual c_not_completed =
  object
    method virtual f : int
end ;;
class virtual c_not_completed : object method virtual f : int end

# class c =
  object
    inherit c_not_completed
    method f = 25
end ;;
class c : object method f : int end
```

Types of definitions must be equal or strictly more general than those of declarations. In example 4.53, the type of the definition of f is `'a list -> 'a`, but must be unified with `int list -> int`.

EXAMPLE 4.53.–

```
OCaml
# class virtual c_v =
  object (s)
    method virtual f : int list -> int
end ;;
class virtual c_v : object method virtual f : int list -> int end
# class d =
    object (s) inherit c_v
    method f = fun l -> List.hd l
end;;
class d : object method f : int list -> int end
```

As shown by example 4.54, introducing virtual "polymorphic" methods using typical syntax for polymorphic types leads to surprising results.

EXAMPLE 4.54.–

```
OCaml
# class virtual c_v =
  object (s)
    method virtual f : 'a list ->'a
    method g l = s#f l + 1
end ;;
class virtual c_v :
  object method virtual f : int list -> int method g : int list -> int end

# class virtual d_v =
  object (s)
    method virtual f : 'a list ->'a
    method g l = s#f l + 1
    method h l = s#f l ^ "oops"
end ;;
Error: This expression has type int but an expression was expected of
type string
```

In the class c_v, the virtual method f is introduced as "polymorphic" but typing method g adds a constraint on the type variable 'a which is instantiated by int. The class d_v is rejected because two incompatible constraints are set on 'a. Thus, 'a does not seem to be universally quantified in the type expression 'a list -> 'a. This is indeed the case. For explicit quantification, it suffices to prefix the type expression by the name of the type variable, followed by a dot: 'a.; this is done in example 4.55, the results of which conform to those expected.

EXAMPLE 4.55.–

```
OCaml
class virtual c_v =
  object (s)
    method virtual f : 'a.'a list -> 'a
    method g l = s#f l + 1
  end ;;
class virtual c_v :
  object method virtual f : 'a list -> 'a method g : int list -> int end

# class virtual d_v =
  object (s)
    method virtual f : 'a.'a list -> 'a
    method g l = s#f l + 1
    method h l = s#f l ^ "oops"
end ;;
class virtual d_v :
  object
    method virtual f : 'a list -> 'a
    method g : int list -> int
    method h : string list -> string
  end

# class c =
  object (s) inherit c_v
    method f = fun l -> List.hd l
end ;;
class c : object method f : 'a list -> 'a method g : int list -> int end

# let o = new c;;
  val o : c = <obj>

# o#f [1;2], o#f ["a"; "z"] ;;
- : int * string = (1, "a")
```

The example 4.56 shows that a definition whose type is less general than that of the declaration is rejected.

EXAMPLE 4.56.–

```
OCaml
# class virtual c_v =
  object (s)
    method virtual f :'a.'a list -> 'a
end ;;
class virtual c_v : object method virtual f : 'a list -> 'a end

# class d =
  object (s) inherit c_v
    method f = fun l -> List.hd l + 1
end;;
Error: This method has type int list -> int which is less general than
'a. 'a list -> 'a
```

Manipulating polymorphic methods may seem a bit complicated. The reason – as explained in Chapter 5 of Volume 1 – is that the generalization of a variable, i.e. its universal quantification, is not done on every expression. Introducing polymorphic methods is often best done with parameterized classes, where the scope of universal quantification of type variables is the whole class.

4.3.3.3. *Parameterized classes*

Parameterized classes of OCaml are parameterized *C-kits*. The parameter can be a type or a value. We saw some of them in example 4.47. The main – albeit small – difficulty is that the developer is sometimes asked to "help" the type inference by providing the types of some identifiers. Let us examine this point in example 4.57.

EXAMPLE 4.57.–

```
OCaml
# class ['a] compare_ex (w, less_than) =
  object (s)
    val min = w
    val mutable current = w
    method set_current y = current <- y
    method choice () = if less_than (w, current) then current else w
end ;;
Error: Some type variables are unbound in this type:
class ['a] compare_ex :
  'b * ('b * 'b -> bool) -> object
                             val mutable current : 'b
                             val min : 'b
                             method choice : unit -> 'b
                             method set_current : 'b -> unit
                             end
  The method choice has type unit -> 'b where 'b is unbound
```

The error message indicates that the typing algorithm failed, pinpointing the sub-expression that triggered the failure. No link seems to be etablished between the type parameter 'a and the formal parameter w. Let us provide the type of w in example 4.58.

EXAMPLE 4.58.–

```
OCaml
# class ['a] compare_ex (w, less_than) =
  object (s)
    val min = (w : 'a)
    val mutable current = w
    method set_current y = current <- y
    method choice () = if (less_than w current) then current else w
end ;;
class ['a] compare_ex :
  'a * ('a ->'a -> bool) -> object
    val mutable current : 'a  val min : 'a
```

```
method choice : unit -> 'a
method set_current : 'a -> unit
end
```

Adding this precision is sufficient. Type inference succeeds and the type of the class is now polymorphic. Note that the universal quantification on 'a applies to all the fields of the class, as shown by the following example where the type variable 'a is instantiated by int in all of the fields.

EXAMPLE 4.59.–

```
OCaml
# let obj = new compare_ex (1, fun (x, y) -> x < y) ;;
val obj : int compare_ex = <obj>
# obj#set_current ;;
- : int -> unit = <fun>
# obj#set_current 25 ;;
# print_int (obj#choice ()) ;;
25- : unit = ()
```

A parameterized class may also contain a polymorphic field which does not depend on the type parameter of the class. In example 4.60, there is an important difference between the universally quantified type variable 'a, whose scope is the definition of pair, and the universally quantified variable 'b, also, whose scope is the whole definition of the class.

EXAMPLE 4.60.–

```
OCaml
# class ['b]  c (x : 'b) =
  object (this)
    val mutable prem = 25
    val mutable w = x
    method pair : 'a.'a -> (int * 'a) = fun y -> (prem, y)
    method f = this#pair w
end ;;
class ['b] c :
  'b ->
  object
    val mutable prem : int
    val mutable w : 'b
    method f : int * 'b
    method pair : 'a -> int * 'a
  end
# let o = new c (true) ;;
val o : bool c = <obj>
```

4.3.4. *Objects*

The notion of object in OCaml is the same as in other object-oriented languages: an object is an *O-kit* created by instantiating a *C-kit*. However, it is possible to create

OCaml objects directly without using classes. An object that has been created directly can be modeled as the unique *O-kit* built from a complete *C-kit* without parameters (families F_a, F_p and F_k are empty) but cannot be inherited. Example 4.61 introduces one unique object whose type contains only the types of its methods.

EXAMPLE 4.61.–

```
OCaml
# let alone =
  object
    val mutable age = 0
    method getting_old v = age <- age + v
    method get_age = age
end ;;
val alone : < get_age : int; getting_old : int -> unit > = <obj>
# alone#getting_old 25 ; alone#get_age ;;
- : int = 25
```

Objects are first-class values. Messages are evaluated using late binding. There is no difference in the treatment of objects according to how they are created.

4.3.4.1. *Closed versus open object types*

Typechecking OCaml objects differs significantly from most other programming languages. As stated at the beginning of this section, object typing was designed (see [RÉM 98]) to maintain consistency with type inference and parametric polymorphism. The greatest benefit of this kind of typechecking is the validity of the strong safety theorem. In concrete terms, this means that if the program is well-typed, then it is logically consistent.

Obtaining this logical consistency proof from typing requires the introduction of two families of types called *object types*: *closed object types* and *open object types*. Types of classes are not object types. We will study their relation with object types later.

An object type that is said to be *closed* is made of a sequence of names n_i which are associated with a type t_i ($i \in [1 \dots p]$). It is denoted by $< n_1 : t_1 ; n_2 : t_2 ; \dots ; n_p : t_k >$. Let us name this type t. An object o has type t if any name m of a public method of o of type s is identical to a name, say n_k occuring in t, s being identical to t_k and, conversely, any name n_i occuring in t is also the name of a public method of o, whose type is t_i. Roughly speaking, names and types of methods are the same in the object o and in the considered type t, forgetting names of private methods of o.

Thus, the closed type of an object is defined in a *structural* manner. This implies that two objects created independently (for example via two different classes, or directly created) have the same type if they have exactly the same public methods, with the same types. Example 4.62 defines two objects, o1 and o2, having the same type < m1 : string; m2 : int >. A function taking a parameter of type < m1 : string; m2 : int > can be applied to o1 and o2.

EXAMPLE 4.62.–

```
OCaml
# class c1 =
  object
    val x = 4.3
    method m1 = "azerty"
    method m2 = 3
end ;;
class c1 : object val x : float method m1 : string method m2 : int end
# let o1 = new c1 ;;
val o1 : c1 = <obj>
# let o2 =
  object
    val y = true
    method m1 = "qwerty"
    method m2 = 25
end ;;
val o2 : < m1 : string; m2 : int > = <obj>
# let affiche (o : < m1 : string; m2 : int >) =
    print_string (o#m1 ^ " ") ; print_int o#m2;print_newline () ;;
val affiche : < m1 : string; m2 : int > -> unit = <fun>
# affiche o1 ;;
azerty 3
- : unit = ()
# affiche o2 ;;
qwerty 25
- : unit = ()
```

The type float of the attribute x of class c1, and thus of o1, does not occur in the closed object type of o1. It is the same for the attribute y of o2. Hence, the type of an object differs to that of its class since it does not include the types of its attributes. However, the name of the class is used as a type abbreviation to designate the type of the object (see section 6.4.1 of Volume 1). This implies that two objects issued from two classes whose names differ, with public methods having the same names and same types, have different type abbreviations but they have the same types (Ans. 1.7).

An *open object type* is built like a closed type with an extra type variable, called a *row variable*, denoted by ρ in the following explanations and printed as .. (called an *ellipsis*) in the examples. Thus, an open object type has the form: $< n_1 : t_1 ; n_2 : t_2; \ldots ; n_k : t_k ; \rho >$. This row variable ρ can be instantiated by (and only by) any set of method names associated with their types. An open object type t_b defined by $< n_1 : t_1 ; n_2 : t_2; \ldots ; n_k : t_k ; \rho >$ is said to be ρ-*instantiated* by a closed type t_s defined by $< m_1 : s_1 ; m_2 : s_2; \ldots ; m_p : s_p >$ if t_s owns the same methods with the same types as those explicitly present in t_b, i.e. if for any name n_i of type t_i in t_b there exists m_j in t_s so that $m_j = n_i$ and $s_j = t_i$. The type t_s can contain method names not present in t_b. Suppose that the methods m_j, for $k < j \leq p$, are not present in t_b. Then, in t_s the variable ρ of t_b is instantiated by the set $\{m_j \mid k < j \leq p\}$.

Open types are used especially to typecheck functions taking an object (or several), say x, as a formal parameter. Its open type t can be inferred in the simple cases, otherwise it must be explicitly stated in the function's declaration. The body of this function can contain messages like x#m as long as the method m is present in the open type of x. Such functions can be applied to any object having a closed object type t_s if t_s is a ρ-instantiation of t. This typing rule ensures that all the messages used in the function's body are present and well-typed, and can therefore be properly executed.

Thus, open object types can be used to define generic functions (as in those of Ada, for example) on objects. In example 4.63, the type of the function f_gen has been inferred. This function can be applied to objects o1 and o2 defined in example 4.62 and to o3, defined in a local declaration. Note the representation of ρ by the ellipsis .. in the type of f_gen.

EXAMPLE 4.63.–

```
OCaml
let f_gen (obj) = print_string (obj#m1); print_newline; ;;
val f_gen : < m1: string; .. > -> unit = <fun>
# f_gen o1 ;;
azerty
- : unit = ()
# f_gen o2 ;;
qwerty
- : unit = ()
# let o3 = object method m1 = "iop" end in f_gen o3 ;;
iop
- : unit = ()
```

4.3.4.2. Subtyping and inclusion polymorphism

The type of objects of a subclass is not that of objects of the inherited class, as shown by the following example where f cannot be applied to an object of type c2. Thus, there is no implicit subclassing in OCaml.

EXAMPLE 4.64.–

```
OCaml
# class c1 = object method m1 = 1 end ;;
class c1 : object method m1 : int end
# class c2 = object inherit c1 method m2 = 4 end ;;
class c2 : object method m1 : int method m2 : int end
# let o1 = new c1 and o2 = new c2 ;;
val o1 : c1 = <obj>
val o2 : c2 = <obj>
# let f (o : c1) = true ;;
val f : c1 -> bool = <fun>
```

```
# f o2 ;;
Error: This expression has type c2 but an expression was expected of type c1
```

In OCaml, an object type t_s is a subtype of an object type t_b if t_s is equal to t_b, or if any method m of t_b is present in t_s, with a type in t_s being a subtype of m in t_b (in other words, t_s is more specialized than t_b).

For instance, type <m : int ; n: bool ; p : string> is a subtype of <m : int ; ..>, of <m : int ; n: bool ; ..>, of <m : 'a ; n: 'b ; ..>.

We previously defined the ρ-instantiation of an open type t_b by a closed type t_s. This is only a particular case of subtyping: t_s is a subtype of the open type t_b. We saw that functions with one formal parameter of open type t_b can be applied to any object of type t_s if t_s ρ-instantiates t_b. This condition is generalized as follows: any function whose formal parameter's type is an open type can be applied to any object whose type is a subtype of this open type.

This subtyping mechanism is called *inclusion polymorphism*. It is compatible with parametric polymorphism. It guarantees consistency between functional, imperative and object features of OCaml. Inclusion subtyping is structural subtyping. It is defined independently of how these objects are built: inclusion polymorphism is not induced by a subclassing relation. It may happen that the type of objects of a subclass d of c is a subtype of the one of objects of c but this is not always the case; for instance, if some methods are binary methods. Example 4.65 illustrates the use of both kinds of polymorphism.

EXAMPLE 4.65.–

```
OCaml
# let f o = o#m1 ;;
val f : < m1 : 'a; .. > -> 'a = <fun>
# let g o = (o#m2 10) + 1 ;;
val g : < m2 : int -> int; .. > -> int = <fun>
# class c =
  object
    method private m1 = "azerty"
    method m2 x = x + 2
end ;;
class c : object method private m1 : string method m2 : int -> int end
# let o1 = new c ;;
val o1 : c = <obj>
# f o1 ;;
Error: This expression has type c1 but an expression was expected of type
  < m1 : 'a; .. > The first object type has no method m1
# g o1 ;;
- : int = 13
# let o2 = object method private m1 = 3 method m2 x = x + 100 end ;;
val o2 : < m2 : int -> int > = <obj>
# g o2 ;;
```

```
- : int = 111
# let o3 =
  object
    method m1 x = 1000 + x
    method m2 x = x + 75
end ;;
val o3 : < m1 : int -> int; m2 : int -> int > = <obj>
# f o3 ;;
- : int -> int = <fun>
# (f o3) (g o3) ;;
- : int = 1086
```

The functions f and g are defined without any previously introduced classes or objects. The function f is polymorphic by inclusion (row variable denoted by .. in its type) and also by parametric polymorphism (type variable 'a in its type). Thus it can be applied to any object whose type is both a subtype and an instantiation (of 'a) of the inferred type. The function g only features inclusion polymorphism. The class c is then introduced and, with the use of the mark private and the application of f to o1, shows the difference between the type of the class (containing the private method m1) and the closed type of the object created from this class (not containing the method). The type of the object o2 (with methods of the same name, type and visibility as the class c1) explicitly shows that object types only include public methods. The applications of f and g to the object o3 illustrate the double possibility of subtyping: the closed type of o3 instantiates both the type variable 'a by int and the row variable .. by m2 :   int -> int in the type of f.

Inclusion polymorphism allows coercions which involves forgetting some fields (Ans. 1.8). There is no implicit coercion in OCaml. In example 4.66, the type pupil has one more component than the type person. The function pupil_is_person converts an object of type pupil into an object of type person by using the coercion operator :>.

EXAMPLE 4.66.–

```
OCaml
# type person = <nom : string ; age : int> ;;
# type pupil = <nom : string ; age :int ; school : string> ;;
# let pupil_is_person (x : pupil) = (x :> person) ;;
val pupil_is_person : pupil -> person = <fun>
# let p = object method nom ="H" method age = 15 method school ="G" end ;;
val p : < age : int; nom : string; school : string > = <obj>
# (p#nom, p#age, p#school) ;;
- : string * int * string = ("H", 15, "G")
# let o = pupil_is_person p ;;
- : person = <obj>
# (o#nom, o#age) ;;
- : string * int = ("H", 15)
# o#school ;;
Error: This expression has type person  It has no method school
```

The ability to use open types, closed types and subtyping together allows one to define generic handling of objects that share method names. Hence, one can define a function dealing with any object of a class and its subclasses, even if they are not yet defined. This maintains a sort of invariant about how to describe families of objects sharing common features. However, this requires careful control of any application of such defined functions. Indeed they can be applied by error to an object whose type is a subtype of the type of the argument of the function.

4.3.5. *Class signatures: confinement and inheritance*

4.3.5.1. *Confinement*

A *class signature* is a class type that only specifies the attributes and methods to be exported. The type inferred for a class is a class signature which shows its attributes with their types, its methods with their types and their possible marks (private, virtual).

A class signature can be created with the keyword class type, by listing the names and types of the methods and attributes which must remain visible outside the class. A class definition may then be constrained by a class signature. Methods confined by a class signature must be defined using the keyword private. They cannot be tagged with virtual. However, a class signature can contain a method marked private. Example 4.67 illustrates these different points.

EXAMPLE 4.67.–

```
OCaml
# class type t_signature =
  object val x : int method m1 : int method private m2 : int end ;;
class type t_signature =
object val x : int method m1 : int method private m2 : int end
# class c : t_signature =
 object
   val x = 1 val y = 2
   method m1 = x - y
   method private m2 = x * y
   method p = x + y
end ;;
Error: The class type
         object val x : int  val y : int method m1 : int
         method private m2 : int  method p : int end
      is not matched by the class type t_signature
         The public method p cannot be masked
# class c1 : t_signature =
  object (s)
    val x = 1 val y = 2
    method m1 = s#p - y
    method private m2 = x * y
    method private p = x + y
```

```
end ;;
class c1 : t_signature
# let obj = new c1 in obj#p ;;
Error: This expression has type c It has no method p
# let obj = new c1 in obj#m2 ;;
Error: This expression has type c1 It has no method m2
```

The class signature t_signature requires an attribute x, a method m1 and a method private m2. The definition of c is rejected because the method p, having no private mark, is not present in t_signature. Once this mark is set on p, the definition is accepted. c has one more attribute compared to the requirements of t_signature. The method p can only be used in c since p is private in c. Likewise, the method m2 being private in t_signature cannot be used outside a class of type t_signature.

4.3.5.2. *Class signature and inheritance*

Let us examine the relationship between confining a class c by a signature and inheriting from this class:

1) any attribute of a class is always inherited. If it is not present in the signature given to the class then it is not visible by a new method, however it remains accessible using the methods of the inherited class. Let us continue example 4.67 by defining the class d. This is rejected because the new method m3 uses the attribute y which is not present in the signature. The occurrence of x is accepted:

```
# class d = object (s) inherit c1 method m3 = x - y end ;;
Error: Unbound value y
```

2) a method absent from the signature of a class c (hence marked private) is not present in the types of its subclasses, and is not visible in them. However it is accessible using the methods of c. In example 4.68, the method p of the class c is not visible in d. The method m1 of c uses p and the method m3 of d uses m1. Thus, p is accessible from d;

EXAMPLE 4.68.–

```
OCaml
class type t_signature =
  object val x : int method m1 : int method private m2 : int end ;;
class c : t_signature =
  object (s)
    val x = 2
    method private p (y) = y
    method m1 = s#p (25) + 1000
    method private m2 = x * 2
end ;;
# class d = object (s) inherit c method m3 = s#p end ;;
Warning 17: the virtual method p is not declared. Error: This class
 should be virtual. The following methods are undefined : p
```

```
# class d = object (s) inherit c  method m3 = s#m1 + 10 end ;;
class d :
  object
    val x : int
    method m1 : int
    method private m2 : int
    method m3 : int
  end
# let obj = new d in (obj#m1, obj#m3) ;;
- : int * int = (1025, 1035)
```

3) any method present in the signature of the class can be inherited. If it is not redefined, a `private` method remains `private` in the subclass. This is the case for method m2, inherited by d in example 4.68. In the remainder of this example, the class d2 redefines the method p without marking it, and m2 remains `private` in d2.

```
OCaml
# class d2 = object (s) inherit c1 method p = x end ;;
class d2 :
  object val x : int method m1 : int method private m2 : int method p : int end
```

Let us take stock of the mark `private` set on a method m of a class c. This mark restricts the scope of m to the body of c. If m is not present in the signature of the class c, then m is absent from the types of subclasses of c, thus it is not visible by subclasses of c but remains accessible using certain methods that have access to it. If it appears in the signature of c, it is inherited by all the subclasses of c and, in this case, if it is redefined it may lose its mark, otherwise it remains `private`.

4.3.5.3. *Confinement by module signatures*

The definition of a class may be contained in a module. If the signature of this module does not mention the class, the latter will not be inherited. In example 4.69, the module signature T contains an object type c and an object o of this type. The module M contains a class (visible in its type). The module X is obtained by constraining the exports of M. The class d1, which inherits from M.c, can be built because the class c appears in the signature of M. Conversely, the attempt to create the class d2 fails. It would inherit from X.c which is impossible because the class c is absent from T (there is only an object type named c).

EXAMPLE 4.69.–

```
OCaml
# module type T = sig
  type c = < m : int >
  val o : c
end ;;
module type T = sig type c = < m : int > val o : c end
# module M = struct
  class c = object method m = 1 end
  let o = new c
```

```
end ;;
module M : sig class c : object method m : int end val o : c end
# module X = (M : T) ;;
module X : T
# class d1 = object inherit M.c end ;;
class d1 : object method m : int end
# class d2 = object inherit X.c end ;;
  Unbound class X.c
```

4.3.6. *Multiple inheritance*

The relationships between inheritance, signatures and the mark private have already been studied. Let us examine some features of OCaml's multiple inheritance. Any class may be inherited, including a class whose fields are all tagged with virtual (hence, similar to a Java interface). Multiple inheritance is controlled at compile-time. The compiler checks that attributes and methods of the same name, inherited from several classes, have the same types. This is required to guarantee the consistency of inheritance with respect to typechecking.

4.3.6.1. *Solving ambiguities*

Let d be a subclass defined by inheriting from several c_i classes. Let m be a method defined with the same type in several of the c_i. The method m inherited by d is then that of the last class in the inheritance clause. If m does not have the same type in all the classes c_i, an error is raised during compilation. The same applies to attributes, with an additional warning that several inherited attributes have the same name.

Example 4.70 shows this check. The class cd cannot be built because of the type conflict on the field f appearing in both c and d. The conflict on x is not yet detected in cd: the compiler emits an error message as soon as the conflict on f is found. This conflict on x is detected in the class ce, the one in f has been resolved. The class cg inherits from c and cf. The compiler warns that c and cf contain two attributes with the same names and types, however the class cg is created anyway.

EXAMPLE 4.70.–

```
OCaml
# class c = object val x = 1 method f = x method g = 10 * x end ;;
class c : object val x : int method f : int method g : int end

# class d = object val x = true method f = true end ;;
class d : object val x : bool method f : bool end

# class cd = object inherit c inherit d end ;;
Error: The method f has type int but is expected to have type bool

# class e = object  val x = true  method f = 25 end ;;
class e : object val x : bool method f : int end
```

```
# class ce = object inherit c inherit e end ;;
Warning 13: the following instance variables are overridden by the class e : x
The behaviour changed in ocaml 3.10 (previous behaviour was hiding.)
Error: The instance variable x has type bool but is expected to have type int

# class cf = object  val x = 100  method f = x + 25 end ;;
class cf : object val x : int method f : int end

# class cg = object inherit c inherit cf end ;;
Warning 13: the following instance variables are overridden by the class cf : x
The behaviour changed in ocaml 3.10 (previous behaviour was hiding.)
class cg : object val x : int method f : int method g : int end

# let o= new cg ;;
val o : cg= <obj>

# (o#f, o#g) ;;
int * int = (125, 1000)
```

4.3.6.2. *Redefinitions*

An attribute or a method can be redefined in a subclass if its type is left unchanged. The semantics of method redefinition is late binding. A method m can just be redeclared in a subclass by marking it virtual: the definition of m in c is no longer accessible. The class d cannot be instantiated. Typechecking redefinitions is performed at compile-time, the binding between the name and the value is done during execution, as explained in section 3.2.1.1.

As shown by example 4.70, the OCaml compiler emits warnings when a method or an attribute is redefined. However, in both cases, it accepts the redefinition if it is well-typed. By using the keywords val! and method!, it is possible to make the intention of redefinition explicit and the warnings then disappear (if redefinitions are legal).

4.3.6.3. *Remark*

A class which is explicitly a function of the family F_a cannot be directly inherited. This is the case for d in example 4.71. Actual parameters must be given for F_a, as in the class e of this example. It also shows the possibility of giving a name to the inherited class with the keyword as.

EXAMPLE 4.71.–

```
OCaml
# class c val_x =
  object
    val x = val_x
    method f = x + 1
    initializer print_string "initial "; print_newline ()
end ;;
```

```
class c : int -> object val x : int method f : int end

# class d = object inherit c end ;;
Error: This class expression is not a class structure; it has type int
-> c

# class e val_x =
    object
      inherit c val_x as my_super
      method f = 2 * my_super#f
      initializer print_int x ; print_newline ()
end ;;
class e : int -> object val x : int method f : int end

# let o = new e 34 ;;
initial
34
val o : e = <obj>

# o#f ;;
- : int = 70
```

Note that the initializer of c is executed when the object o of e is created (display of initial), then the interactive system displays its feedback val o : e = <obj>. The evaluation of o#f requires that of my_super#f.

4.3.7. *Other features*

Due to lack of space, we have provided relatively little detail on the use of coercions required to meet subtyping constraints. Several other aspects have not been studied: pure functional classes and objects, mutually recursive classes, cloning objects, binary methods, etc. These points are covered in the reference manual of OCaml, which contains many examples, but they are also addressed in various dedicated books [CON 14, DUB 04, MIN 13].

4.4. Presentation of Python

Chapters 3, 4, 5 of Volume 1 use Python to implement most of the semantical concepts studied therein. Chapters 6, 7 and 8 of the first volume also present some of its features. The present section completes the overview of this language and is dedicated mostly to Python's classes.

Thanks to its interpreter, Python can be used as a calculator, allowing the use of numbers and functions but also lists, sets, arrays, etc. Such use only requires an intuitive understanding of these features, without needing to delve into the underlying computational concepts. But Python is also a language which provides very rich libraries and, to use them wisely, developers need to master Python's semantics, which is described in the reference manual [FOU 19b]. Since the general objective of this book is also to help with the reading of a reference manual, we do the exercise with Python. The examples provided are of minimum size, designed to highlight a semantical point and to identify some possible difficulties. They are absolutely not representative of programs commonly written in Python. We answer questions from Chapter 1 and clarify some terminology.

4.4.1. *Getting started*

Like Java, Python is an object-oriented language compiled into a *bytecode* which is then interpreted. In contrast to Java, Python's expressions and constructs are not typechecked at compile-time but during execution : Python is a *dynamically typed* language. We will come back to the notion of types in Python later (Ans. 1.1). Let us verify this point with example 4.72.

EXAMPLE 4.72.–

```Python
# --- File calculator.py
a = [3]
print ("running line 2")
b = 5
print ("running line 4")
c = a + b       # Attempt 1
```

In the program `calculator.py`, the variable a points to the list [3] and the variable b points to the integer 5. Expressions like a + b or a(4) will clearly cause a typing issue. When will it be detected?

To compile example 4.72, it suffices to import the module `py_compile` containing the compiler, then to compile the program. The result is a bytecode file suffixed by .pyc. During the compilation the error is not detected: typechecking is not performed statically.

```
$ python3
Python 3.7.0a1 (v3.7.0)
>>> import py_compile
>>> py_compile.compile ('calculator.py')
'__pycache__/calculator.cpython-37.pyc'
>>> exit ()
```

Let us now execute the generated file:

```
$ python3 calculator.cpython-37.pyc
running line 2
running line 4
Traceback (most recent call last):
  File "calculator.py", line 6, in <module>
    c = a + b
TypeError: can only concatenate list (not "int") to list
```

The typing error (line # `Attempt 1`) is detected after the execution of lines 1 to 4, as shown by their messages in the output. Typechecking is thus performed block by block (which only contain one line in this example) during the execution : Python is clearly a dynamically typed language. Let us replace `c = a + b` by a (4) in the line # `Attempt 1` and recompile the program. The execution now provides the following diagnostic:

```
Traceback (most recent call last):
  File "calculator.py", line 5, in <module>
    a (4)
TypeError: 'list' object is not callable
```

A typing error is still detected: a is not a functional expression (`callable` is a property of functions and methods).

4.4.2. *An overview of classes, modules and types*

Python provides functions, classes, packages and modules. Roughly speaking, classes are *C-kits*, objects are *O-kits*, and modules and packages are weak *kits* (Ans. 1.2). Definitions and instructions introduced during interactive use of Python form a module called `__main__`. The text of this module is often called a *script*.

4.4.2.1. *Entities*

The reference manual [FOU 19b] refers to all the manipulated values (numbers, functions, programs, classes, objects, modules, etc.) using the term *object*, which we replace here by the term *entity*. We keep the term "object" for *O-kits* defined by the user. If an entity is named n.a then a is said to be an *attribute* of n, whether n is a class, a package, a module, etc. We will only use the term *qualified identifier* and retain the meaning of *attribute* given in section 3.2.

Any entity a has one identity, one type and one value: type (a), id (a) respectively provide the type of a and its identity which is an integer encoding the address of its value in memory. Neither the identity nor the type of an entity can be changed. The name given to an entity is bound to a value, which is a pointer to this entity. Thus this entity is said to be the *pointed value*. Pointers are not typed. In example 4.73, we use `type` and `id` to show certain features of the language. The comments # Part have been inserted to aid explanation.

EXAMPLE 4.73.–

```Python
>>> type (25), id (25)                        # Part 1
(<class 'int'>, 4304981184)
>>> a = 25
>>> type (a), id (a)
(<class 'int'>, 4304981184)
>>> def f (x):                                # Part 2
...     print ("function f's body", x)
 >>> type (f), id (f)
(<class 'function'>,  4320816664)
>>> type ('program'), id ('program')          # Part 3
(<class 'str'>, 4326463600)
>>> type ((1, 2, 3)), id ((1, 2, 3))          # Part 4
(<class 'tuple'>, 4326458856)
>>> type ([1,2]), id([1,2])                   # Part 5
(<class 'list'>, 4327511048)
>>> type (list), id (list)                    # Part 6
(<class 'type'>,4304636800)
>>> type (float), id (float)                  # Part 7
(<class 'type'>, 4304631008)
>>> type (type), id (type)                    # Part 8
(<class 'type'>, 4304664256)
>>> type (class)                              # Part 9
                ^ SyntaxError: invalid syntax
>>> import numbers                            # Part 10
>>> type (numbers), id(numbers)
(<class 'module'>,4326550488)
```

An integer is an object of the class `int` (Part 1). The instruction a = 25 declares the name a, which is a pointer on 25, type (a) returns the type of the pointed entity and id (a) returns the encoding of 25 (the pointed value). Part 2 defines a function f whose type is `function`, without information about the types of the arguments and of the result.

Python calls any entity containing references to other entities (for instance a tuple, a list, a dictionary – i.e. an association list –, etc.) a *container*. Parts 3, 4 and 5 show the types of some containers, particularly those of strings, tuples and lists.

Parts 6, 7 and 8 show that the (so called) types of Python are also objects of the class `type`, as well as the entity denoted by the identifier `type`. Part 9 reminds us that `class` is a keyword used to introduce a class definition. Part 10 is the import of the module `numbers` of the standard library. Once its name is known, its type and identity can be requested.

In our model (see Chapter 1), the name of a variable is bound to a set of informations. To reduce the comments in the examples, we restrict displayed information to the value pointed by a variable in the current environment (if no other information is relevant). Thus, when analyzing the assignment x = 5, we only state that x is a pointer to 5 if necessary, otherwise we simply say that x is bound to 5.

4.4.2.2. Types

Example 4.73 shows that in Python 3, a type is defined by a class whose name it bears. All the types displayed by type () in example 4.73 are defined as classes (Ans. 1.5 and Ans. 1.6). Entities are thus objects that share the methods of their class, a point which justifies the use of the term "object" to denote entities. For instance, the module numbers introduces a hierarchy of abstract classes, whose root is numbers.Numbers (Ans. 1.37). This module is used in example 4.74.

EXAMPLE 4.74.–

```
Python
>>> issubclass (int, numbers.Integral)        # Part 1
True

>>> issubclass (bool, int)                     # Part 2
True

>>> True + True + 25 + False                   # Part 3
27

>>> isinstance (4, bool), isinstance (4, numbers.Integral) # Part 4
(False, True)
```

The type int is that of the class int, which defines the fields of the abstract class numbers.Integral. This class inherits from numbers.Rational, itself inheriting from numbers.Real, etc., and finally from numbers.Numbers (Part 1). The type bool is defined by the class bool, inheriting from the class int (Part 2). bool cannot be inherited. Its only objects are True and False, behaving like the objects 1 and 0 of the class int, which explains the output of Part 3. It is possible to test whether an object is an instance of a class or of one of its subclasses with the function isinstance (Part 4).

4.4.2.3. Functions

A function is an object of the class function (see example 4.73) and thus owns certain attributes. A function can be directly defined at the top level of a script or as a method of a class. Python is dynamically scoped. Indeed let f be a function whose body contains a free variable a. To evaluate the application $f(v)$ in an environment Env, the binding of a in Env is used, as shown in example 4.75.

EXAMPLE 4.75.–

```
Python
>>> a = 5
>>> def f () : print (a)
>>> f ()
5
>>> a = "zz"
>>> f ()
zz
```

Dynamic scoping may lead to unexpected results. In example 4.76 that follows, the expression f ("z") is first rejected, then accepted once the variable a has been redefined, i.e. after the introduction of the new binding for a in the current environment.

EXAMPLE 4.76.–

```
Python
>>> a = 5          # id (a) returns 4304980544
>>> def f (x) : print (a + x)
>>> f (0)
5
>>> f ("z")
Traceback (most recent call last):
  File "<stdin>", line 1, in <module>
  File "<stdin>", line 2, in f
TypeError: unsupported operand type(s) for +: 'int' and 'str'
>>> a = "rr" # id (a) retourne 4354740272
>>> f ("z")
rrz
```

The arguments of a function may receive default values which are evaluated once and for all when the function is defined, in other words, they are not evaluated each time the function is called. Providing a default value for a function parameter may lead to some surprises if this value is mutable. In example 4.77, the default value of the formal parameter 1 of f is the mutable value []. The message 1.append physically modifies 1 which points to [5] after the execution of f (5). This is clearly shown by the value of f (6). The default value is not used for the evaluation of f (7, ['a']).

EXAMPLE 4.77.–

```
Python
>>> def f (x, 1 = []) :
        1.append (x)
        return 1
>>> f (5)
[5]
>>> f (6)
[5, 6]
>>> f (7, ['a'])
['a', 7]
```

4.4.2.4. *Classes*

Python's classes have already been widely used in this book. A class is a *C-kit* whose name defines a type (Ans. 1.5), which is also the type of *O-kits* issued from this class. Typechecking is nominal (Ans. 1.6). Using our terminology, fields of classes can be attributes, methods, class variables and class methods. We use example 4.78, to detail some aspects of classes.

EXAMPLE 4.78.–

```
Python
>>> class C (object) :                    # Part 1
...     x = 3
...     def __init__ (self, v) :
...         self.y = v
...         self.z = self.meth_obj (v)
...         print ("initialization")
...     def meth_obj (self, b) :
...         print ("the meth_obj")
...         return (C.meth_clas (b))
...     @classmethod
...     def meth_clas (cls, a) :
...         print ("the meth_clas")
...         return ([a])
>>> dir (C)                               # Part 2
[..., 'meth_clas', 'meth_obj', 'x']
>>> o = C ("w")                           # Part 3
the meth_obj
the meth_clas
initialization
>>> dir (o)                               # Part 4
[..., 'meth_clas', 'meth_obj', 'x', 'y', 'z']
>>> o.x, o.y, o.z
(3, 'w', ['w'])
```

Part 1 defines the class C, inheriting from the class object. The class object is inherited by all classes (implicitly if the declaration of the class does not state it). A class variable x is defined with no particular keyword, then the object constructor __init__ is introduced. Its body defines two attributes y and z, using the parameter v and the method meth_obj defined afterwards. The parameter self denotes the object under construction.

An attribute cannot be directly introduced into a class, even by a definition self.y = ... which is rejected. This definition has to be placed in an object constructor or it may be done by extension during the execution (this point will be covered later).   Next, the definition of the method meth_obj is stated, it calls the class method meth_clas expliciting the namespace C. A method must always have a formal parameter, referred to here as self, acting as V_this, introduced in section 3.2 to model late binding in case of redefinition. Since the evaluation is fully dynamic in Python – late binding being a particular case of dynamic evaluation – the use of

V_this must be explicit (Ans. 1.4). Any other name may be used instead of self to denote V_this but it must be the first parameter of any method. As self is widely used, we use it in the rest of this section.

The label @classmethod introduces the class method meth_clas, its parameter cls denotes a class. The class C under construction is indeed itself an object of a class named class (called *metaclass*). cls can be instantiated later, for example by a subclass of C which is also an object of class. The constructor and all the methods perform side effects (displaying a message) used in the explanations. However, inserting such side effects in constructors is not recommended.

dir(C) (Part 2) lists all the methods and attributes of its actual parameter (the ... partially hides this rather long list).

The object constructor __init__ is called in Part 3 to create the value of the *O-kit* o: the name of this object o is bound to the parameter self (whose presence is mandatory), the effective value "w" is bound to the argument v (Ans. 1.10). The call to meth_obj, then to meth_clas to obtain the value of the attribute z, perform the expected side effects : print the meth_obj, then the meth_clas and finally initialization at the end of the constructor's execution.

In Part 4, the attributes y and z of o are present in the result of dir (o) although they did not appear in dir (C) (displayed in Part 2): these attributes are not present in the entity C. Let us continue this example by calling C's methods.

```Python
>>> C.meth_clas (5), o.meth_clas (10), o.meth_obj (8) # Part 5
the meth_clas
the meth_clas
the meth_obj
the meth_clas
([5], [10], [8])
```

In Part 5, during the evaluation of the message C.meth_clas (5), the parameter cls is substituted by C and the parameter a by 5. While executing the message o.meth_clas (10), cls is instantiated by o. Note that all objects of a class share class methods. In a same way, during the execution of o.meth_obj (8), the parameter self is bound to o and b is bound to 8. Let us continue this example.

```Python
>>> id (o.meth_clas), id (C.meth_clas), id (o.meth_obj)  # Part 6
(4320642376, 4320642376, 4320642376)

>>> def f (this, a) :                                     # Part 7
...        print ('here is f')
...        return (this.x + a)
>>> C.meth_clas = f
```

```
>>> id (o.meth_clas), id (C.meth_clas), id (o.meth_obj)  # Part 8
(4320642376, 4320816664, 4320642376)

>>> o.meth_clas (8)                                      # Part 9
here is f
11

>>> C.meth_clas (8)                                      # Part 10
TypeError: f() missing 1 required positional argument: 'a'
>>> C.meth_clas (C, 8)
here is f
11

>>> o.meth_obj (25)                                      # Part 11
the meth_obj
Traceback (most recent call last):
  File "<stdin>", line 1, in <module>
  File "<stdin>", line 9, in meth_obj
TypeError: f() missing 1 required positional argument: 'a'
>>> o.meth_obj (o, 25)
Traceback (most recent call last):
  File "<stdin>", line 1, in <module>
TypeError: meth_obj() takes 2 positional arguments but 3 were given

>>> a = C ('a')                                          # Part 12
the meth_obj
Traceback (most recent call last):
  File "<stdin>", line 1, in <module>
  File "<stdin>", line 5, in __init__
  File "<stdin>", line 9, in meth_obj
TypeError: f() missing 1 required positional argument: 'a'
```

In Part 7, a function f is defined then assigned to C.meth_clas. A comparison of the evaluation results in Parts 6 and 8 shows that only the identity of the method C.meth_clas was changed by the assignment. However, the evaluation of the message o.meth_clas in Part 9 shows that it is really C.meth_clas, i.e. f, which is executed: the field meth_clas is searched for in C and not in o since meth_clas is a class method. The formal parameter this of f has been correctly bound to o, as shown by the display of the value 11.

Part 10 shows the execution failure of C.meth_clas (8): the interpreter does not perform the binding of C to the parameter this of f. It suffices to make explicit the effective parameter in the message C.meth_clas (C, 8), the first occurrence of C simply indicating the namespace in which meth_class must be looked up.

In Part 11, the call o.meth_obj (25) requires the evaluation of the expression C.meth_clas (25) which fails for the same reason as above. Making the parameter explicit, as we did for Part 10, is no longer sufficient. In the call o.meth_obj (o, 25), the first occurrence of o denotes the receiver of the message meth_obj and is bound to the formal parameter V_this of o.meth_obj. The second occurrence of o, i.e. the one in (o, 25), is bound to the formal parameter b of o.meth_obj and there remains a third effective parameter, 25, with which the interpreter does not know what to do. It then raises an error.

In Part 12, the attempt to create an object from C fails. The call to the constructor __init__ (self, y) triggers the evaluation of self.meth_obj (y) which prints the meth_obj, then calls C.meth_clas (b), with y then b being bound to 'a'. But C.meth_clas has been assigned with f and we get the same error. The assignment of C.meth_clas outside the definition of C does not enable the interpreter to perform all the required bindings. Assigning a function to a method is a *programming error*, which may be detected (too) late.

Let us end this example by going back to the definition of C given in Part 1.

```
Python
>>> C.x = "change"                                    # Part 13
>>> print ("C.x  is " + C.x + " ; o.x is " + o.x)
C.x is 'change' ; o.x is 'change'

>>> C.m = "add"                                       # Part 14
>>> o.m
'add'

>>> o.p = "one more attribute for o "                 # Part 15
>>> dir (o)
[..., 'm', 'meth_clas', 'meth_obj', 'p', 'x', 'y', 'z']
>>> dir (C)
[..., 'm', 'meth_clas', 'meth_obj', 'x']

>>> obj = C ("new")                                   # Part 15
initialization
>>> dir (obj)
[..., 'm', 'meth_clas', 'meth_obj', 'x', 'y', 'z']
```

The class variables can be modified: Part 13 shows an assignment to the attribute x of C. The feedback of this modification acts in the objects of this class already created: the values of both C.x and o.x are now 'change' of type str. A class variable m is added to C in Part 14, it is *de facto* added to all the objects of the class, as shown by the value of o.m. A new attribute p is added to the object o in Part 15 but this attribute remains unknown by C. A new object obj, created in Part 15 (see example 4.73), does not own the attribute p.

This lengthy example highlighted some features of Python: no type declarations for fields (Ans. 1.9), the ability to redefine attributes and methods outside an inheritance mechanism, the ability to extend classes by adding fields shared by all the objects of these classes, and the ability to add fields to an already created object.

Note that creating an object constructor as we did in Part 3 is not mandatory, fields can be created on demand.

As seen in the study of *C-kits*, the definition of a class method cannot use attributes and methods belonging to the class. An attribute or a class masks the class variable or the method having the same name, there is no field overloading (Ans. 1.9).

It is possible to remove a field from a class or an object with the function del. Example 4.79 again uses the class C and the object o from example 4.78. The object a is created by the assignment a = o. The field z is removed by the instruction del (o.z). Thus, o.z disappears, as does a.z because a is an *alias* of o.

EXAMPLE 4.79.–

```
Python
>>> o.z
  ['w']
>>> a = o
>>> a.z
  ['w']
>>> del (o.z)
>>> o.z
Traceback (most recent call last):
  File "<stdin>", line 1, in <module>
AttributeError: 'C' object has no attribute 'z'
>>> a.z
Traceback (most recent call last):
  File "<stdin>", line 1, in <module>
AttributeError: 'C' object has no attribute 'z'
```

Python provides the possibility to define so–called *static* methods. Defining a static method *f* does not introduce a formal parameter to denote the object (of the class) calling it. Thus, the method cannot use attributes and methods of the class. Example 4.80 takes the class C from example 4.78 and adds a static method meth_static to it.

EXAMPLE 4.80.–

```
Python
class C (object) :
    ...
    @staticmethod
    def meth_static (d) : return d
o = C ('w')
o.meth_static (89)
89
```

Let us consider the expression o.meth_static (89). The occurrence of o makes it possible to access the binding of meth_static but there is no binding of o created during the evaluation of o.meth_static (89). A static method differs from a class method since it does not own a parameter representing the class (the parameter cls in the class method `method_clas` of C in example 4.78). Its main advantage is that its name belongs to the namespace of the class.

4.4.3. *Names and assignment*

4.4.3.1. *Namespaces, environments, bindings*

Some presentations of Python (see the reference manual [FOU 19b]) use *namespace* to refer to what we call "environments" and the word "scope" is sometimes used in the sense of "visibility". In this book, a namespace was defined in Chapter 1 as a set of identifiers built by syntactical analysis. We retain this terminology. In Python, classes, modules and packages have their own namespace. The function `dir (arg)` returns the list of the names of the namespace `arg` (Ans. 1.3). Moreover, in the Python reference manual, any entity definition is considered an instruction because its evaluation records the entity's name in the current module's namespace and binds it in the current environment.

As seen in Chapter 1, an environment is a set of bindings, partitioned into subsets that group the bindings of certain names of the same namespace. We have decided to bind a name to all its known information and use only the items relevant for the current analysis. Here, we only mention the value accessible via the name to simplify the explanations. A Python environment can be modeled by a list containing (in this order):

1) the bindings of local names (formal parameters, local variables);

2) bindings of the global variables, functions, classes defined in the current script P, which defines the module `__main__`. These bindings can be mutually masked;

3) bindings of names coming from flattened imports performed by P (see below);

4) bindings of module names imported by P (Ans. 1.5).

Example 4.81 shows an example of masking:

EXAMPLE 4.81.–

```Python
>>> def fact (n) :                                          # Part 1
      return 1 if n == 1 else n * fact (n - 1)
>>> type (fact), fact
(<class 'function'>, <function fact at 0x1018a6e18>)

>>> class fact (object) :                                   # Part 2
        def f (self, x) :
            print ('a terrible fact')
            return (x + x)
>>> type (fact), fact, fact.f
```

```
(<class 'type'>, <class '__main__.fact'>), <function fact.f at 0x10401dd90>

>>> fact ()                                              # Part 3
<__main__.fact object at 0x101d04828>
>>> fact ().f (20)
a terrible fact
40
```

Part 1 introduces the definition of `fact` and shows its type and value. After the execution of this first definition, the name `fact` belongs to the namespace of `__main__` and is bound in the current environment to the value of this recursive function (Ans. 1.11). Part 2 introduces a new definition for `fact`, now defined as a class. The name `fact` of the class is added to the namespace of `__main__` (`<class '__main__.fact'>`) and is bound in the current environment to the value of this class (itself an object of the (meta-) class `class`). This binding masks that of `fact` to the value of the recursive function. Moreover, the evaluation of the new definition of `fact` creates a new namespace. In Part 3, the expression `fact ()` is a call to the (implicit) constructor of the class `fact`, returning an (unnamed) object of the class `fact`, which can call the method `f`.

4.4.3.2. *Scope*

The scope of an identifier defines the lifespan of its binding during the execution, thus its presence in the sequence of environments created during the execution. The scope of an identifier declared locally in a function is the body of the function. Let us consider example 4.82.

EXAMPLE 4.82.–

```
Python
>>> x = 'aa'                                             # Part 1
>>> def g (y) :
...         print ('binding effective param., formal param.:', y)
...         z = x
...         return (z)
>>> g (5)
binding effective param., formal param.: 5
'aa'

>>> x = 25                                               # Part 2
>>> g (6)
binding effective param., formal param.: 6
25
>>> z
Traceback (most recent call last):
  File "<stdin>", line 1, in <module>
NameError: name 'z' is not defined
```

Let us examine Part 1. The binding $(x, 'aa')$ is present in the environment Env where the definition of g is evaluated. After this definition, the binding of g to its value v is added at the head of Env. The current environment at the moment g (5) is evaluated is $(g, v) \oplus$ Env. This evaluation creates the binding $(y, 5)$ at the head of $(g, v) \oplus$ Env. While evaluating the right-hand side of the assignment z = x, the binding of x is searched for in $(y, 5) \oplus (g, v) \oplus$ Env to get $(x, \text{'aa'})$. The variable z is local to g, its binding $(z, \text{'aa'})$ is created then destroyed after the execution of g (5). Likewise, the binding $(y, 5)$ is deleted, as explained in Chapter 3 of Volume 1.

In Part 2, the assignment x = 25 creates the binding $(x, 25)$. The current environment becomes $E = (x, 25) \oplus (g, v) \oplus$ Env. The application g (5) is evaluated in E as is x: Python is a language with dynamic scope, the free variable x is evaluated in the environment present at the moment the application of g is encountered. This example also shows that the scope of the local variable z, defined in the body of a function, is restricted to this body.

In Python, it is possible to specify the scope of an identifier in the body of a definition. The tagged declaration global a indicates that a must have a global scope (i.e. spanning all along the program). Below follows an illustration showing that the global variable x is not masked by the redefinition of another global variable in f's body.

EXAMPLE 4.83.–

```
Python
>>> x = 0
>>> def f () :
...       global x ; x = x + 1 ; return (x)
...
>>> f () ; print ("and then") ; f ()
1 and then 2
>>> x
2
```

The tag nonlocal widens the scope of a variable to the block encompassing the one where the variable is located. In example 4.84, the scope of the local variable x of f is widened to the scope of g, and is thus bound to 25 which is the value of the local variable x of g. As is the case for any local variable of a function, x is allocated at each execution of g as shown by the value 26, returned by the two successive evaluations of g ().

EXAMPLE 4.84.–

```
Python
def g ():
    x = 25
    def f () :
        nonlocal x ; x = x + 1 ; return (x)
    return f ()
>>> g ()
26
```

```
>>> g ()
26
```

Variables introduced in a loop, like j in example 4.85, are not local to the loop. j remains accessible after the execution of the loop.

EXAMPLE 4.85.–

```
Python
>>> x = 0
>>> while x < 2 :
        j = 20
        x = x + 1
        print (x)
1
2
>>> x, j
(2, 20)
```

4.4.4. *Assignment and typechecking*

Some of the assignment examples already given may have been surprising. We now examine the links between assignment and typechecking.

4.4.4.1. *Assignment*

Binding declarations are performed with the syntax name = exp. The operator = is called an *assignment* in the reference manual but its semantics is a bit different from that described in Chapter 4 of Volume 1.

If name is a non-qualified variable name, with no index (i.e. name does not denote a *container*), an assignment creates a binding of name to a pointer on the value w of exp. If name was bound to a value v, this binding (name, v) is destroyed: in other words, name was pointing to v before the assignment, it points to w afterward. Pointers are not explicit in Python and are not typed. During the execution of a block, a name can denote values of different types. After an assignment, the scope of name is the current block, except if its scope was set by global or nonlocal. The assignment of name thus acts as a new definition.

Let us now examine an assignment of the form obj.x = exp, where obj denotes an object of a class C. If exp contains an occurrence of obj.x, it denotes either the attribute obj.x or the class variable x of C. After the evaluation of exp, in any case, obj.x (the *l-value*) denotes a new attribute of obj, reusing the name obj.x, if it was already denoting an attribute of obj before the assignment. Example 4.78 illustrated some of these points.

If obj denotes a *container*, it can only be assigned if its type is mutable, which we will address later in this section. Note that the same entity can be pointed to by several identifiers. The question of *aliasing* has already be addressed in Chapter 7 of Volume 1.

4.4.4.2. *Typechecking*

The description of an assignment allows for a better understanding of the typing mechanism of Python. As shown in example 4.73, any entity has a type. However, the previous examples have also shown that the notions of type and typechecking are not those studied earlier in this book. As depicted in example 4.72, compiling into bytecode does not involve any typechecking. The evaluation triggers a typing analysis but this typing may seem lax for those from the strong typing world.

In example 4.78, the type of the class variable x seemed to change from int to str after the assignment C.x = "change". In fact, x is a pointer, first pointing to an entity of type int, then to an entity of type str after the assignment. The supposed "typing error" is due to the absence of pointer types. However, example 4.72 contains two errors, diagnosed as type errors.

In example 4.86 that follows, one defines expression assuming that the type of (thus the class of) the object passed as a parameter will define the method speak (). If the latter is missing at runtime, an error will occur.

EXAMPLE 4.86.–

```Python
>>> def expression (person) :
...      person.speak ()
>>> expression
<function expression at 0x1018a6e18>
>>> expression (1)
Traceback (most recent call last):
  File "<stdin>", line 1, in <module>
  File "<stdin>", line 2, in expression
AttributeError: 'int' object has no attribute 'speak'
```

4.4.4.3. *Mutability*

The type of an entity defines its mutability. Numeric types are not mutable. Containers include lists, arrays, sets built with set () and dictionaries that are mutable. Tuples, strings, sets built with frozenset () are not mutable. Beware, mutable elements in an immutable container remain mutable. Example 4.87 illustrates some of these points.

EXAMPLE 4.87.–

```Python
>>> a = [3, 4], 5                          # Part 1
>>> id (a), type (a), a
(4325405256, <class 'tuple'>, ([3, 4], 5))
>>> id (a[0]), type (a[0]), a[0]
(4325388680, <class 'list'>, [3, 4])

>>> a[0].append (6)                        # Part 2
>>> id (a[0]), type (a[0]), a[0]
```

```
(4325388680, <class 'list'>, [3, 4, 6])
>>> id (a), type (a), a
(4325405256, <class 'tuple'>, ([3, 4, 6], 5))

>>> a[0] + [7]                                    # Part 3
[3, 4, 6, 7]

>>> a[0] = a[0] + [7]                             # Part 4
Traceback (most recent call last):
  File "<stdin>", line 1, in <module>
TypeError: 'tuple' object does not support item assignment
```

Part 1 defines the variable a pointing to the couple ([3, 4], 5). The first component a[0] is an object of the class list. In Part 2, the message append is sent to a[0] and executed. The identities of a and a[0] remain unchanged, the execution of append only changed the value pointed by a[0]. Part 3 shows that a[0] can be read. However, Part 4 and the related error message show that a[0], being the first component of the couple pointed by a, cannot be modified because a couple is not mutable. In other words, it is not possible to modify the pointer of a to its first component but, if this component has a mutable type, it is possible to modify the value pointed by this first component.

4.4.5. *Overloading*

Python provides operator overloading, the resolution being done at runtime as the language is dynamically typed. Any Python operator is associated with a function that is said to be a *special method* that can be redefined in any class. For instance, the + operator is associated with the special function __add__. The expression author + 100 is equivalent to author.__add__ (100).

In example 4.88, the class Person overloads the addition operator + by redefining __add__.

EXAMPLE 4.88.–

```
Python
>>> class Person :
...      def __init__ (self, age) : self.__age = age
...      def __add__ (self, i) : return self.__age + 10 * i
>>> author = Person (15)
>>> author + 10
115
>>> author.__add__ (10)
115
>>> Person.__add__
<function Person.__add__ at 0x101f091e0>>>>
>>> 25 + 10
35
```

The interpretations of the expressions `author + 10` and `author.__add__ (10)` are the same. They differ only in concrete syntax. The name of the method `__add__` belongs to the namespace `Person` and is not accessible in the current environment of `__main__`. The evaluation of `25 + 10` is clearly done without the addition defined in `Person`.

Functions directly defined in a module, attributes and methods cannot be overloaded (except special methods). Unlike in C++, it is possible to define two functions with the same name in the same namespace but the most recent definition masks the older one.

Since types are not stated in Python, the compiler has no way of determining that two functions differ by the types of their arguments. However, as Python is dynamically typed, it is possible to get the type of an expression at runtime. It is then sufficient to define the body of a function `f` by case on the formal parameters' types to obtain a quasi-overloaded function. Indeed the code executed during a call to `f` will be chosen according to the types of its actual parameters. This process does not necessarily simplify the rereading of the code. It is better to introduce two names rather than have to analyze each call of the pseudo-overloaded function to check the result of the call. Example 4.89 shows a definition given by case on the type of the argument.

EXAMPLE 4.89.–

```
Python
>>> class ArgErr (Exception) :
...      pass
>>> class Person :
...      def __init__ (self, name, age) :
...          self.age = age
...          self.name = name
...      def __add__ (self, v) :
...          if type (v) is float :
...              return self.age + v
...          elif type (v) is str :
...              return self.name + " " + v
...          else :
...              raise ArgErr
>>> a = Person ("A", 15)
>>> a + 15.7, a + "zz"
(30.7, 'A zz')
>>> a + True
Traceback (most recent call last):
  File "<stdin>", line 1, in <module>
  File "<stdin>", line 11, in __add__
__main__.ArgErr
```

The program starts by a user-defined exception `ArgErr` (see section 8.3.2 of Volume 1 on Python exceptions). The special function `__add__` is redefined in the class Person per case on the type of the argument v. If v is of type float, the returned result has type float. If v has type str, result has type str. Otherwise the exception ArgErr is raised.

Instead of testing the types of the effective parameters, it is also possible to test their number by giving a default value to some of the formal parameters, using the notion of the "undefined" variable: None (representing "no value"). This is done in example 4.90 where the body of work is defined per case on the effective values of the parameters in order to select the code to execute for each call.

EXAMPLE 4.90.−

```Python
>>> class Person :
...        def __init__ (self, name, age) :
...            self.__name = name
...            self.__age = age
...        def work (self, x = None, y = None) :
...            if x is None and y is None :
...                return "Neither x nor y provided."
...            elif x is None :
...                return "No x, but y provided."
...            elif y is None :
...                return "No y, but x provided."
...            else :
...                return "x and y provided."
>>> a = Person ("T", 20)
>>> a.work ()
'Neither x nor y provided.'
>>> a.work (1, 'H')
'x and y provided.'
>>> a.work (1)
'No y, but x provided.'
>>> a.work (None, "P")
'No x, but y provided.'
```

In the call a.work (), the actual parameters are set to None by default. The call a.work (1) can instantiate either x or y. By default, Python considers that the n provided arguments are associated with the n first parameters of the function. Thus, the call a.work (1) binds x to 1. To give a value for y, the "value" None must be explicitly given for x (see a.work (None, "P")).

Typical operators can be redefined with a different number of arguments but, in this case, they can no longer be used with their usual syntax. Such a practice greatly reduces the readability of the code.

4.4.5.1. *Duck typing*

Python does not have static typing rules for function application because the declaration of a function states neither the type of the formal parameters nor that of the result. Python's typing method is often described by the term *duck typing*, the meaning of which is given by the joke: "If it walks like a duck and it quacks like a duck, then it must be a duck". This means that any expression that contains an operation, an instruction, a method call, etc., that can be executed, is accepted by the typechecker. Let us investigate this aspect using example 4.91.

EXAMPLE 4.91.–

```Python
>>> class C (object) :                         # Part 1
...      def f (self, x) :
             print ("In C", x)

>>> class D (object) :
...      def f (self, x) :
             print ("In D", x)

>>> def which_one (o) :
         o.f (1)

>>> for y in [C (), D ()] :                    # Part 2
         which_one (y)
In C 1
In D 1

>>> class E (object) :                         # Part 3
...      def g (self, x) :
         return (x)

>>> for x in [C (), E ()] :
         which_one (x)
In C 1
Traceback (most recent call last):
  File "<stdin>", line 2, in <module>
  File "<stdin>", line 2, in which_one
AttributeError: 'E' object has no attribute 'f'
```

Part 1 defines two classes C and D, and then the function which_one. The expression o.f (1), which is the body of the function which_one, requires the existence of a name f in the environment accessible from its effective parameter o. Moreover, this name f must be *callable* since o.f is applied to an int. In the iteration of Part 2, y first denotes an object of C having a method f, then an object of D. Part 3 defines the class E then iterates. The error message obtained shows that the absence of the method f in E has been detected after the loop started by printing In C 1.

Note that the function hasattr (o, 'n') returns False if an object o does not own a field named n. This function can be used to avoid raising of an exception during the execution. It could be used here to handle the error case, hence only calling the function which_one on objects coming from classes with a method f.

4.4.6. *Modules and packages*

A module is a file with the .py suffix. It groups definitions of functions, classes, exceptions, etc. and may contain a block of instructions which is executed during the first import of the module (see example 4.72 which is actually a module).

Thus, a module can be modeled by a weak *kit* defining a namespace. Any module can be exported. The only *kit* operation on a module is the import. The execution of the instruction import name_module proceeds in several steps, as follows:

1) check that name_module.pyc (or name_module.pyc) exists in the current directory or in the one denoted by the environment variable PYTHONPATH. A module is, in effect, a known file of the operating system (or it is obtained by an interaction with the external environment, for instance via an url);

2) if necessary, compile name_module.pyc as name_module.py.c;

3) load the bytecode file name_module.pyc;

4) create a module entity from the execution of the bytecode file name_module.pyc, introducing its name into the module namespace and its binding in the corresponding sub-environment.

Let us consider the example 4.92 whose content is stored in the current directory under the name Helloworld.py.

EXAMPLE 4.92.–

```Python
print ("Hello")
def f (x) : print ('Bye', x)
```

This program is then used as follows:

```Python
>>> import Helloworld                    # Part 1
Hello

>>> f                                    # Part 2
Traceback (most recent call last):
  File "<stdin>", line 1, in <module>
NameError: name 'f' is not defined
>>> Helloworld.f
<function f at 0x101cfdd08>

>>> def f () : print ('f from main')     # Part 3
>>> f
<function f at 0x101cfde18>
```

```
>>> Helloworld.f ('f not masked')        # Part 4
Bye f not masked
>>> f ()
f from main
```

Part 1 shows the side effect (printing `Hello`) caused by the import and thus confirms the loading of the module. Part 2 shows that the name `f` is unknown but is accessible using the qualified name. Part 3 defines a new function `f`. The execution of this definition adds this function to the module `__main__`. Part 4 shows that this definition did not mask `helloworld.f`. The visible name `f` is the one introduced in Part 3. The two occurrences of the name `f` are not bound in the same sub-environments because they are not in the same namespace.

A module `name` can be flattened, this operation is done with the construct `from name import n1, n2`, where `n1, n2` are fields of the module `name`. The addition of the bindings for the non-qualified names `n1, n2` of `name` is performed at the head of the current environment, with a risk of masking bindings that have already been introduced, as shown in example 4.93.

EXAMPLE 4.93.–

```
Python
>>> def f (x) : return [x]        # Part 1

>>> from Helloworld import f      # Part 2
Hello
>>> f (5)
Bye 5
```

Part 1 defines a function `f`. Part 2 shows that this function is masked by `helloworld.f` because of the flattening.

Packages are modules that have a field `__path__`. They are *W-kits* whose fields are files that define *kits* or *C-kits*. They are used to structure namespaces. Let O be a package containing two packages P1 and P2. P2 contains a module M which owns a class C. C has a method m. Access to m is done using the dot-notation O.P2.C.m and access to f from P1 is done by O.P1.f. Packages can contain a field `__init__.py`, executed when the package is imported. Import clauses for packages are slightly different to those of the module. We do not delve any deeper into the description of packages but instead invite the reader to consult the reference manual.

4.4.7. *Confinement*

By default, functions, attributes and methods are public. Python does not use marks as Java does to confine fields and does not provide real confinement. A field m of a class

C can be made not directly usable by naming it __m (without _ after the name). Its name m is removed from the namespace of C and is replaced by _C__m. However, the name _C__m remains visible. This is illustrated in example 4.94.

EXAMPLE 4.94.–

```
Python
>>> class C (object) :
...     x = 3
...     def __init__ (self, x, y) :
...         self.__y = y
...         self.x = self.__confin (y)
...     def __confin (self, x) : return (x + x)
>>> o = C (5, 6)
>>> o.x
12
>>> o.__confin (20)
Traceback (most recent call last):
  File "<stdin>", line 1, in <module>
AttributeError: 'C' object has no attribute '__confin'
>>> o._C__confin (20)
40
>>> o._C__y
6
```

The fields y and confin of C are confined. Their names are not directly usable. However, it is easy to bypass the confinement, as shown by this example.

4.4.8. *Inheritance*

As already seen, Python allows simple and multiple inheritance. The names of the inherited classes are written between parentheses in the header of the class: class C (A) in the case of simple inheritance, class C (A, B, ...) in the case of multiple inheritance (Ans. 1.37). If the constructor A.__init__ of the inherited class A has been defined and if C does not define a constructor, then that of A is called. The class C can define its own constructor without calling that of A and whithout an implicit call to the latter.

Example 4.95 defines a class C that inherits from A without defining a constructor. The error raised when building o_C shows the call to the A constructor. The class D inherits from A, defines its own constructor without calling the A constructor. A call to the D constructor does not trigger a call to the A constructor.

EXAMPLE 4.95.–

```python
Python
>>> class A (object) :
...      def __init__ (self, xx) : print ("Cstr A") ; self.x = xx
...
>>> o = A (2)
Cstr A
>>> class C (A) :
...      y = 5
...
>>> o_C = C ()
Traceback (most recent call last):
  File "<stdin>", line 1, in <module>
TypeError: __init__() missing 1 required positional argument: 'xx'
>>> o_C = C (6)
Cstr A
>>> class D (A) :
...      def __init__ (self) : print ("Cstr D")
...
>>> o_D = D ()
Cstr D
```

Attributes and methods can be reintroduced without constraints or notifications (Ans. 1.38). There is no notion of redefinition in Python since the evaluation is dynamic. Reintroducing a field masks its previous value which remains visible by its qualified name (Ans. 1.39). The method C.__bases__ returns the list of classes directly inherited by the class C.

Python resolves multiple inheritance by searching a path in the inheritance graph traversing all the nodes only once. The details of this algorithm are outside the scope of this book. Example 4.96 illustrates this resolution mechanism.

EXAMPLE 4.96.–

```python
Python
>>> class C(object) :
    x = 3
    def __init__ (self, y) :
        self.y = y
>>> class D :
    x = 'aa'
    def __init__ (self, z) :
        self.z = z
    def m (self, p) :
        return ([p, p])
>>> class E (D, C) :
    def __init__ (self, y, z, w) :
        D.__init__ (self, z)
        C.__init__ (self, y)
        self.w = w
    def m1 (self, p):
        return (D.m (self, p))
```

```
      def m (self, p) :
          return (p + p)
>>> a = E (1, 2, 3)
>>> a.x, a.y, a.z, a.w, a.m1 (5), a.m (6)
('aa', 1, 2, 3, [5, 5], 12)
```

The class E is built by multiple inheritance from C and D. The value of a.x is that of x in D, this latter being located at the beginning of the inheritance clause. The definition of m1 uses some inherited methods. The method m of D is redefined but remains accessible by the name D.m (see m1's body). Let us continue this example:

```
Python
>>> class F (C, D) :
...        def __init__ (self, y, z, w) :
...            C.__init__ (self, y)
...            D.__init__ (self, z)
...            self.u = w
>>> b = F (1, 2, 3)
>>> b = F (1, 2, 3)
>>> b.x, b.y, b.z, b.u
(3, 1, 2, 3)
>>> class G (E, F) :
...        def __init__ (self, y, z, w) :
...            E.__init__ (self, y, z, w)
...            F.__init__ (self, y, z, w)
Traceback (most recent call last):
  File "<stdin>", line 1, in <module>
TypeError: Cannot create a consistent method resolution
order (MRO) for bases D, C
```

A new class F is introduced, also inheriting from C and D. The value of b.x is that of x in C. The attempt to define the class G fails as the resolution process was unable to determine the origin of the field x in G.

It is recommended that multiple inheritance be used sparingly, checking for name conflicts and dealing with them by renaming those inherited from several different classes.

4.4.9. *Incomplete* C-kits *and abstract classes*

It is possible to define incomplete *C-kits* in Python, known as *abstract classes*, even if they are not really part of the language's features. The module abc of the standard library, containing the class ABC, must be imported. In the abstract class, one declares a method called *abstract*, i.e. *not defined*, by the annotation @abc.abstractmethod and the body pass (Ans. 1.29). The definition may be given in a class extending the abstract class. As seen in section 3.2, an incomplete *C-kit* cannot be instantiated as is the case for abstract classes.

In example 4.97, the class C is abstract since the method f is only declared. The class D remains abstract since f is not defined inside it. Thus, it cannot be instantiated. Classes E and G provide two definitions for the method f, with different numbers of parameters. Note the creation of an attribute y thanks to the method g, which changes each time g is called.

EXAMPLE 4.97.–

```Python
>>> import abc
>>> class C (abc.ABC) :
...        @abc.abstractmethod
...        def f (self,x, y) : pass
...        def g (self, y) : self.y = y
>>> class D (C) :
...        def h (self, x, y) : return (x + y)

>>> a = D ()
Traceback (most recent call last):
  File "<stdin>", line 1, in <module>
TypeError: Can't instantiate abstract class D with abstract methods f

>>> class E (D) :
...        def f (self, x, y) : return (x + y)
>>> a = E ()
>>> a.g (8)
>>> a.y
8
>>> a.f (3, 4)
7
>>> class G (D) :
...        def f (self, x) : return (x)
>>> b = G ()
>>> b.g (4)
>>> b.y
4
>>> b.g (a)
>>> b.y
<__main__.E object at 0x1092e1c10>
```

4.4.10. *Other features*

4.4.10.1. *Reflection, metaclasses*

Python is mostly implemented in Python and makes its internal compilation and interpretation tools available to users. For instance, a Python developer can use the expression o.m (where o is an object) or go to a lower level by using the native function getattr (o, 'm') which "interprets" o.m. Thanks to these tools, a programmer can obtain a lot of information about the entities (functions, classes, modules, fields, etc.), even if their source code is not available, and they can also modify them.

A user-defined class C is an entity defined as an object of a metaclass, which is generally class. The metaclass class has many class methods, which are then also methods of the class C. The evaluation of dir (C) can be used to list them. Example 4.98 is based on the class C of example 4.78.

EXAMPLE 4.98.–

```python
Python
>>> dir (C)
['__class__', '__delattr__', '__dict__', '__dir__', '__doc__',
 '__eq__', '__format__', '__ge__', '__getattribute__', '__gt__',
 '__hash__', '__init__', '__init_subclass__', '__le__', '__lt__',
 '__module__', '__ne__', '__new__', '__reduce__', '__reduce_ex__',
 '__repr__', '__setattr__', '__sizeof__', '__str__',
 '__subclasshook__', '__weakref__',
 'meth_clas', 'meth_obj', 'meth_static', 'x']
```

The list obtained with dir (C) contains (among others) the function __delattr__ which is called by del. This explains why it is possible to remove class fields during the execution.

Functions and methods whose names are enclosed between __ are called *special functions* (or *special methods*). They are predefined. They are used to define certain instructions (like dir, which calls the function __dir__), to create classes and objects, to define tools to manipulate class fields, etc. Example 4.99 illustrates these points.

EXAMPLE 4.99.–

```python
Python
>>> import numbers
>>> numbers.__doc__
'Abstract Base Classes (ABCs) for numbers, according to PEP 3141 ...
>>> numbers.__cached__
'/opt/local/Library/.../lib/python3.7/__pycache__/numbers.cpython-37.pyc'
>>> numbers.__all__
['Number', 'Complex', 'Real', 'Rational', 'Integral']
```

Execution of the instruction import numbers loads the file numbers.cpython-37.pyc then it evaluates its content. It creates the namespace defined by numbers then the entity numbers as an object of the native class module. Being an object of this class, numbers owns some methods, like __doc__ (which returns the documentation string present in the first line of the file or before a definition), __cached__ (the file's location), __all__ (the components of the module, which are classes here).

It is not possible to present all of these special functions here. Their description, present in the reference manual [FOU 19b], allows one to understand the implementation of classes, how the interpreter works, and the reflection tools used to acquire information about entities.

4.4.10.2. *Evolution of the language*

Python has evolved since its first public release in 1995. Evolution requests and studies are documented in the *Python Enhancement Proposals*, abbreviated by PEP. For instance, PEP 484 and 526 deal with the introduction of a type language, which differs from the class mechanism, along with an algorithm for static typechecking based on this language. We strongly recommend reading PEP 483 [FOU 19a] at least.

Appendix: Questions to Guide Learning

In Chapter 1, we created a set of checks – in the form of questions – for grasping the precise meaning of syntactic constructs and keywords offered by a programming language. This appendix groups these questions into a list. The reader will thus find a plan for investigating the semantics of the language they wish to appropriate, by analyzing documents and reference manuals of this language.

QUESTION 1.1.– How is the source language under consideration – referred to here as MYL – translated into binary code: is it compiled, interpreted or compiled to bytecode and then interpreted on a virtual machine? Does it offer both a compiler and an interpreter of the source code? Is MYL a typed language? Is it strongly typed (i.e. does every expression have one unique type)? Is it statically typed (typing done only by the compiler)? If not, does the language offer a notion of a type that prohibits certain operations or that determines the size of memory allocation?

QUESTION 1.2.– Does MYL offer at least one syntactic construct for the notion of *kit*? If not, how can this notion emerge from the functionalities of the language, using for example its file management, as we would do in C? (see the introduction of the concept of a weak *kit* in section 2.3.2 of Chapter 2).

QUESTION 1.3.– Does MYL have multiple namespaces? How is the membership of an identifier of a given namespace determined (syntactic construct, naming convention, etc.)?

QUESTION 1.4.– What is the general mechanism of scoping adopted by MYL? What forms of masking are accepted by MYL? Write – if needed – a program such as (exaggerated) example 1.2 to show prohibited/allowed masking.

QUESTION 1.5.– Does MYL possess a notion of type of a *kit*? If so, what is the link between the name of a *kit* and the name of its type?

QUESTION 1.6.– Are the fields of *kits* typed? Are their types declared by the developer or synthesized by the compiler?

QUESTION 1.7.– Let $P1$ and $P2$ be two *kits* having the same fields associated with the same types. Do $P1$ and $P2$ have the same type? Or, is MYL typing strictly nominal?

QUESTION 1.8.– This question covers all types (if any) in MYL. Is it possible to make explicit a conversion of a type t_1 to a type t_2? Does MYL perform implicit conversion of types, at least in some cases? Identify these cases.

QUESTION 1.9.– May two components of a *kit* having different types be named by the same field? In other words, if MYL accepts some form of overloading of fields, is it allowed?

QUESTION 1.10.– In MYL, is the order of the fields of a *kit* important? Can a field use a field that is defined after it in the source code?

QUESTION 1.11.– May a field have a recursive definition without mentioning it using a keyword like rec? Is there a possibility of mutual recursivity between several fields?

QUESTION 1.12.– Apart from its fields, can a *kit* contain a block of instructions declaring, for example, local variables to the *kit* and performing any side effects? When is this block executed?

QUESTION 1.13.– Are the functions of MYL first class values?

QUESTION 1.14.– Are the *kits* of MYL first class values? (see Chapters 2 and 3 for further explanation).

QUESTION 1.15.– The file management made jointly by the language and the operating system may offer some form of export/import. Does MYL allow for confining values or types apart from a kit mechanism? See the definition of weak *kits* in Chapter 2.

QUESTION 1.16.– How is confinement of *kits* defined in MYL? Is there some interaction between confinement and the management of language libraries through some marks (as protected, for example)?

QUESTION 1.17.– Is the name of the confined *kit* different to that of the original *kit*? Is it possible that the two names are identical?

QUESTION 1.18.– Is it possible to define several confinements for the same *kit*?

QUESTION 1.19.– Does MYL consider that the type of the confined *kit* is the same as that of the original *kit*?

QUESTION 1.20.– In MYL, can a *kit* P be imported under two different names RP_1 and RP_2 in the same source code?

QUESTION 1.21.– If the answer to the previous question is yes, does the typing consider that the type of the *kit* RP_1 is different from the type of the *kit* RP_2?

QUESTION 1.22.– Does MYL accept some form of compatibility between types RP_1 and RP_2?

QUESTION 1.23.– If P exports a type t whose definition is confined, does the typing consider that the type $RP_1.t$ is different from the type $RP_2.t$? Apply the same question to other exported fields.

QUESTION 1.24.– Does MYL have an explicit syntactic construct for exporting a *kit*? For importing a *kit*? Otherwise, how does the language handle these operations?

QUESTION 1.25.– Is it possible to flatten a *kit*? Can this operation mask bindings in the source being written? Is there a way to remedy this masking?

QUESTION 1.26.– Can flattening a *kit* overload an identifier?

QUESTION 1.27.– Does MYL offer the possibility to build incomplete *kits*? What is the syntax of such a construct?

QUESTION 1.28.– What are the uses of incomplete *kits* provided by MYL?

QUESTION 1.29.– Must the type provided in the declaration of a field and the type of its definition be the same?

QUESTION 1.30.– Can a *not-defined* field of an incomplete *kit* be confined? Can this confinement be modified or removed when this field is completed?

QUESTION 1.31.– Can an incomplete *kit* be completed in several steps? Is it needed to indicate that there are still fields to be defined?

QUESTION 1.32.– Which forms of parametrization of *kits* are offered by MYL?

QUESTION 1.33.– If it is possible to parameterize by a type, is it also possible to parameterize by a value? What are the dependencies between type and value parameters?

QUESTION 1.34.– Does MYL offer a notion of functor? If it does not, but if parametrization of a *kit* is possible, how do we maintain the invariants that would have been guaranteed by a *kit* passed as an actual parameter to a functor?

QUESTION 1.35.– Is it possible to use an incomplete *kit* as an actual parameter to a functor? Can the result of the application of a functor be an incomplete *kit*? A parameterized kit?

QUESTION 1.36.– What are the interactions between confinement and parametrization?

QUESTION 1.37.– In MYL, are the actions of definition and extension of *kits* distinguished by different syntactic constructs?

QUESTION 1.38.– Is it possible to extend a *kit* P by reintroducing some fields of P? Is there a syntactic mark to indicate that it is a reintroduction?

QUESTION 1.39.– What is the semantics of such a reintroduction: with or without back-update? Can its reintroduction hide the corresponding field of P? If so, is it possible to use a qualified identifier to denote the hidden field?

QUESTION 1.40.– Are certain types of fields changed during the extension? Can the type t of a field of P not reintroduced in the extension be modified in the extension (perhaps becoming a subtype of t)?

QUESTION 1.41.– Identify all interactions between the confinement and development of *kits*. Distinguish between the interactions of the confinement with exports/imports and those with extensions.

List of Notations

References

[ABA 96] ABADI M., CARDELLI L., *A Theory of Objects*, Springer, 1996.

[ANS 11] ANSSI, *LaFoSec : sécurité et langages fonctionnels*, Agence Nationale de la Sécurité des Systèmes d'Information, 2011.

[APO 96] APONTE M.-V., DI COSMO R., "Type isomorphisms for module signatures", *Programming Languages Implementation and Logic Programming (PLILP), Lecture Notes in Computer Science*, Springer-Verlag, vol. 1140, pp. 334–346, 1996.

[AUT 19] AUTHORITY A.C.A., *Ada 2012 Language Reference Manual*, Ada Conformity Assessment Authority, 2019.

[BRU 96] BRUCE K.B., CARDELLI L., CASTAGNA G., *et al.*, "On binary methods", *Theory and Practice of Object Systems*, vol. 1, no. 3, pp. 221–242, 1996.

[BRU 99] BRUCE K.B., CARDELLI L., PIERCE B.C., "Comparing object encodings", *Information and Computation*, vol. 155, no. 1–2, pp. 108–133, 1999.

[CAS 19] CASTAGNA G., "Covariance and contravariance: A fresh look at an old issue (a primer in advanced type systems for learning functional programmers)", *Logical Methods in Computer Science*, 2019.

[CAU 15] CAUDERLIER R., DUBOIS C., "Objects and subtyping in the lambda-Pi-calculus modulo", *20th International Conference on Types for Proofs and Programs (TYPES 2014)*, LIPIcs, vol. 39, pp. 47–71, 2015.

[CON 14] CONCHON S., FILLIÂTRE J.-C., *Apprendre à programmer avec OCaml : algorithmes et structures de données*, Eyrolles, 2014.

[DUB 04] DUBOIS C., MÉNISSIER-MORAIN V., *Apprentissage de la programmation avec OCaml*, Hermes, Lavoisier, 2004.

[FOU 19a] FOUNDATION P.S., *Python Enhancement Proposal 483*, Python Software Foundation, 2019.

[FOU 19b] FOUNDATION P.S., *The Python Language Reference*, Python Software Foundation, 2019.

[GOG 78] GOGUEN J., THATCHER J., WAGNER E., "An initial algebra approach to the specification, correctness and implementation of abstract data types", *Current Trends in Programming Methodology*, vol. IV, Prentice Hall, 1978.

[GOS 19] GOSSLING J., JOY B., STEELE G., *et al.*, *The Java Language Specification*, Oracle, 2019.

[HAS 19] HASKELL.ORG, *Haskell*, Haskell.org, 2019.

[IGA 01] IGARASHI A., PIERCE B., WADLER P., "Featherweight Java: A minimal core calculus for Java and GJ", *ACM Transactions on Programming Languages and Systems (TOPLAS)*, vol. 23, no. 3, 2001.

[INR 19] INRIA, *OCaml*, Inria, 2019.

[JAE 14] JAEGER E., LEVILLAIN O., CHIFFLIER P., "Mind your language(s): A discussion about languages and security", *LangSec Workshop at IEEE Security & Privacy*, ANSSI, 2014.

[KEN 06] KENNEDY A.J., PIERCE B.C., "On decidability of nominal subtyping with variance", *FOOL-WOOD '07*, 2006.

[LER 00] LEROY X., "A modular module system", *Journal of Functional Programming*, Cambridge University Press, vol. 10, no. 3, pp. 269–303, 2000.

[LIS 81] LISKOV B., ATKINSON R.R., BLOOM T., *et al.*, *CLU Reference Manual, Lecture Notes in Computer Science*, vol. 114, Springer, 1981.

[MIL 19] MILNER R., TOFTE M., HARPER. R., *SML Family*, MIT Press, 2019.

[MIN 13] MINSKY Y., MADHAVEPEDDY A., HICKEY J., *Real World OCaml*, O'Reilly, 2013.

[PAR 72] PARNAS D., "On the criteria to be used in decomposing systems into modules", *Communications of the ACM*, vol. 15, no. 12, pp. 1053–1058, 1972.

[PIE 05] PIERCE B.C. (ed.), *Advanced Topics in Types and Programming Languages*, MIT Press, 2005.

[RÉM 98] RÉMY D., VOUILLON J., "Objective ML: An effective object-oriented extension to ML", *Theory and Practice of Object Systems*, vol. 4, no. 1, pp. 27–50, 1998.

[RÉM 14] RÉMY D., CRETIN J., "From amber to coercion constraints", *Essays for the Luca Cardelli Fest*, no. MSR-TR-2014-104 TechReport, Microsoft Research, 2014.

[WEI 99] WEISS P., LEROY X., *Le langage Caml*, Dunod, 1999.

[WIL 18] WILLIAMS T., RÉMY D., "A principled approach to ornamentation in ML", *Proceedings of the ACM on Programming Languages*, vol. 2, no. POPL, pp. 21:1–21:30, ACM, January 2018.

Index

Other titles from

in

Computer Engineering

2021

DELHAYE Jean-Loic
Inside the World of Computing: Technologies, Uses, Challenges

DUVAUT Patrick, DALLOZ Xavier, MENGA David, KOEHL François,
CHRIQUI Vidal, BRILL Joerg
*Internet of Augmented Me, I.AM: Empowering Innovation for a New
Sustainable Future*

HARDIN Thérèse, JAUME Mathieu, PESSAUX François,
VIGUIÉ DONZEAU-GOUGE Véronique
*Concepts and Semantics of Programming Languages 1: A Semantical
Approach with OCaml and Python*

MKADMI Abderrazak
*Archives in The Digital Age: Preservation and the Right to be Forgotten
(Digital Tools and Uses Set – Volume 8)*

2020

DARCHE Philippe
Microprocessor 1: Prolegomena – Calculation and Storage Functions –
Models of Computation and Computer Architecture
Microprocessor 2: Core Concepts – Communication in a Digital System
Microprocessor 3: Core Concepts – Hardware Aspects
Microprocessor 4: Core Concepts – Software Aspects
Microprocessor 5: Software and Hardware Aspects of Development,
Debugging and Testing – The Microcomputer

LAFFLY Dominique
TORUS 1 – Toward an Open Resource Using Services: Cloud Computing
for Environmental Data
TORUS 2 – Toward an Open Resource Using Services: Cloud Computing
for Environmental Data
TORUS 3 – Toward an Open Resource Using Services: Cloud Computing
for Environmental Data

LAURENT Anne, LAURENT Dominique, MADERA Cédrine
Data Lakes
(Databases and Big Data Set – Volume 2)

OULHADJ Hamouche, DAACHI Boubaker, MENASRI Riad
Metaheuristics for Robotics
(Optimization Heuristics Set – Volume 2)

SADIQUI Ali
Computer Network Security

VENTRE Daniel
Artificial Intelligence, Cybersecurity and Cyber Defense

2019

BESBES Walid, DHOUIB Diala, WASSAN Niaz, MARREKCHI Emna
Solving Transport Problems: Towards Green Logistics

CLERC Maurice
Iterative Optimizers: Difficulty Measures and Benchmarks

GHLALA Riadh
Analytic SQL in SQL Server 2014/2016

TOUNSI Wiem
Cyber-Vigilance and Digital Trust: Cyber Security in the Era of Cloud Computing and IoT

2018

ANDRO Mathieu
*Digital Libraries and Crowdsourcing
(Digital Tools and Uses Set – Volume 5)*

ARNALDI Bruno, GUITTON Pascal, MOREAU Guillaume
Virtual Reality and Augmented Reality: Myths and Realities

BERTHIER Thierry, TEBOUL Bruno
From Digital Traces to Algorithmic Projections

CARDON Alain
Beyond Artificial Intelligence: From Human Consciousness to Artificial Consciousness

HOMAYOUNI S. Mahdi, FONTES Dalila B.M.M.
*Metaheuristics for Maritime Operations
(Optimization Heuristics Set – Volume 1)*

JEANSOULIN Robert
JavaScript and Open Data

PIVERT Olivier
*NoSQL Data Models: Trends and Challenges
(Databases and Big Data Set – Volume 1)*

SEDKAOUI Soraya
Data Analytics and Big Data

SALEH Imad, AMMI Mehdi, SZONIECKY Samuel
*Challenges of the Internet of Things: Technology, Use, Ethics
(Digital Tools and Uses Set – Volume 7)*

SZONIECKY Samuel
Ecosystems Knowledge: Modeling and Analysis Method for Information and Communication
(Digital Tools and Uses Set – Volume 6)

2017

BENMAMMAR Badr
Concurrent, Real-Time and Distributed Programming in Java

HÉLIODORE Frédéric, NAKIB Amir, ISMAIL Boussaad, OUCHRAA Salma, SCHMITT Laurent
Metaheuristics for Intelligent Electrical Networks
(Metaheuristics Set – Volume 10)

MA Haiping, SIMON Dan
Evolutionary Computation with Biogeography-based Optimization
(Metaheuristics Set – Volume 8)

PÉTROWSKI Alain, BEN-HAMIDA Sana
Evolutionary Algorithms
(Metaheuristics Set – Volume 9)

PAI G A Vijayalakshmi
Metaheuristics for Portfolio Optimization
(Metaheuristics Set – Volume 11)

2016

BLUM Christian, FESTA Paola
Metaheuristics for String Problems in Bio-informatics
(Metaheuristics Set – Volume 6)

DEROUSSI Laurent
Metaheuristics for Logistics
(Metaheuristics Set – Volume 4)

DHAENENS Clarisse and JOURDAN Laetitia
Metaheuristics for Big Data
(Metaheuristics Set – Volume 5)

LABADIE Nacima, PRINS Christian, PRODHON Caroline
Metaheuristics for Vehicle Routing Problems
(Metaheuristics Set – Volume·3)

LEROY Laure
Eyestrain Reduction in Stereoscopy

LUTTON Evelyne, PERROT Nathalie, TONDA Albert
Evolutionary Algorithms for Food Science and Technology
(Metaheuristics Set – Volume 7)

MAGOULÈS Frédéric, ZHAO Hai-Xiang
Data Mining and Machine Learning in Building Energy Analysis

RIGO Michel
Advanced Graph Theory and Combinatorics

2015

BARBIER Franck, RECOUSSINE Jean-Luc
*COBOL Software Modernization: From Principles to Implementation with
the BLU AGE® Method*

CHEN Ken
*Performance Evaluation by Simulation and Analysis with Applications to
Computer Networks*

CLERC Maurice
Guided Randomness in Optimization
(Metaheuristics Set – Volume 1)

DURAND Nicolas, GIANAZZA David, GOTTELAND Jean-Baptiste,
ALLIOT Jean-Marc
Metaheuristics for Air Traffic Management
(Metaheuristics Set – Volume 2)

MAGOULÈS Frédéric, ROUX François-Xavier, HOUZEAUX Guillaume
Parallel Scientific Computing

MUNEESAWANG Paisarn, YAMMEN Suchart
Visual Inspection Technology in the Hard Disk Drive Industry

2014

BOULANGER Jean-Louis
Formal Methods Applied to Industrial Complex Systems

BOULANGER Jean-Louis
Formal Methods Applied to Complex Systems:Implementation of the B Method

GARDI Frédéric, BENOIST Thierry, DARLAY Julien, ESTELLON Bertrand, MEGEL Romain
Mathematical Programming Solver based on Local Search

KRICHEN Saoussen, CHAOUACHI Jouhaina
Graph-related Optimization and Decision Support Systems

LARRIEU Nicolas, VARET Antoine
Rapid Prototyping of Software for Avionics Systems: Model-oriented Approaches for Complex Systems Certification

OUSSALAH Mourad Chabane
Software Architecture 1
Software Architecture 2

PASCHOS Vangelis Th
Combinatorial Optimization – 3-volume series, 2nd Edition
Concepts of Combinatorial Optimization – Volume 1, 2nd Edition
Problems and New Approaches – Volume 2, 2nd Edition
Applications of Combinatorial Optimization – Volume 3, 2nd Edition

QUESNEL Flavien
Scheduling of Large-scale Virtualized Infrastructures: Toward Cooperative Management

RIGO Michel
Formal Languages, Automata and Numeration Systems 1: Introduction to Combinatorics on Words
Formal Languages, Automata and Numeration Systems 2: Applications to Recognizability and Decidability

SAINT-DIZIER Patrick
Musical Rhetoric: Foundations and Annotation Schemes

TOUATI Sid, DE DINECHIN Benoit
Advanced Backend Optimization

2013

ANDRÉ Etienne, SOULAT Romain
The Inverse Method: Parametric Verification of Real-time Embedded Systems

BOULANGER Jean-Louis
Safety Management for Software-based Equipment

DELAHAYE Daniel, PUECHMOREL Stéphane
Modeling and Optimization of Air Traffic

FRANCOPOULO Gil
LMF — Lexical Markup Framework

GHÉDIRA Khaled
Constraint Satisfaction Problems

ROCHANGE Christine, UHRIG Sascha, SAINRAT Pascal
Time-Predictable Architectures

WAHBI Mohamed
Algorithms and Ordering Heuristics for Distributed Constraint Satisfaction Problems

ZELM Martin *et al.*
Enterprise Interoperability

2012

ARBOLEDA Hugo, ROYER Jean-Claude
Model-Driven and Software Product Line Engineering

BLANCHET Gérard, DUPOUY Bertrand
Computer Architecture

TRUCHET Charlotte, ASSAYAG Gerard
Constraint Programming in Music

VICAT-BLANC PRIMET Pascale *et al.*
Computing Networks: From Cluster to Cloud Computing

2010

AUDIBERT Pierre
Mathematics for Informatics and Computer Science

BABAU Jean-Philippe *et al.*
Model Driven Engineering for Distributed Real-Time Embedded Systems

BOULANGER Jean-Louis
Safety of Computer Architectures

MONMARCHE Nicolas *et al.*
Artificial Ants

PANETTO Hervé, BOUDJLIDA Nacer
Interoperability for Enterprise Software and Applications 2010

SIGAUD Olivier *et al.*
Markov Decision Processes in Artificial Intelligence

SOLNON Christine
Ant Colony Optimization and Constraint Programming

AUBRUN Christophe, SIMON Daniel, SONG Ye-Qiong *et al.*
Co-design Approaches for Dependable Networked Control Systems

2009

FOURNIER Jean-Claude
Graph Theory and Applications

GUEDON Jeanpierre
The Mojette Transform / Theory and Applications

JARD Claude, ROUX Olivier
Communicating Embedded Systems / Software and Design

2005

GÉRARD Sébastien *et al.*
Model Driven Engineering for Distributed Real Time Embedded Systems

PANETTO Hervé
Interoperability of Enterprise Software and Applications 2005

Printed and bound by CPI Group (UK) Ltd, Croydon, CR0 4YY
05/11/2021

03090625-0006